# The Guest

## A Backroads Journey By Bicycle

Quinten Dol

For my family and my friends.

*"The Road goes ever on and on*
*Down from the door where it began.*
*Now far ahead the Road has gone,*
*And I must follow, if I can,*
*Pursuing it with eager feet,*
*Until it joins some larger way*
*Where many paths and errands meet.*
*And whither then? I cannot say."*

— Bilbo Baggins in *The Fellowship of the Ring*

# PROLOGUE

It was late in the afternoon, but the day's heat still smothered the highway when we found the man. The bike gang had split in two by this point — Robbie and I were riding ahead, and we hadn't seen Jamie or Alejandra for about an hour. We had just crested a hill, sweating and sucking the humid air, and were celebrating with the usual hooting and ringing of handlebar bells when I spotted a figure sitting in a drain just off the road.

We often shared the highway with pedestrians on this stretch of Oaxacan coast, and it was common to see sack-slung laborers trudging, women promenading, farmers resting atop rumbling tractors, even the odd shepherd strolling with his goats on the edge of the asphalt. So a man sitting alone on a remote patch of highway wasn't especially remarkable — it was his unsettling stillness that made me touch my brakes and look again.

There wasn't much daylight left, and we still needed to find food and drinking water before embarking on the night's round of "Where Are We Sleeping Tonight?" I considered pedaling on and pretending I'd never seen him until I saw Robbie watching me, his faltering Hilltop Grin broadcasting an awareness that something was up.

"There's a man down there," I blurted, pulling my brakes and planting a foot on the road.

Robbie stopped his bike, squinted through his sweat and then scanned the hillside above us. From the side, I could see his eyes darting behind his sunglasses. Now that we had both seen him, neither dared to broach the option of riding away. I propped my bike in the gutter and walked slowly down the concrete drain, which ran at an angle of the highway. No birds gossiped in the thick scrub around us, still and leafless at the end of the dry season. The only sound came from the man's feet shuffling around in the gutter.

Upon closer inspection, he was more of a boy than a man. His right eye had been swallowed by purple swelling and his right arm was covered in cuts, road rash and bruises. His right hand hung pale and stiff, apparently broken. Blood ran slick from his mess of a mouth and dripped into a wet stain in the crotch of his torn jeans. There was more blood in his hair and shining on his black t-shirt. "Fuck," I muttered. "*Fuck.*" Rob warned not to get too close.

I asked for his name, where he was from, what had happened to him. I asked if he wanted water. He groaned, rocked back and forth. When he tried to stand, his right leg gave way beneath him and he fell. A single shoe sat in the gutter with the twigs, drifts of dry dirt and old Coke bottles. When he sat up again, he slipped it on and off his left foot with his good hand.

Jamie and Alejandra rolled up after a while, and Alejandra took over the questions.

"What's your name?" she asked and then, softly, "Where's your family?" He rocked some more and gave a wet sigh.

Jamie had trained as a physiotherapist, which gave him more medical knowledge than the rest of us combined. He crouched, clicked his fingers in the boy's face and tried several of the Spanish phrases he knew. The boy ignored him and became preoccupied with his shoe again. Jamie stood.

"If he can't tell us his name and age, that might indicate swelling in the brain," he said. "He needs to get to hospital right away."

This stirred us into action. Alejandra had the only working cell phone, but there was no signal. As the group's fluent Spanish speakers, she and I left the others with the boy and ventured up the road to wave down motorists.

Large pickup trucks are used as a kind of public transport on this southern leg of Highway 200. The driver shares his cab with a friend or elderly passenger while the rest stand in the back and hold on, and they commute to work, take their produce to market, keep doctor's appointments and visit one another like this, up and down the coast. It was one of these trucks that stopped first — two shiny, late-model sedans had swerved around us and driven on — and we begged the driver to take the boy to the nearest hospital. He had room in the back, where about ten passengers stared from the flatbed. A woman shut her eyes, began muttering a prayer.

"Pues…," the driver sighed. Silence reasserted itself as he stared out at the road ahead, considering his options, until two passengers piped up to say that they'd seen the boy in the same place when they'd passed by that morning. He'd been in a similar state then, they said. Now passengers were shaking their heads. The praying woman's brow tensed as she squeezed her eyelids together. Her incantations became louder and faster, as if someone had fiddled with the knobs on a turntable.

"What's the fucken holdup?" Jamie fumed once I'd translated, glaring at the idling truck, the watching passengers, the glum driver. "He needs a lift right now. It's not rocket science."

My voice shook as I translated a watered-down version of Jamie's sentiments to the driver. I'd never seen anyone as badly hurt as this boy and I was scared of being left alone with him, of what might happen in the night. Why wouldn't they take him? If we had been back home, I was convinced the first motorist along would've bundled him into their car and driven straight to the nearest hospital. Eight months of cycling in Canada, the United States and Mexico had taught me a rather obvious lesson: that people on this continent were generally inclined to do the same.

Since leaving Mexico City we had seen plenty of teenage boys draped and drowsing like lambs atop piles of agave piñas or hay bales in the back of sooty trucks. We sometimes speculated about what might happen if a rowdy dream or a typical Oaxacan pothole jostled one from his perch. It was possible — perhaps likely — that this kid had fallen in his sleep. A patch of blood that Robbie had found baked onto the highway, the boy's missing shoe and the one-sided nature of his injuries suggested such an impact. If he'd been alone up there, or his companions were sleeping, nobody would have missed him for some time.

"If the police get involved, I don't want any trouble for myself," the driver of the pickup was saying. He looked at Alejandra. "You understand." But he did promise to call an ambulance.

Then a stern, gray-haired woman in the flatbed spoke. She said that she, too, would call an ambulance, and something else: She would "dar parte."

"It means she's going to report this to the police," Alejandra explained, watching the woman swaying in time with her fellow passengers as the pickup lurched away.

And then she said something that explained the curious air of resignation that had pervaded that truck, a ponderous shifting of feet and inspecting of fingernails that mocked our urgency.

"If somebody did this to him on purpose, it could be dangerous to help." Alejandra shrugged her little shoulders. "You never know who might be watching."

# CHAPTER 1

The idea for a bike trip had germinated two years earlier. I was hiking in central Colombia's Valle del Cocora, famous for its meadows dotted with tall, thin palms and happy cattle. I walked with an Englishman in his late twenties named James, who had a moppish haircut and used the word "splendid" in a way I found endearing. We strode up the valley's grassy slopes together into a forest filled with toucans and hummingbirds and, in the backpacking custom, exchanged notes on our travels thus far.

By this point I had spent six months living in Bogotá, the Colombian capital, on a study abroad program. I felt that I knew the country quite well, and typically took on an air of authority when discussing it with travelers like James, who were "only passing through." So as we walked I talked about Bogotá's enormous sprawl, mortifying mispronunciations I'd committed during my Spanish studies and Colombia's outdated narco state image — common conversational fodder throughout the country's growing network of backpacker hostels — before ceding the silence to James.

"I came here by bicycle," James said. "From Buenos Aires."

My feet squelched in soft coffee country mud as I paused mid-stride. "By bicycle?"

James had a sheepish smile on his face. "Eight months in the Andes, mate. My legs are bloody ripped."

He talked about the character of individual villages, the texture of the landscape and how it changed from one valley to the next. He had stumbled into beachside paradises, slept in village squares, spent days laboring up Peruvian mountain ranges. As he spoke I saw him in my mind's eye: a solitary man inching across vast high-altitude desertscapes carrying just enough food, water and spare inner tubes to reach the next village, living every inch of the continent. He'd spent months pedaling through Colombian villages and landscapes that, for me, had been little more than darkness and smudged streetlights through night bus windows.

By the time we dropped our packs for lunch, I'd made the full transformation from aloof authority to slavish disciple. I kept pestering him for stories and just about fell to pieces when, a day later, we returned to our backpacker hostel and I actually saw his bicycle. It was like meeting a celebrity, especially since I was now planning my own bike trip.

"It is quite difficult, you know," James cautioned when I revealed this nascent plan over post-hike beers. He pointed out that he and his cycling companion, a childhood friend named Tom, hadn't traveled well together over the preceding eight months. "It's very uncomfortable from a physical perspective, but the mental game is the real challenge. You have to choose your partner carefully because you won't always get along — and if you can't disagree in a constructive sort of way, it can be hell.

"We haven't said anything about it, but I think there's some kind of agreement between Tom and I that we're not going to be friends anymore once we get back to England," he went on. "At least not for a while. But then if you try doing it on your own, the mental challenge gets worse — much worse."

They'd originally planned to ride as far as Alaska, but had long since abandoned the idea. They would now fly home from Cartagena, just a fortnight's ride away. I met Tom later that day and found him pleasant, but I never saw him and James in the same room.

* * *

When I returned to Brisbane six months later, a friend gifted me an old steel-framed mountain bike that, in the hipster fashion, had a milk crate zip-tied to the rear rack. This, I decided, would be my touring bike.

As my fellow students chased up connections and jostled for jobs, I puzzled over digital maps of North and Central America and trawled through the blogs of those who had gone before. I was always drawn to the early photos of clean, nervous-looking cyclists in bright clothes on the lush Oregon and California coasts. From there I liked to skip forward to photos of the same people half a year down the road, their clothes now faded, squinting at the wide Atacama Desert or utterly alone deep in the Southern Cone.

I turned to a friend named Kelsey for guidance. She was quiet and competent, the kind of semi-feral kid whose parents had started taking her into the bush before she'd learned to walk. She'd recently returned from three months of cycling alone in Patagonia, and I probed her for tips on tents, handlebar arrangements, meal planning, V brakes versus cantilevers, handlebar configurations, anything that wandered into my increasingly frantic mind as the departure date approached.

"How would you fix a broken spoke in the middle of nowhere?" I asked one evening.

Kelsey thought for a moment. "I don't know the first thing about fixing spokes."

"Me neither, that's why I'm asking."

"I did meet this old German fella who knew a bit about bikes. He was cycling, like me, and he would stop every thousand kilometers — didn't matter where or when — to mark the occasion with a beer..." and off she went into a tale of midday beers on the Patagonian steppe, which led into a night she'd spent huddled in her tent while Antarctic winds stormed overhead, which neatly segued into a story about hitching rides with Argentine truckers.

"Kelsey," I interrupted. "The broken spokes — what did you do?"

"You're still worried about spokes?" she frowned. "You'll figure it out. That's the point: you'll have no choice."

\* \* \*

Packages began arriving on the doorstep of my share house: waterproof panniers, racks, a handlebar bag, a fold-out camping stove — sturdy, lightweight gear that made me wide-eyed with the realization that paper plans would soon become real.

Some of these items were second-hand, but most came brand new — paid for with wages I earned selling overpriced travel gear in a retail chain and supplemented with cash from a student welfare program.

I removed the bike's milk crate. A mechanic sandblasted the frame, repainted it a dark British racing green and built a pair of wheels. Over a couple of June afternoons my friend Karl and I assembled it all below his Dutton Park share house. We stood back once it was finished.

"Looks like a Baxter," Karl declared, and so Baxter he was.

* * *

"So," Robbie said, ice cubes tinkling in his glass as he took a sip of his cuba libre, "I'm thinking you should probably try out this cycle touring thing before you actually go to Canada."

I turned away from the pot of pasta sauce on the stove and faced him.

"Shit, you're right." *More sound advice from Responsible Rob*, I thought.

In the living room, the horns of Willie Colón set a frantic pace from my housemates' sound system. Hector Lavoe's silky voice was advising us to keep our wits about us when venturing through dangerous barrios at night.

Robbie and I had become friends in Bogotá, where he had also studied abroad. Upon our return to Brisbane he regularly rode his bike across the river from West End and up the hill to Paddington, where I lived in a drafty old share house. We would cook dinner, sip rum, smoke joints and listen to cumbia or salsa, telling ourselves we were "homesick" for Colombia.

Watching me from across the kitchen, Robbie wore a mischievous grin I associated with impending adventure. He was tall, solidly built, good-looking in a non-threatening kind of way with messy black hair and a gentle smile that put strangers at ease. "Now, don't hold this against me, but I have a bit of an ulterior motive: I want to go with you."

"Just on the practice ride or…"

"Just the practice ride," he nodded. "For now."

So a month later we spent two weeks riding Australia's paradisiacal east coast from Newcastle back to Brisbane. Though I'd covered it on countless surf missions and family road trips since childhood, I barely recognized the country as I now saw it from these small roads and dirt tracks. The landscape became a resource, from the beaches and creeks where we washed to the fallen trees we used as camp stools to the blessed small-town public toilets.

Like me, Robbie had grown up in a mid-sized country town and moved to Brisbane for university. He was the Nice Boy, the kid your parents wanted you to be friends with, but he was careful to surround himself with people who would drag him away from his responsibilities and off to some backpacking trail or unsavory nightclub. Before Colombia he had lived in Canada, Japan and northern Australia. He had worked at hotels in the Whitsundays, driven catering trucks all over outback Queensland, led Canadian summer camps and once, on a university field trip, accepted a snow globe containing the figure of an erect penis from the princess of Bhutan, where such imagery is a symbol of good luck. He could move with confidence among the crew-cut legions of a Brisbane law school soiree, but he loved the life of a dirtbag traveler — we'd been bedraggled Andean through-hikers and Caribbean beach louts together — and I saw my awakening love of bike-based travel reflected in him as we settled into life on the road.

By the time we crossed back into Queensland, I was convinced that there is no more dignified method of travel. There were no departure times to rush for, no unexplained delays and no snoring, stinking or loud fellow passengers. There was no insulating cocoon of steel and glass, no traffic, no engine noises interfering with the world around us. I had felt the folds and ripples of the country, tasted the salt water, agricultural chemicals and eucalyptus tang in the air. It didn't quite match my lonesome imagination of James on the Bolivian altiplano, but in my mind the towns and beaches I'd been visiting my whole life were now linked by the landscape that swelled around them. I felt I had experienced the country as it was.

We returned to Brisbane in time for Karl's 23rd birthday party, and all night I heard him telling his guests that "Robbie and Quinten just rode in from Newcastle!"

"No, I'm not going to Canada," I heard Robbie saying later. "I've got a job."

For my part, I spent the evening confirming that yes, what they'd heard was true: I'd be off to Vancouver soon. And now I knew how to fix a flat tire!

* * *

Karl, who had named Baxter, was one of my oldest friends. We had known each other since we were five years old. He had moved in with my family after I finished high school and my dad, a manager at a tomato greenhouse nearby, got us jobs on his maintenance crew. We fixed shoddy wheels on pickers' trolleys, reinforced truss wires that tended to snap in summer heat and fished drowned feral foxes out of the slick-banked water reservoir. We paid my parents minimal rent, saved everything else and, on my 19th birthday, skipped onto a plane bound for Amsterdam.

This was our gap year, a middle-class Australian rite of passage almost as important as getting drunk in a paddock or learning to use a clutch. We wandered Europe together by bus and train, occasionally drifting apart and then organizing rendezvous in famous cities over email. Feeling an increasing confidence on the backpacker trail and the financial pinch of life in 15 euro-a-night hostels, we tacked south and east towards cheaper, more exotic locales. To me, this was life as it should be — new sights, sounds, tastes and people every day, parties every night, cities brimming with history — a life of color and excitement after my quiet little hometown. In February I would start university in Brisbane but, like a child on summer holidays, the thought of going back was scary and alien enough to be unthinkable.

One night, over a hostel dinner of pasta and sauce in some medieval Albanian village, Karl wondered aloud at how my parents had stayed together all this time. "I mean, I lived with them for five months and they seem to be on totally different wavelengths."

"I guess," I shrugged. "It's not like they haven't had their problems. But hey, maybe the sex is just really good."

Karl spluttered and sprayed canned bolognese across the hostel kitchen.

We parted ways again in Turkey. I took a series of night buses eastward and crossed into Iraqi Kurdistan, mainly to say that I'd been there. I met Karl again in Istanbul, then checked my email to find a two-word message from Mom: "Call me."

This was in 2010, when young travelers still purchased prepaid cards to call their families from payphones. Karl and I found a row of them in the city's central train station and I dialed my parents' landline. Mom's voice was terse and brittle when she answered the phone.

When I hung up half an hour later, I found Karl waiting for me on a bench with his hands behind his head, serenely watching passengers milling about the platforms.

"What'd she want?" he asked.

I squeezed everything I knew into a 20-second summary. When I started, I was sitting upright on the bench. By the time I'd finished, I was sobbing into his lap.

"Maybe the sex wasn't so good, after all," he was drunk enough to say later that evening, and I was drunk enough to laugh. We parted ways a week later — Karl was headed home.

In Amman I called Mom again.

"Do you want me to come back?" I asked. There was a pause.

"You... you do what you need to do, mate." I had already changed my ticket before it had all happened, pushed my return date right up against Christmas. And without any explicit request to do otherwise, I left it there.

I kept moving south until visa requirements prevented further overland travel. I flew out of Cairo as its first Arab Spring protesters took the streets. I returned to the same central European cities I had passed through months earlier, only now the hostels were empty and the streets were flush with snow. I got drunk on the plane back to Australia and walked into the arrivals hall to find my two little sisters and red-eyed mother.

* * *

Three-and-a-half years went by: Brisbane, Bogotá, Brisbane again. When I finished university, a central structure dictating the shape of days disappeared. Its replacement was the yawning chasm of a work life that would not end, now, until retirement or even death. With a degree in hand, it no longer felt acceptable to wait tables or sell hiking boots or make coffees for a living. It was time to stop dicking around and do something. And when I looked around at my friends and fellow students — all suddenly taking 8:05 trains to the city or disappearing into the bush on long research missions — everyone seemed to be succeeding but me.

Under such conditions, my so-called "Great Expedition" was the perfect antidote. It was simple enough to fit into one tight, impressive sentence. It was more exciting than a job. It was also unique enough to stand out from the crowd of new graduates. And when compared to the abstract goals of white-collar work, the Great Expedition — with a beginning, a destination and lots of territory in between — was a more satisfying story to tell.

In the week before I left, a wave of guilt had me half-heartedly looking around for reasons to stay in Brisbane. A drooping sadness in Mom's eyes showed that she was still barely holding on. My sisters had each grown their own emotional armor against the family's split, but as they took their first steps into the wider world these shields showed signs of calcifying into something harder, and more permanent. And while my dad's career was flourishing, his personal life appeared to have settled into a quiet delusion.

As a child and teenager, nobody I knew seemed to have a vocabulary for expressing real emotion. Unbridled joy, hope or pride made you an object of ridicule, and open displays of grief or depression were sources of intense embarrassment for all involved. We never admitted to our demons, but watched each other for subtle clues — the tensing of facial muscles at the mention of a name, the steering of a conversation into safer territory.

If you happened to spot some wordless distress signal, you had two choices. Option One was the risky work of asking someone if they were okay and if there was anything they needed to talk about. It meant coaxing an admission out of someone who had been culturally trained on phrases like "you'll be 'right" and "harden up." Robbie — the great listener — was the first Australian I ever met who was any good at Option One.

Option Two was far easier and therefore more popular: you took someone at their word. Everything was fine because they said it was.

So when I straight up asked, everyone was doing fine. Getting through it. Yeah, you know. Na, I'm good. And if I chose to listen to their words and ignore the inconsistencies I saw in their faces, it became easy to run away with some savings, a scheme and a bicycle.

# CHAPTER 2

I rose at 3 a.m. on the fourth day in Vancouver. I crept out of my host's apartment, loaded my bags onto Baxter and rolled past the street people swarming around Chinatown drugstores, letting my legs fall into a rhythm as the road began to climb a large hill.

*The first!* I thought triumphantly.

At the top I took a break from pedaling (*Oh dear*, I puffed) before barreling down, rolling through a set of lights onto the Lougheed Highway. I plowed on, bursting through the city limits, wading through the suburbs and industrial estates, gunning for the countryside as the sun rose and the traffic thickened around me.

I had been talking about Vancouver for months, name-dropping it whenever I mentioned my "flight to Vancouver," or dramatically revealing that I'd be cycling from Vancouver to Ushuaia — and then explaining, in a matter-of-fact tone, that Ushuaia was at the bottom of Patagonia. But now I was here, I was only excited to leave.

A cyclist pulled up beside me at a set of lights at Maple Ridge and eyed my bags.

"Where're you goin'?"

"Trying to get to Agassiz by this afternoon," I replied.

"Oh," he said, sounding deflated. "Well, you're not far…" "

"…and then Argentina?" I added. He flashed his teeth.

I pedaled east on the Lougheed, which ran parallel to the Fraser River. Lawns and offices soon gave way to yellowing trees and wet leaves coating the forest floor. There were sawmills on the river and a piney scent of butchered wood spiced the crisp Canadian air. The wobbly weight of Baxter's bags made him feel flimsy for a great expedition such as this, but within days we would settle into it and the added weight would give the bike a sense of momentum and purpose.

As the light dimmed, I made my camp behind a toilet block at a rest stop outside Agassiz. I pulled a microfiber towel from a pannier and scooted across the highway on foot, down and across a bed of smooth stones to the river's edge. Dark slopes jutted skyward on either side of the river, the high edges of no-nonsense mountains. I stripped and plunged into the shallow, icy water, shrieking and huffing at the shock of immersion until I noticed a group of fishermen that had appeared upstream. I scrambled out and stumbled across the rocks to my piled clothes, bent over in an attempt to hide my cold-shriveled manhood. I heated microwave mac 'n' cheese over my camping stove for dinner and then lay awake inside my tent, watching its synthetic walls lift and fall with a breeze in time with my own deliberate breaths. I'd cycled 120 kilometers, but I couldn't sleep. I felt nervous and slightly nauseous.

"This is it," I whispered to myself. "All the way down."

It was raining when I woke, so I ate a hurried bowl of porridge and scampered up into the town of Hope, bustling in defiance of the wet weather that had settled over the feet of what I thought were the Rocky Mountains.

"These aren't the Rockies, man," a pale kid called Josh said later that morning. He looked concerned. "These are the Cascades. The Rockies are, like, a thousand kilometers away."

"Oh."

He and his friends Jay and Jarney were the first cycle tourists I met. It had taken them three weeks to ride here from Saskatoon, and their stories about the joys and frustrations of mountain riding made my chest feel light — it sounded like serious stuff.

"It's my second day," was all I said.

"Yeah, you look clean," Jarney smiled. I felt filthy, despite yesterday's swim, but there was a sense of ragged competence to the group and their worn gear — Jarney's left shoe was wrapped in duct tape, for example — so I kept quiet.

The Saskatoonians were headed for the coast, the opposite direction to me. When they offered a spare map of British Columbia, I walked with them across town to retrieve it from their hotel room. As we walked, my new friends mentioned another Australian cyclist they'd met in town. *More cyclists?* I thought excitedly. We met him as we passed the Greyhound station, where he'd just purchased a ticket to Penticton.

"Yesterday I rode here from Vancouver, and that was the hardest thing I've ever done. And now, these mountains? No way. I'm done."

"I'm heading the same way," I offered. "We could ride together."

He wore a kind of utility belt around his waist stuffed with knives, gadgets and, crucially, bear mace. This was the first I'd learned of the existence of bear mace — and now that I knew about it, I dearly wanted to be camping with someone who had some.

Between the unexpectedly dark stillness of the evergreen forests, the gray weather and now the rather late realization that large, toothy predators lived in these hills, the Canadian countryside grew more menacing by the hour. Crossing the Cascades alone now seemed quite daunting.

"Just one more day," I tried, with my best helpful smile.

He eyed me for a moment, but conviction soon settled on his face.

"I've already got my ticket," he shrugged.

So I left alone, laboring in the rain up the great asphalt ramp of the Lougheed Highway into the first of the Cascade Mountains. The road leveled, then leaned down a little, and as Baxter's wheels sped up water flecked off his fender and soaked my shoes. The sky was dark and fuzzy with low clouds, and what light there was died in the silent, staring evergreens crowding the roadside. The forest thinned at the cruelly named hamlet of Sunshine Valley, where I met a tall middle-aged man with a long, gray-flecked ponytail in a small store. He sat alone at a plastic table, munching on a sandwich. His name was Peter.

"Hope you've got some dry socks in those bags," he said in a slow, deep voice. The faintest possible smile played at the edges of his face. "Are you having fun?"

"More so now that I'm over that hill," I replied, pulling out a loaf of bread and a jar of peanut butter. "It's only my second day, though, and now that I'm here I'm getting pretty scared by all the warning signs and the stories about bears and mountain lions."

The smile edged further onto Peter's face, dimpling the dark skin of his cheeks, and he allowed it to linger for a moment. "Lucky for you, I give classes in wilderness survival," he deadpanned.

"I've been making sure to cook well away from the tent," I said, slathering peanut butter over four slices of bread.

"You don't need to worry about that," Peter replied in an even voice. "Just hang your food bag from a tree. High up, if you can, and away from your campsite."

"What are you supposed to do if you meet a bear or something?" I asked. Now that I had food in hand, I was rifling through my handlebar bag for a pen and scrap of paper to take notes.

"Never look an animal in the eye. They take it as a challenge, just

15

like you would."

*Would I?* I thought.

"But that's the obvious stuff. Really, the most important thing to remember is this: when you're in the woods, never assume you're alone. Know and accept that you are surrounded by creatures at all times — bears, deer, cougars, raccoons. They know you're there, so you should know that they're all around you." I ceased scribbling and stared at him.

"That's supposed to make me feel better?"

"I think you'll find it will help you lose your fear," Peter said. "Do you meditate? No? Well, when you're lying in your tent at night, concentrate on thinking about nothing."

"Think… about… nothing…" I repeated, and looked up from my notebook, frowning.

"Clearing your mind raises your vibrations to the same level as those of Mother Earth."

I looked up from my scribbling again. This sounded a bit New Agey to me.

"It essentially allows you to blend in with your surroundings," Peter went on, dead serious. "Once you achieve that, you'll find bears and deer will walk right up to you, walk right past you like a part of the forest. Because," and he paused for effect, "you *are* part of the forest.

"And there you have it," he shrugged. "People come a long way and give me lots of money to essentially learn what I just told you." He snorted softly.

"Geez, Peter, thanks for this."

"You have a calm energy," he said. "You'll be fine. Good luck."

I hadn't really finished eating, but it felt like I was being dismissed so I hastened outside and put my squelchy feet to the pedals, somehow both calmed and alarmed at the same time.

\* \* \*

In these early evenings I only ever stayed outside long enough to eat, then ducked inside the tent as the sun went down. Despite Peter's advice, the forest still unsettled me — the fungi fusing with trees crawling with moss and insects, the insects snapping inside the mouths of mammals and reptiles which themselves fed larger mammals — and all of it happening in silence, or out of sight, or at a pace slow enough to seem malevolent. Trees communicated over the air and under my tent, small animals skittered and foraged in the fallen needles and maple leaves, faceless birds gave their watchful calls to the night and I lay awake in my portable bedroom, pretending to think about nothing.

I reached the town of Penticton two days later, proud at having camped out four nights in a row without surrendering a bite of human rump steak to a hungry bear. The town sat on an isthmus between lakes Skaha and Okanagan, pooling end-to-end between parallel ranges. I spent a few uneventful days hanging out in town and plotting my route into the United States until I woke to a gray morning, a reminder that winter was on its way. I packed up and rolled out heading south.

"Well, Baxter," I murmured. "We're cyclists again."

By the afternoon I'd reached Osoyoos, situated along a lakeshore in the country's only patch of arid territory, thereby earning a droll billing as "The Warmest Welcome in Canada." Here, I had organized to stay with a couple through Couchsurfing, a website that matches travelers with locals who are happy to host them free of charge. Having never used the service before, I was drawn to its idealistic mission — but slightly nervous about who I might meet.

Scott, a portly white-haired man in his 60's, welcomed me at the door of his third-floor apartment, and over several trips we squeezed Baxter and my bags into his laundry. I was sitting on the couch when his husband, a skinny, bearded man named Kel, came through the door from a walk with their miniature poodle, Fagin.

We made small talk for quite some time — or rather, Scott and Kel talked while I listened, sitting on the couch in their small, cozy flat. The conversation moved from Couchsurfers they'd hosted to life in San Francisco in the 1970's, illnesses they'd suffered and an assortment of culinary passions and fads they'd succumbed to over the years.

"But enough about us!" Kel cried in sudden dismay. "You're the guest — you're here to entertain us! Tell us about yourself."

So I told them about my plans for Patagonia and the life I'd left in Australia. They said they'd hosted cyclists before, and soon enough we were back onto Scott and Kel's life stories, which suited me fine. I found them fascinating.

Both had grown up in small Alberta towns in the 1950's and 60's, long before rural Canadian society ever considered it "okay" to be gay.

"My family owned a ranch, and every season when it came time to round up the cattle my father hired groups of young cowboys to help out," Scott said. "They all slept on these cots in the barn, and my father made me sleep out there with them. He thought he was toughening me up, making a man out of me." Scott snickered for a second, a sly expression on his face. "Little did he know, he was actually helping me live out my wildest teenage fantasies with older boys."

"At what point did you feel comfortable coming out in a place like that?" I wondered.

"We were in our 40's," Kel said. "We were living in another small town. We rounded up all the gay men we knew locally and had big party, kind of presenting ourselves to the community. We invited everyone, and they all knew Scott — he was the high school principal then — so he stood at the door to put them at ease as they came in." Kel was beaming. "You were great, that day," he added, looking at Scott.

"It helped that I knew several of my pupils' parents from our local BDSM community," Scott added, as if he were discussing a minor workplace drama. "We had an understanding."

Later, I asked about Kel's career during the same period.

"I was a hospice nurse in a retirement home," he said. "There were a lot of people who lived alone — no friends or family to speak of, no-one to visit. I took care of their basic needs each day, but the job was more than that. I was also their friend — their last friend." He paused. "It's like being a guide, someone to shepherd them through their last few months on Earth."

"Must have given you a different perspective on death."

"Maybe, I'm not really sure. I'm still afraid of dying, if that's what you're talking about. It's a funny thing, to be the one left behind over and over again."

There was a moment of silence, and Scott reached over to take Kel's hand.

"But now, to business!" Kel piped up suddenly. "First: we're making pizza. Is there anything you don't eat? Second: we'd like your help in the kitchen. How good are you at taking or" and he looked over his glasses, "*giving* instructions? And third: do you toke?"

My answers were, "I eat everything; I'm better as a follower than an instructor; and not tobacco."

"Oh good. We have a pissy neighbor, so we have to smoke under the bathroom fan."

This was my first experience with the famous BC bud, and by my second turn on the pipe everything had become quite strange. Later, once I'd sunk back into the couch, I became intensely aware of my stiff quad muscles and the road grit flecking my skin and excused myself for a long-overdue shower.

Overwhelmed by the weed, which was far stronger than anything I'd encountered before, I became distracted in the shower by the hot rivulets of water running over my skin and completely missed out on pizza-making. Then, confirming my status as a terrible guest, I completely forgot to help with the washing up.

But Scott and Kel were gracious about it. We spent the night talking, smoking, drinking whiskey and listening to old Yes albums. We went to bed at four in the morning and when I woke, I bid them a fond and quiet goodbye. Head throbbing and stinking of scotch and marijuana, I set out with Baxter to ride the short distance to the U.S. border.

# CHAPTER 3

There is something strange about being a foreigner in the United States for the first time. Many of us grew up with some basic exposure to its culture through music, movies, television and news, and our eyes are drawn to the stereotypes: the flabby, oversized SUVs, the enormous restaurant portions, the farmers shouldering hunting rifles by a busy highway and the ubiquitous stars and stripes, which fly proudly from the glitziest city skyscrapers and the most run-down demountable homes outside some dingy Washington State border town.

Entering the United States was doubly strange for me because I am technically a citizen. My Australian mother and Dutch father were living in Pennsylvania when I was born, and a quirk of U.S. law gives me citizenship in a country where I have no familial ties, and which I hadn't lived in since I was five years old. This benevolent law of birthright citizenship regardless of parental immigration status is common throughout the Americas — a continent full of immigrants — but surprisingly rare elsewhere. So while I felt no real sense of connection to the United States, my mom still had my Lehigh County birth certificate and an old, expired U.S. passport bearing a photo of me as a bowl cut-wearing toddler.

So it felt weird to approach this border as a foreigner in the country of my birth. A customs official checked my bags, stamped my Australian passport and explained that I would need to leave the U.S. within three months, by December 23rd.

*Christmas in Mexico*, I thought. It seemed unfathomably far away in both space and time.

Over the following four days I pedaled deeper into the so-called

Evergreen State which, on this side of the Cascades, was more brown than green as the land readied itself for winter. In the evenings I stayed with people I'd met online through a site called Warmshowers, a lesser-known Couchsurfing-style community that caters specifically to traveling cyclists.

On the outskirts of Wenatchee, I stayed with a family of four. Knowing that I had likely not showered in days, a small middle-aged woman named Judith led me from the front door to the granny flat in their backyard with very little introductory small talk. I spotted clean sheets swaddling a cloud of a bed, but Judith pointed me straight to the shower.

"Take your time, and come up to the house when you're ready," she said. "We're having lentil curry for dinner."

For this anticipation of a cyclist's very specific needs — shower, bed, hot dinner — Warmshowers hosts deserve a collective Nobel Peace Prize. For the shower alone I was willing to forgive all the times I'd had to hastily explain myself to startled senior citizens after saying something like "I'm Warmshowering with a couple over in Ellensburg" or "I've organized a Warmshower with a guy in Omak."

I stood in the shower for far too long, watching the water turn black at my feet, and then dried off with the fluffy towel Judith had left on the bed. I found a clean pair of underwear in my panniers and pulled on a clean (if slightly musty) shirt along with my one pair of long pants.

After dinner, Judith and Peter pulled out a large atlas and had me point out places I'd been to their 13 year-old daughter and 15 year-old son. The son was particularly taken with my stories about the mud-brick Iranian city of Yazd, while the daughter only wanted to hear stories of Istanbul.

"We love living here," Judith said, putting the atlas away after the kids had gone to bed, "but when the time comes, they must leave this town."

I was ecstatic to be in bed by 9:30 — once again, Judith and Peter had anticipated the cyclist's desires — and drifted to sleep listening to coyotes howl and yip in their backyard.

Between the nightly dinner parties, I shadowed the Okanogan River until it joined the larger Columbia. The riverbanks lifted, turning the waterway into a sparkling corridor flanked by brown, bare hills. Later, I climbed out to camp on the shores of Lake Chelan.

Mountains darkened the horizon as I followed Route 12 westward, back to the Cascades. As I pushed up into the tiny town of Rimrock, Baxter's odometer clicked into four digits — my first thousand kilometers since Vancouver. Thinking of Kelsey, I entered its only store.

"One thousand kilometers at the Rimrock Grocer, whooda thunk it," a mountain of a man chortled from behind the counter, his beard like an avalanche down his chest. He handed me a canned pale ale when I asked for his "most local beer." I then sat in a patch of sun outside to drink it down with a pile of chocolate-and-almond Mr. Goodbars, summoning my strength for the coming climb up a long finger of granite reaching down from distant White Pass. I spent the afternoon scratching over the ledge, then hurtled back into a turbulent landscape where all but the steepest peaks were coated with the fluffy moss of evergreen forest.

I had covered more than 100 kilometers by the time I rolled into the small town of Randle, and decided to reward myself with a rest day and a large meal. However, camping close to a town would complicate a game I played on nights when I hadn't organized a Warmshower stay, which I called "Where Am I Sleeping Tonight?"

The game started in the late afternoon, when I knew that within an hour or two I would be setting up camp somewhere — but for now I had no idea where that might be. Safety was paramount, of course, and to me safety meant solitude. I still felt vulnerable alone in my tent, and despite the weariness of mounting days in the saddle I was usually tossing and turning until late at night. Cracking twigs in silent forests still put me on high alert.

In time I figured out that advanced players of "Where Am I Sleeping Tonight?" considered the softness of the ground beneath their tent, shelter from the wind and unexpected storms, proximity to unlocked bathrooms and water taps and, crucially, a place to sit — ideally a rock or log sculpted to comfortably accommodate a pair of skinny human buttocks. A picnic bench was a rare treat. Living on a tight budget, I took pride in not having paid for accommodation thus far.

For the cyclist looking to camp near one of Randle's handful of highway diners, the main "Where Am I Sleeping Tonight?" offerings came from its extensive variety of churches. Proximity to other homes disqualified the Reconciled Christian Fellowship, the Church of the Nazarene and the Abundant Life Fellowship, and there was something about the dirty drawn curtains of the Family Worship Center that seemed downright sinister. After some hesitation, I set up my tent behind the United Methodist Church because it had a soft lawn out the back and no neighbors.

In the morning I woke to veterans, retirees, mountain hippies and farmers working at a food bank the Methodists were operating in the building. The organization gathered every first and third Friday of the month, according to Jim Mahitka — an Air Force veteran, according to his hat — who let me inside to cook porridge on a gas stove.

"Whichever way you're going, you sure came up a long way to get here," he chortled.

Eager to repay my hosts, I asked if I could help the volunteers with their tasks.

"Anyone need an extra set of hands?" Jim addressed the room.

"Not unless he can satisfy my wife!" someone shouted back.

"Carol, you're needed in the tent!" chimed another. Carol and I blushed.

After a lazy day of wandering Randle's expansive meadows and gawking at the local elk herd, I entered a small gas station to buy some Mr. Goodbars and use the bathroom. By this point, around two weeks out from Vancouver, my body had accepted its new role as an engine and demanded ever-increasing quantities of fuel in return. A cycle tourist's appetite is famous, but less so are a cycle tourist's bowel movements. Put simply: the sheer volume of matter going in means large volumes of matter coming out, and this increasingly unstable arithmetic came to a head at the Randle One Stop.

The usual satisfaction of producing a redwood-sized log quickly turned to terror when I tried and repeatedly failed to flush it. Each new wave lapped uselessly at the unmoving mass, like a Greenpeace volunteer splashing buckets of seawater over a beached whale. Defeated, I washed my hands and left, hoping that slow decay might achieve what force could not.

After a heavy bout with the kitchen at the Tall Timber Diner, I walked back along the highway through the quiet twilight. Inside the One Stop, the cashier sounded stressed.

"No, you can't use the restroom, Greg," she was saying to a man standing by the door. "It's out of order and I can't get a hold of Bill to come help me fix it."

"What happened in there?" Greg was concerned.

The cashier moaned, and her voice shook with dismay. "Some asshole blocked it up," she said, stomping with frustration. "There's water all over the floor and leaking into the parking lot, and I can't get this one down, Greg. It's not moving."

"Oh boy."

"Yep, and I should've closed fifteen minutes ago but I can't just leave it like that can I?" As Greg walked outside, the cashier turned to me as I reached the counter, my face burning. "That'll be $2.85, sweetie," she said with a smile and a glance over my two dessert Mr. Goodbars and packet of chips. My cheeks turned a darker shade of maroon as I realized there were only two dollars in my wallet. I tried to return one of the chocolate bars to the shelf.

"Oh no, don't you worry about that. Take it anyway," she smiled, reaching into the tip jar. "Where're you from, anyway? You're camping behind the church, aren't you?"

"I'm from Australia and yeah, I'm camping behind the church." I tried to slink towards the door and out of there. "Please don't worry about the chocolate. I'm fine without it."

"Hoooweee!" Greg had opened the bathroom door. He sounded impressed.

"No, no," the cashier protested, thrusting the second Mr Goodbar back at me. "First time I ever had an Ostralyun in here, and we can't have anyone going hungry in Randle — least of all visitors. You're most welcome," and she smiled again.

*Nice town, Randle,* I thought as I speed-walked into the dark and the desperate cashier began yelling at Bill's voicemail through her phone. *Pity I can never, ever return.*

With fresh legs on the pedals next morning, Baxter sped south across a flat valley floor. Once an early fog lifted, the steaming, silent Pacific Northwest woods glittered in crisp September sunshine. Baxter positively skipped up the slopes as we left the valley.

Around lunchtime I stashed the bike behind a bush and hitched a ride up a side road onto the feet of Mount St. Helens. The area is still a moonscape decades after a violent 1980 volcanic eruption produced landslides, pyroclastic flows and avalanches of ice, snow and water called lahars. Together, these forces scrubbed all life from the landscape, leaving it dotted with the remains of decapitated trees, their corpses speckled with pebbles like bullets in the dead timber.

There is something frightening about the slow and sometimes sudden power of natural forces. Mount St. Helens began to bulge out of the Earth's crust almost 40 millennia ago and yet, in the space of an afternoon, this apparently immovable fixture had shed its northern flank, wiped out hundreds of square kilometers of forest and poisoned the once-paradisiacal Spirit Lake. Then, having expended its energy and thoroughly rattled every living thing in the vicinity, the landscape went back to its usual, seemingly inert state of slow growth and recovery.

I had assumed that the turn-off for Mount St. Helens would mark the day's altitudinal high point, but it was not to be. The road was like a mountain goat skipping ever-upward, finding a way across steep hillsides and bare expanses where the mountains showed their granite bones. Aside from the snow-swaddled peaks of mounts Hood, Adams, Rainier and St. Helens gleaming against the clear sky, this ridge was the highest crest on an unmarked ocean of evergreen.

But I only saw these things when I stopped for breaks. On the bike, my horizons collapsed to encompass little more than Baxter, my body and the few meters of road ahead. I listened to the gentle buzz of Baxter's rear wheel hub and the click of his chain shifting gear, felt the texture of the road through his wheels and constantly wondered if the rear tire was too flat.

If the bike is configured correctly, the cyclist rarely feels any real pain. But over time, a heavy weariness begins to weigh upon one's legs. With time, I would gain a sixth sense for mountain roads and anticipate the false peaks without premature celebration. But these were early days and rounding a bend to reveal yet more asphalt sloping skyward was a knife in my soul. When the incessant low buzz of the bike and my own irregular breathing began to bother me, I switched on an old mp3 player hooked up to a portable speaker I'd rigged on my handlebar bag and played James Brown's *People Get Up And Drive Your Funky Soul* on repeat. I bobbed and bucked in the saddle, moaned through the horn solos and pedaled more or less in time with the song's unceasing beat, which drove me on until, at last, the road ran out of mountain.

I parked Baxter against a tree and walked to the spot where the shoulder dropped out of sight. I felt I could see half of Washington State from up here and beyond the north-eastern horizon, which I'd come from, I felt the land calm into a drier country crisscrossed by highways and broad rivers. Portland waited to the south and, beyond that, Oregon's famed Highway 101.

From this height, there was nowhere else to climb. I basked in anticipation of the coming flight downhill, the rest and showers that waited in Portland and the confidence that came with knowing I was apparently capable of mountain riding. A solitary happiness seemed to vibrate within me like water boiling under a heavy lid until, unable to hold it all in, I began to scream.

It started as a guttural yell that found joy as it climbed into higher registers, then morphed into a hoot as my lungs emptied. The echoes took their time to answer and did so only as a whisper. If the mountains had noted my presence, they showed their disinterest in silence. My face was sore with grinning as I walked back to Baxter, who watched me with one of his handlebar-end eyebrows raised.

# CHAPTER 4

Thick Pacific northwest woods peeled back from Highway 101 as I approached town. In their place, weatherboard houses and mossy businesses stooped under gray skies. Up ahead, I spotted a man in a gray t-shirt standing by the road and straddling a bike loaded under two bulky panniers: another bicycle tourist.

He was slathering sunscreen on himself as I pulled up alongside. He was short and solidly built with messy black hair and the pale skin I soon learned to associate with his hometown of Seattle. His name was Miki.

"I'm in a hurry," Miki said once I'd introduced myself. He spoke quickly. "I want to make San Francisco in ten days." Then he looked over his glasses at me, and said, "Do you know anything about fires? Because I bought this flint from a camping store, and I'm desperate to use it to start a fire." Then he said, "I heard there's great ice cream up ahead in Florence, we just have to find the place."

Florence was a town of weatherboard houses and wharves on a bend in the Siuslaw River. We spent almost an hour going in and out of stores asking after the best ice cream in town. I let Miki make the inquiries because he seemed comfortable in conversation with anyone, especially when he revealed to shopkeepers that he, too, was a small business owner — a bike store in Seattle. Eventually, someone mentioned a name he recognized: BJ's Ice Cream Parlor.

"Aha!" he cried.

We sat on a picnic bench by the river, taking its time through the last couple of bends before the ocean. Miki had ordered salted caramel while I tried huckleberry, mostly because I hadn't known that huckleberry was anything other than a Mark Twain character.

"Have you been cycling down the coast for long?" Miki asked.

"A couple of days," I replied. "I was staying in Portland for about a week and then took this road over the coast range. It was actually a dirt road for the last section, running alongside a river."

Miki eyed my bike. "Your rig looks solid enough to handle it. In fact, you look pretty prepared all around. You have quite a lot of gear."

"I'm hoping to go a long way," I shrugged.

"Was it difficult to get out of Portland? I know it's a really bikeable city, but I've never tried to get in or out by bicycle."

"Freeways and suburbs," I sighed. "But at some point, when I spotted the Coast Range, I pulled over to ask this guy if I was on the right road. He was one of those half-hippies, half-rednecks that live out here, you know what I mean?"

"I'm not sure he'd appreciate that description," Miki smiled, "but yes, I understand."

"So I pulled up to ask him for directions and he turned around, liquor stinking on his breath, and shouts, 'Shoot, yew got some climbin' to do before you get to Beaver!'"

Miki chuckled. "I gotta tell you: your rural American accent needs some work."

I snorted. "That's fair. I don't know why I tried to make him sound southern."

In the moment of silence that followed, I cast an eye over Miki's bike. His two small panniers looked overloaded and awkward, as if they'd been stuffed with several irregular-shaped objects "You're traveling light, hey."

He looked at me over his glasses. "I must admit: I'm quite underprepared." He had no stove and no pad or bedroll — just a sleeping bag and a pile of clothes to sleep in. He said he was cold at night. Later, I would learn that he had also forgotten to bring long pants or a rain jacket and relied on his seldom-charged phone for navigation. As for his bike, it had a rare titanium frame.

"Titanium is more flexible than aluminum or steel, and it's very strange to ride. I can feel it bending on the bumps in the road, flexing when I pedal. Quite fun, but very inefficient."

Even though Miki kept saying he was in a hurry, we'd spent two hours seeking and then consuming ice cream by the time we'd left Florence. We left town together, chatting about his bike shop.

"I grew up south of downtown, a kind of working-class neighborhood," he said. "No bike shops down there, but my friends and I were big cyclists. So I started fixing my friends' bikes in my parents' garage."

We were rolling behind sand dunes and through thickets of cedar and fir, blackberries running riot beside the road. Highway 101's traffic was constant, but the shoulder was wide enough in places to ride side-by-side.

"Eventually, the community actually demanded that I open a real bike store in our neighborhood." So he did, at the age of 20. He'd never been to college, a fact that he wore as a badge of honor. Now, at the age of 28, he employed several people and owned his home.

"The store basically runs itself now," he said. "When I turn up to work and start tinkering, my employees tell me I'm getting in the way. So I stay home and play video games. I have no real economic incentive to do anything anymore. I don't know what to do next."

We drank beers on the beaches, stole into county campgrounds after dark and snuck into the showers without paying, wandered through small-town supermarkets and then made our own deli sandwich feasts on bluffs overlooking the kelpy Pacific. We watched retirees in thick fleeces and walking shoes stomping along the dark sand beaches. Offshore, pelicans glided in single file, riding the updrafts off the steepening faces of waves. Splashes belied the presence of dark-headed seals beyond the breakers. Occasionally, we spotted the puffs of spray that heralded the arrival of gray whales along this section of coast.

This watery new world — rain, fog, ocean spray — felt like a new country. The winding, bucking 101 followed the contours of Oregon's varied coastline, a sort of cycling variety show after the unending climbs, white-knuckle descents and deathly quiet of the mountains. Fog descended on the highway at times, sharpening our other senses to compensate for the temporary blindness it caused. I sniffed the unfamiliar combination of fir forest with the kelpy brine of cold seawater. I listened for the distant slap of waves against the cliffs. And when I stuck my face over the edge, I felt a breeze moving up the wall of rock.

A self-described "troublemaker," Miki liked to offer up opinions that he deemed "controversial" for debate.

"If a relationship is going to work, you have to be friends," he was saying late one afternoon. We'd just raided a dumpster and were strapping timber off-cuts to our bikes. We planned to use them for firewood. "Friendship means you're fundamentally compatible. Passion, though, passion is very unstable. It's essentially a chemical reaction in your brain — it's not actually real. It's just your brain telling you to spread your genes with this person. Once it disappears, what are you left with?"

"Didn't you say your girlfriend is 18?"

Miki looked over his glasses and gave a mischievous grin. Every time he did so, it reminded me of my Nanna. "That's right."

"So are you friends with her, or is this just an unstable passion-driven relationship?"

Here was Miki on Japan in the Second World War, a special fascination as his father had emigrated to the U.S. from Japan in the 1960's: "So you have these people brutally rampaging across a continent, subduing nation after nation, stealing resources and imposing their laws. What do you get at the end of that? Well, you get the United States. That's how Japan would've ended up."

"Ahhh... you sure about that?"

"Oh yes," he looked over his glasses at me. "Forget the merits of democracy or fascism, the U.S. simply didn't want Japan to become an imperial competitor."

"I have my own theory," I offered, steering the conversation away from the depressing realm of conquest and genocide. Miki perked up. "I'm not sure if you've experienced this, but I feel like there is a difference between being a Cyclist and being a Human."

Miki was riding behind me in a narrow segment of highway shoulder, and there was silence for a moment as he considered this.

"I think I know what you're getting at, but explain."

"Like, when I was in Portland for a week, I was a Human. I felt self-conscious about how I dressed and smelled in public. If I was in a public place and felt like sitting down, I would use a bench or some other appropriate amenity, you know what I mean?"

"Sure," Miki said. "Humans see the street as a set of clearly demarcated zones designated for automobiles, wheelchairs, children, pedestrians. There are special rules and conventions governing one's behavior within each space."

"Right. And then yesterday, you remember we were in that cafe? We were the only ones there. And I don't think I said anything to you at the time but after we'd been there for like an hour, I noticed the woman behind the counter wrinkling her nose at us and I realized: 'Holy shit, we smell awful!' I had no idea. And I almost didn't care."

"I can smell you right now," Miki said. He was still riding behind me. "I can confirm: you stink."

"But the slipstream isn't bad, hey?"

I glanced back. Miki had his mischievous smile on. "Cyclists and Humans. Continue."

"Right. So, for example, sometimes I'll catch myself squatting in the gutter gorging on a pile of fried chicken. And then later, I'll be laid out on some grassy median strip sweating it out as my body attempts to digest that chicken. It's like an urban environment is just another landscape, like a forest or mountains, filled with potential resources. You know, water taps, a wall to lean the bike on, a sunny place to rest, a stranger to endear yourself to."

We had crested a small hill as I spoke, and remained silent as we zoomed down the other side, wind and the noise of passing traffic buffeting our ears.

"We've got bike lanes and highway shoulders," Miki said at last. "But the Cyclist is still essentially an outlaw in car country."

We stopped for stove fuel in Coos Bay late in the afternoon ("We can use it to start fires!" Miki said), and ended up poking around a sporting goods store that, along with soccer boots and hockey sticks, was heavily stocked with lethal firearms. This, of course, raised an issue that every Australian is constitutionally required to rant about while visiting the United States: guns.

"I understand the hunting rifles and the scopes," I said a little too loudly as we walked back into the parking lot, "but what are you hunting with a pistol? Or a semi-automatic?"

Miki laughed. "It's our right, man. Welcome to the United States."

At that moment, a bald man in purple overalls sidled up to us. He glared at me over his rimless sunglasses and growled, "Guns are the only thing that keep people at bay."

He then stepped into a waiting minivan, which immediately pulled away. Utterly bewildered, I turned and gaped at a still-chuckling Miki.

"Once again, welcome to the United States," he laughed. "By the way: I mostly agree with you about the guns. It's an insane way to run a society. But watching that guy stand up to you on it makes me weirdly proud to be American.

"That's why no-one would ever invade us," Miki said as we rode out of town. "Even if you could beat the world's most powerful military, our civilian population is armed to the teeth! You think it's tough in Iraq or Afghanistan? Try a nation that collects AR-15s for fun."

Baxter's odometer clicked over its 2,000th kilometer outside Brookings, the last town in Oregon, and after celebratory beers we passed a sign that read, *Welcome to California.*

"We're basically there!" Miki cried. "Nothing but sunshine and palm trees from here on!"

But another sign appeared a little way along. *San Francisco*, it read, *390 miles.*

"That's at least seven days of riding!" I groaned.

It was now late in October, and southbound motorists spoke of winter as a wet wall of cloud and rain following us down the coast. "I hope the weather doesn't catch us," Miki said.

# CHAPTER 5

We were riding on a smooth side-road that had branched off Highway 101. Miki was riding ahead — he'd been telling me about the so-called Seattle Dog, a hot dog that allegedly came smothered in cream cheese — but the conversation had died off and he'd pulled away. I could have sworn he was only 20 meters or so ahead of me, but he looked tiny. Something was off. Was he really riding that fast?

I pushed on the pedals to catch up and as I approached, he swiftly regained his normal size. When I let him roll ahead again, he seemed to shrink alarmingly quickly.

An approaching car appeared around a bend in the road. It was a typically obese American SUV but, like Miki, it looked comically small — like a European hatchback.

"Wait, holy shit!" I yelled, pulling on my brakes.

Miki looked back. "What?"

I was looking up now. "The trees," I stammered. "Oh my god, the trees!"

Miki looked up. "Aha, it appears we've found the redwoods. I was just wondering when we were going to encounter them."

We pedaled on among these immense, arrow-straight monarchs of northern California, the sounds of our awestruck shouts muffled in the thick bed of needles gathered on the forest floor. The ancient red trunks were like earthen pillars holding up the sky.

Beyond Crescent City the coastline climbed high above the ocean as it had in Oregon — so high, in fact, that we emerged on a sunlit hillside forested with redwoods high above the clouds. On this joyous road we quickly began catching up to other cycle tourists, and by the time we reached the campground at Elk Prairie we were a veritable bike gang.

I had never been around so many of them, but quickly learned that unlike backpackers and other types of travelers, cycle tourists were always happy to meet other cycle tourists. Suddenly, you weren't a weirdo in padded pants anymore, nor did you have to smile and nod through some well-meaning motorist's explanation of "the conditions" on a road that he had traveled on his ass, in air conditioning, at 100 kilometers per hour.

A full 19 cyclists camped at Elk Prairie that night. During introductions, Miki irreparably estranged himself from Jack, an Englishman in his late 20's who wore John Lennon glasses and mutton chops, when he asked where Jack was from.

"Jerseh," Jack replied with an unmistakable British accent.

"Oh cool," Miki said eagerly. "Where in Jersey? Closest I've been is Newark Airport."

Jack glared at him. "Not *New* Jerseh," he spat. "The *original* Jerseh."

Martin from Toronto was obsessed with weight.

"Look at those savings!" he kept saying as he admired others' gear. Later, he explained that his relentless pursuit of a lighter load had driven him to cut the handle off his toothbrush.

"Half a gram is half a gram," he shrugged as the rest of us groaned.

Jack and Martin had teamed up with Sue-May, a camp cooking extraordinaire and self-professed "terrible cyclist" from Malaysia.

"I only go about 30 kilometers per day," she sighed.

"Gives us plenty of time to drink beer while we wait," Martin added, smirking at Jack.

There was a young German couple towing a trailer behind their tandem bike, and an older Australian called Brad who had recently quit the Darwin police force. Brad was traveling from Alaska to Patagonia, though he had covered a large portion of the Canadian leg in a canoe.

Then there were Jeff, Ryan, Hamilton and Katie from Vancouver, who were raising money for cancer research by riding a four-person tandem bike to Mexico. A fifth friend drove a support car, carrying their gear and fetching supplies. Their combined weight slowed them down on the climbs, but when their pedaling powers combined on the flats they flew along at incredible speeds. As the smallest rider, poor Katie had to sit at the back and deal with the unwashed stench of her male teammates.

Last to arrive were Ron and Sue, a fluoro-clad couple in their 50's from Connecticut. They were the only ones who had actually paid to camp in the cyclist's campground.

"There's nobody else in there, you'll have it to yourself," a ranger had told them, so they were surprised to find the campground chock-full of cyclists who'd sneaked in through the bush.

The Oregon and California parks services give tacit acknowledgement to the "otherness" of cycle tourists by segregating campgrounds into separate areas for "hiker-bikers" and the general public. In the latter, elderly couples retired to their electrically lighted and heated RVs. Families bonded over wholesome camping activities, like burning store-bought firewood to make s'mores, playing cards and drinking Bud Light.

Meanwhile, in the hiker-biker district, joints and pipes packed with Northern California's most famous crop orbited a communal picnic table as strangers pooled the offerings from their food bags — a potato here and another there, an onion over here, a bit of forgotten pasta found at the bottom of a pannier, some cheese that needed to be used right now, a few pinches from someone's spice bag (I made a mental note to start a spice bag) and someone else — legend! — had a jar of pesto. A tin of Spam appeared, but under vegetarian objections it quickly disappeared with a sigh from its owner, who had been looking forward to canned pork all day.

Several cyclists ventured into the forest to find wood for a fire. Others debated the merits of each cyclist's camping stove (noise, reliability and the ability to simmer were all important considerations), and a few helpful cyclists volunteered for chopping, stirring and washing up duties. Two dominant "head chefs" emerged — Sue May and Miki, who had once run a sushi restaurant with his brothers — and they debated every culinary option in front of them.

"Thoughts on stirring in the cheese now, or upon serving?"

"Let's save some pasta water to splash on right at the end. Keeps it nice and creamy."

"This zucchini: fry or steam?"

Feeding cyclists was a perilous (but never thankless) job.

Most cyclists carried narrow little cooking pots to save weight, but mine was large enough to make a decent-sized meal and was therefore commended by all except the weight savers, who made sly comments about inefficiency.

As dinner came together, Jack the Englishman returned from the bathroom.

"What's going on in the normie section?" Martin asked.

"Oh, just a bunch of RV drivers fantasizing about murdering cyclists," Jack quipped, prompting a collective wince from the table.

You see, large sections of the Pacific coast highways — winding, dipping, narrow and full of hairpin turns — would be challenging enough for a sensibly-sized vehicle. But large numbers of gray nomads routinely took them on in 40 foot-long, triple-axle buses weighed down with 12 hurtling tons of furniture, plumbing and faux wood grain.

"My favorites are the ones that tow trailers behind the giant bus," Martin said. "You've seen 'em towing golf carts, right?"

"We saw one pulling a giant SUV," Katie gasped.

"Wanna know something really messed up?" Sue from Connecticut said. She was sitting at the end of the table, still in her fluoro-pink jacket. "Lots of states don't require any special license to drive an RV at all."

There was momentary confusion at the table. "What do you mean?" someone asked.

"It means," said Ron, Sue's husband, who wore a matching fluoro jacket in yellow, "that in more than 30 states — including Florida, where Americans often go to retire — you can pass your driving test in a two-door hatchback and then legally get behind the wheel of a 26,000-pound bus."

"The worst part is the lack of noise," Miki said. "I can basically tell what type of vehicle is approaching — even how close it's going to pass — based on the engine noise alone, but the RVs are completely silent!"

Sue-May was nodding. "You know that shockwave of compressed air that breaks over you a millisecond before it appears at your shoulder?" The table collectively shuddered and observed a moment's sober silence.

As the pot simmered, Miki took a moment to find a large stone and drop it into the fire.

"I'm camping without a sleeping pad," he explained to the group. "Every morning I lie on my pile of clothes, shivering and imagining Quinten in his tent, fast asleep on his cushy mat, tucked into his sleeping bag. That kind of resentment is not good for our cohesion as a duo.

"But I remember reading that if you heat a rock in the fire and wrap it in a towel, it will stay hot for hours," Miki went on, dusting off his hands as he resumed his seat at the table. "So, ah, does anyone have a towel?"

Bicycles and their workings were discussed at length over dinner and, as the resident mechanic, Miki was in high demand. Mechanically minded cyclists gathered around a troublesome steed, while the gear nerds produced obscure gadgets to sort minor niggles.

The good-looking, inexplicably clean German couple retired soon after dinner had finished. Meanwhile, off in the trees, Brad from Darwin sat brooding at his own fire. Marijuana lapped the table again and stories were told of strange, forgotten towns on Saskatchewan prairies and nights spent in enormous Wyoming barns. Eventually, everyone drifted off to brush teeth and clamber noisily into sleeping bags. Hours later, I woke to Miki calling my name.

"Wssup?" I murmured.

"This rock is still warm!" he cried. "This is incredible! I'm so excited, I can't sleep!"

# CHAPTER 6

Pastel San Francisco sunshine bathed the brown hills above the stadium, up where university buildings jammed against the hills that ring the metropolis by the Bay. I pulled into the parking lot only a few minutes late but, finding no-one there, took Baxter up a side road by some football fields, scanning the faces of passersby for a look of recognition. My phone didn't work without a WiFi signal, so I had no way of knowing whether she had cancelled or not.

As I rolled back towards the stadium, I spotted a woman in a hairband that struggled to tame a mane of brown curls. She spoke first: "Quinten?"

I'd never heard of anyone wearing exercise clothes — jogging shoes, running shorts, a tank top made from some moisture-wicking material — to a date before. But I quickly learned that Hailee doesn't just go on walks — this was an opportunity to elevate her heart rate, and she wasn't going to pass it up. A Tinder outing was just an add-on to the walk, not the other way around.

"So. How's the bike trip going?" she asked as we began huffing up the busy fire trails into the hills.

I thought back over the preceding month: screaming at the Cascade mountains, skulking after a campsite on the wide streets of Randle, spotting whales off the Oregon coast, waiting out a rainstorm by some dollar store with Miki and a handful of drifters. I summoned it all up and then shoved it through a filter of nonchalance: "It's been great," I said. "A fantastic way to travel. And it's a wonderful country. I didn't realize I would like America so much."

"And you're planning on going to Patagonia, huh?"

"That's the idea. I saw in your bio that you'd studied in Buenos Aires?"

"I got back a few months ago."

Observing a sort of custom among former Latin American exchange students, we switched to Spanish long enough to convince one another that we weren't pretending, then switched back to English.

"Did you do any traveling outside the city?"

"As much as I could," she said. "Lots and lots of overnight bus rides. I've got a list of things to do in Buenos Aires and Argentina. I could share it with you, if you're interested. Not sure if B.A. is on your way, but you'll love Patagonia. I could probably make a list for parts of Chile too, though I spent less time there."

"Sure! I mean, it's a long way away. Maybe I need some inspiration."

"What have you been doing since you arrived in San Francisco?"

"Honestly? Not much. Resting. It was a rough couple of days getting here."

"What does 'a rough couple of days' look like for you?"

"Well, I was riding with this guy who was supposed to finish here, but his bike fell apart a few days out. So his friend came up to drive him back to the city. We'd been together since Oregon. The night after he left, I camped by this beach in a state park. At 3 a.m. I woke to this cop shining a spotlight on my tent screaming to 'Show me your hands!'"

"What? Oh my god!"

"Yeah," I said. "I cranked up the accent and that helped. She didn't move me on. But then she said, 'Somebody was murdered in this parking lot a few weeks ago, I was just making sure you weren't dead or something.'"

"What? Come on, that's a bit dramatic."

We reached a bench overlooking half of the Bay, Oakland's skyline in the foreground, the tall buildings of San Francisco and the Golden Gate Bridge silhouetted against a hazy afternoon sun in the distance.

"So do you prefer it down here, or back in Seattle?"

"I mean, it's beautiful up there but the winters can be tough. After I moved here, it took a long time to accept that I don't have to go outside every time the sun comes out," she said. "Otherwise, you end up exhausting yourself."

"How do you spend those sunny afternoons inside?"

"You mean if I'm not studying? I do a lot of reading. Historical fiction, mostly. I've loved it ever since I was a little kid. I used to spend entire family road trips hunched in the back of the car with a book."

"Doesn't historical fiction usually feature a romp in the hay barn or a breathy scene in a meadow?"

"Well, my main criteria is that it has to be believably set in a historical period, and there has to be a strong female character in there somewhere," Hailee said, and then grinned. "But yes, 'romps' is putting it mildly. Let's say I was a little young to be reading *Clan of the Cave Bear* when I did. My parents must've wondered why my face turned maroon every time they saw me with it."

We remained on the bench for a couple of hours, chatting and watching the orange orb of the sun sinking into the Golden Gate, a watery mile-wide keyhole in the continent. After the sun had set she said, "There's a Brazilian sandwich place near the university. Want to get some dinner? President Obama once ate there."

We ate greasy, delicious sandwiches and she seemed impressed at my cyclist's appetite. She led me around the University of California campus — dropping a historical anecdote for almost every building — and then into a bar called Jupiter, where a band with a horn section soon had the crowd on its feet. Later, we walked up to the sorority house where she lived — "We think of ourselves as the anti-sorority sorority, if that makes sense" — and where I'd chained up Baxter. It was very late by the time I kissed her.

She spent her days at school, working multiple internships and squeezing in periods of study ahead of a testing season. I spent mine eating and half-heartedly seeking out the city's many hilltop spectacles — the stadium of the Golden Gate, the low sweep of waterfront along Fisherman's Wharf to the tall buildings of the Financial District, the coastward neighborhoods tumbling toward a swirling mix of bay water and Pacific Ocean. I did some long-overdue bike maintenance and gorged on unhealthy food: mac 'n' cheese, burritos and Capn' Crunch cereal.

But really I was just filling time until the evenings, when I met Hailee at dive bars and student district restaurants. Later we would go back to the place I was staying. Mercifully, my hosts had gone on vacation and left me alone in their apartment for four days.

One night, a car almost hit us in an Oakland crosswalk.

"What the fu-" I started at him, scared and furious.

"Are you okay?" Hailee cut in. The driver looked sheepish. "Are you fine to drive?" He nodded.

"I'm fine," he mumbled. "I'm sorry."

"Be careful, alright? Get home safely."

I lay awake in the early hours, watching a landscape of gentle curves and forests of curls taking shape from the gloom of a gray autumn morning. Later, she was pulling on t-shirts and plotting her day's movements before I could peel the curtains away and let in pale Bay Area sunshine.

My hosts returned to Oakland, and I planned my departure. On my last day in the Bay I rode a loaded Baxter to the Berkeley waterfront to meet Hailee for the last time. I made sure she saw me arrive with Baxter loaded under his bags, and was rewarded with an arched eyebrow.

"Okay, I'm impressed," she shrugged.

My stomach did cartwheels.

"Did you decide whether you're going to Big Sur or back to the mountains?

"The coast is tempting, but I can't come all the way to California and not see the Yosemite Valley."

"I want to say I support that decision — but I'm not the one who's gonna be pushing Baxter up all those hills."

"You said you have a test this afternoon? Do you need to study or anything?"

"I prepared yesterday; I think I'm okay."

We spent most of the day sitting on the grass, picnicking on snacks and listening to her music: Blue Scholars, Alabama Shakes, Los Cafres. We filled each other in on our details — families, hometowns, friends, past travels, future plans — and yet there always seemed to be some powerful current beneath it all, some unspeakable thing that needed no acknowledgement, as if we were close friends from multiple past lives exchanging postcards on our latest bodily incarnations.

"I'm saving up to do some traveling after I graduate next summer," she said. "Have you ever been to India? How about Southeast Asia? No?" I was shaking my head. "Well, I've got some trips lined up there. Although my travel partner for India just got into a program in D.C. so I'm not sure if that one's actually going to happen."

"You graduate in May?" I said, and she nodded. It was now October.

"I suppose I'll be in Panama by then. I know you've already been…"

"Only briefly."

"… so if you end up looking for something to do, maybe you should come find me."

"Palapas, jungles, Caribbean beaches," she listed them on her fingers and shrugged. "Count me in," she grinned.

She was already late for her test when we said goodbye. She cocked her head and said, "I feel like I know you quite well, somehow." Her expression seemed to mirror my own sense of happy confusion. We kissed and she ran to catch her bus. We'd known each other for five days.

I didn't have time to dwell. Having exhausted my welcome with my hosts (who never learned that I'd brought a stranger into their home), and with Hailee living in a women-only sorority house, I took a train east out of town. While the other passengers clustered around a radio to hear the San Francisco Giants win a World Series, I sat alone and wondered why I was leaving the city. It was very dark when I hopped off in a town called Tracy, and once I found its edge — a black void fringed with floodlit industrial parks — I struggled through a challenging round of "Where Am I Sleeping Tonight?"

Eventually I found an empty water reservoir, no more than a pit beneath a tree and lined with cracked-dry mud. A road ran beside it to a glowing military facility a mile or so away, and trucks rumbled by all night.

I was hungry and uneasy in that hole, but I had found my home for the night and so allowed Hailee to wander back into my mind. Regular pilgrimages to the San Juan Islands (her "favorite place in the world"), coaching elementary school basketball, babysitting jobs — these were some of the tangible things I had learned about her. And yet I felt like I knew far more — that she always gave her honest self to the world, for example, and expected nothing more than honesty in return. I knew that she cherished her friends, yet also loved to be alone.

"Sometimes, when I'm going to meet someone, I'll text and say 'I'm going to be late,'" she said one evening. "Even though I'm ready, I just want a few more quiet minutes to myself."

There was nothing particularly special about that, and yet there was something in it that moved me — my stomach had dropped like a rollercoaster ride. I had stared at her for a moment, stunned. Something ancient and elemental had happened, as if we had bumbled into an old magic that allowed direct communication between souls where words were little more than decoration. Miki would have rolled his eyes and said my chemical-sniffing brain was lying to me.

But I knew she'd felt it, too. I caught her confused glances every now and then, and at the end there was no question in her voice when she'd said, "We'll see each other again."

If she'd asked, I might have followed her anywhere. I was sure she knew it, too, and yet she was wise enough not to do so. She knew it wasn't time. We would see each other again.

A passing truck threw a shower of pebbles into my pit, reefing me back into the squalid, uncertain present. But I felt peaceful now, and settled back into my jacket-and-t-shirts pillow.

# CHAPTER 7

The campground was a small flat littered with picnic tables, fire pits and a handful of old RVs among the trees, their curtains drawn against the cold. Glimpses of sky through the forest canopy revealed a single mass of gray cloud. Pine trees sucked the light away, magnifying the day's gloom.

I wore a flannel, a fleece and my thrift store down jacket over several t-shirts, thermal leggings under my synthetic hiking pants and fresh woolly socks under my shoes: evening wear. They felt clean against my salty skin — the padded pants, riding jersey and rank little ankle socks I'd been wearing in the saddle hung from Baxter's frame and handlebars.

A woman emerged from an RV in a pink onesie and approached me.

"Just wanted to let you know that there's a snowstorm on the way," she chirped, prompting me to choke on my noodles. "Enjoy your night!"

From Tracy it had taken a day to cross the Central Valley, once a wide marshland until settlers pulled down the trees, dammed the rivers draining the Sierra Nevada and replanted it all with a grid of orchards and crops, irrigation canals and chemical tanks, muddy pickup trucks and gangs of hooded laborers forming ragged lines across the fields. I spent a second day climbing dry, scrubby foothills onto a spur, where gray pine thickened and morphed into ponderosa, and gaps in the forest allowed views across the blackened scars of the summer's wildfires.

At the first campground inside the national park, a ranger told me snow had swamped the road up ahead overnight, and so I set up my tent among the other travelers who had been stranded on this wooded shoulder of the range.

I had just finished dinner when the storm announced its arrival with the sighing, clicking and groaning of tree trucks beneath the wind, like whale song in the forest. My stove and pot clattered into my bags, and my riding clothes flew into the open tent. I stuffed panniers under the vestibules to block the wind. The forest was thrashing around me now, and thick droplets hit the earth in haphazard bursts as the storm began to seep into the forest. Fingers clumsy with cold, I drew a plastic bag around Baxter's leather saddle, dashed around the tent tightening straps, then dived inside and zipped the fly home as the rain settled into a rhythmic din.

I woke to snow falling, and news that the road into the Yosemite Valley would remain closed for another night.

"Are they going to clear Tioga Pass?" I asked the ranger. The pass was one of the only paved roads over the Sierra Nevada for several hundred kilometers to the north or south, and I'd been dreaming of riding through the deserts that waited on the eastern side of the mountains.

The ranger winced. "You're a day late," she said. "They won't plow it 'til spring."

"Are there any other options to go over the range?" I asked. "I'm headed to Death Valley."

"The only one that'll be plowed goes to Lake Tahoe, way up north. Otherwise, you'd have to go all the way south to Bakersfield and loop around." She smiled. "Long trip."

I stumped back to my tent through the frigid forest.

Snowflakes gathered piece-by-piece on the disorderly forest floor like a poorly played game of Tetris. I dozed in the wan light of day and lay awake at night, wondering if this mountain detour had been a mistake.

The road was plowed and reopened on a sunny morning a day later, though thick banks of snow now gathered between the trees and pulled at their branches. I was glad to be working uphill in the cold. At a fork in the road, a police officer confirmed that the Tioga Pass was no longer an option.

"What is up there that will physically stop me?" I asked, still drawn to the desert and dreading a return to the Central Valley.

"Well, firstly: the snow. There's a foot or two of it on the road up there." He frowned. "And secondly: the law."

And so down I went, the still air turning to knives as Baxter picked up speed. The road swung high and wide onto the edge of the Sierra, dry foothills in a dusty distance to the right, while the asphalt weaved in and out of the range, probing for an opening. At last it found a large gash in the granite that ran straight into the heart of the mountains and, clinging to the cliff face, Baxter and I barreled in.

The Yosemite Valley is like a fenced garden writ large. Proud towers, smooth domes and imposing walls of granite protect yellowing deciduous and evergreen pine forests, steaming logs caught in beams of sunlight, and all of it dotted with grassy meadows home to the happiest deer on the planet.

The parks service has done an impressive job of accommodating Yosemite's hordes of bucket-listing tourists in a series of discrete lodges and campgrounds. There's a sort of village consisting of a visitor's center, administrative buildings, lodging for the staff and even a supermarket. Between the pitched roofs and log cabin aesthetic of the buildings, the multitudes of shuttle buses, children dragging parents, the military-style uniforms of the rangers and the looming acres of vertical granite overhead, the place felt like a theme park.

The next day I hiked a trail that would've taken me to the top of Yosemite Falls if there had been any water running this late in the year. Still, it was a nice, huffing workout up between two giant shards of granite, like a vulnerable approach to castle gates. The rim of the canyon sat above the snow line, and I found bear prints in the drifts.

I sat down to rest at the edge of the cliff, with the smooth sentinels of El Capitan and Half Dome facing one another to my left and naught but air beneath my toes. I munched on the peanut butter-and-jelly sandwiches I'd brought along — I was a recent convert to that particular bedrock of American cuisine — and, as is custom with such a view, tried to open my mind long enough to let it leave a mark.

The sparkling bones of the range showed themselves here and there while, in sheltered places, soil collected to support sturdy forests of fir and pine. Clouds drifted in from the west and I watched their shadows mosey across the flats or dart up and down steeper faces of sheared rock. Half Dome's titanic vertical face presided over all, stained black with moisture and the lichens feeding off it.

With all these stories playing out in front of me — most of them far too large and slow for an impatient human mind to grasp — it was easy to feel small in the world, and small in time. This, of course, is a familiar emotion to anyone who has taken a moment to really look at a mountain, a star-filled sky, an ancient ruin, an old tree or any other obvious reminder of how small and petty our daily dramas really are.

But while contemplations of deep time and space had always calmed me in the past, something in the sheer beauty of this day — the harsh clarity in the light, the dark and serrated edges of the woodlands, the glittering crystals within the snow drifts — seemed almost menacing.

For two months now I had been moving only for movement's sake. I was wandering the edge of humanity's great cooperative project, using its amenities without contributing to its advancement. Cycle touring was engaging for the body, not the mind, and this potent combination — aimless wandering, mental space and new surroundings bombarding the senses — left me to uselessly ponder my lack of purpose. What was I doing out here?

"Great," I told the valley, feigning good humor. "And what am I supposed to do now?"

The valley seemed to ignore that question and, unable to come up with anything myself, I batted the thought away and spent the rest of my hike looking down, absorbed in the placement of my feet on the trail.

# CHAPTER 8

I felt the road ease forward beneath Baxter's wheels, felt the momentum of my pedal strokes begin to build behind the bike in a way that signaled my departure out of the Yosemite Valley. I stopped, pulled on my gloves and raincoat and did a couple of jumping jacks to warm up, then threw a leg over Baxter's saddle and let his weight carry him forward.

The road snaked between giant fir trees, and I squinted against the cold air as Baxter picked up speed, picking out potholes and drifts of fallen leaves and needles across the road. I wasn't steering with my hands anymore, just leaning into the curves with subconscious shifts of my hips. I kept an eye on my toes, careful that they wouldn't catch Baxter's front wheel during a turn. We entered a smooth realm of fresh asphalt and, feeling confident, I began swooping from the outside onto the inside line of each bend, drifting out into the middle of the road, half an eye on the river of pavement rushing a few inches past my knee.

The landscape shed its foliage as I dropped onto the last foothills and finally bottomed out at Oakhurst, where I climbed over a small range and found myself in the Central Valley once more. At dusk I turned off the highway and found Lake Millerton, which had formed behind a dam in the San Joaquin River. I was alone. As night fell, the moon appeared and I lingered by my campfire, watching the coals, using a forked stick to cook cheese on toast. In the morning I stripped and swam in the lake, then sat on a rock to dry, feeling invisible.

The next day I skirted around a metropolis of malls and asphalt called Fresno. At dusk I rolled into the small community of Orange

Cove. It was surrounded, unsurprisingly, with orange orchards. Fruit pickers filled the main street with the low-level bustle of a working town on a weeknight, men in baggy pants and boots loitering outside stores or strolling, fatigued, to beat-up sedans while their kids roamed on BMX bikes. Overhead, the early-evening sun lit the Central Valley's ever-present haze to a luminous orange. Instead of butchers, diners and supermarkets, Orange Cove had carnicerías, taquerías and mercados. Workers greeted each other in chingada-heavy Mexican street Spanish while the kids conversed in California Spanglish.

"I'll text you más tarde, I got hella homework from Ms. Brown."

"Okay chamaco, no'vemos mañana."

I busied myself with "Where Am I Sleeping Tonight?" and ended up talking with a bald, mustachioed man who'd been loitering outside a mercado.

"You mean in a house?" he replied when I'd repeated my query in Spanish.

"Well, yeah. If the owners are okay with it, I could pitch my tent in the backyard."

"Espérate."

He dialed a number on his phone and spoke briefly before handing it to me. A woman named Stella gave directions to her house, several blocks away.

"Down that way," the man said — his name was Fernando — tossing a thumb over his shoulder when I returned his phone. "I'll be around in a bit. You'll find it, no es difícil. Muchos doggies," he added.

Stella was a bushy-haired abuela who strode out to greet me flanked, as promised, by a tumbling, scampering horde of chihuahua puppies and their snarling mother.

"There's a kind of party out back," she said in English, "but you must be starving. Come eat first."

The house was small and cluttered with old furniture decomposing into the carpet. Paths of cleared floor wound between sagging couches and tables piled with old newspapers, stacks of car manuals and catalogs, a battered guitar or two. A ceramic virgin of Guadalupe leaned against a cabinet along with some wilted Kim Possible-themed birthday balloons. Mattresses stood against almost every wall.

Stella sat me at a small kitchen table and fed me string beans and carne asada, watching me eat from the stove and replenishing my pile of fried corn tortillas. She asked cursory questions about my trip, but Stella's attention was in short supply in this house full of children, dogs and a sound like heavy metal thundering from the backyard. The place was an orbital center for what seemed like several extended families. Cousins and nieces kept popping in and out, asking after dinner or chasing down truant children, and none of them seemed surprised to see me munching away at the kitchen table.

I had my first warm shower since leaving the Bay Area, and then Stella took me into the backyard to meet her sons, Ray and mustachioed Carlos, and a buzz-cut, solidly built nephew named Eric. They wore oversize jeans, work boots and t-shirts that billowed around their bodies. An extension cord ran from the house to an amplifier, which broadcast the heavy riffs and chaotic solos Eric was playing on a black electric guitar. At intervals, he and his uncles swigged from a bottle of El Presidente brandy.

"Siddown and take a glass," Eric said, pouring me a drink. He was covered in tattoos. When I asked him about them, he showed me an Aztec pyramid representing his Mexican family on one arm, a dream catcher for his Apache family on the other and the logo of a video game company over his heart.

"I love Grand Theft Auto," he explained.

Carlos lived with his mom, Stella, and worked at a Walmart outside town.

"They treat me like shit, but they pay me on time," he shrugged.

Eric was forming a metal band with his uncle, Carlos' brother Ray. Ray was a large man with a soft voice who wore his hair in a single long, black braid straight out of an L.A. gangster movie. He had lived and worked in Los Angeles for most of his life — most recently as a guitar salesman — but had been staying with his mom as he recovered from a bout with bowel cancer.

"I'm in remission," he beamed. "I just got the news recently." We celebrated with a round of shots of El Presidente. Fernando appeared and joined us for a drink. He didn't show any sign of understanding the English conversation around him, but he sat in companionable silence.

"I knew some people through the hospital who had to say 'goodbye' to their families," Ray said, taking a sip from his glass. "Honestly, that's what I'm thankful for. That I didn't have to say goodbye."

I mentioned an uncle who was diagnosed with pancreatic cancer when I was in high school, a gravitational center of my extended family. His beer belly and his quiet, devastating humor were already gone when I saw him for the last time, hours from the end.

"You still think about him, huh."

"When I've got a tailwind pushing me along, I like to think it has something to do with Uncle Kev. He never stopped you from doing something stupid or intervened in any overt way. But he always seemed like he could subtly guide you in the right direction."

Ray nodded. "I don't know if you believe in a higher power or something but man, maybe he guided you here," he replied mysteriously. He picked up an acoustic guitar to play what he called an original composition, a series of gorgeous overlapping melodies building upon one another.

As his brother played, eyes closed, Carlos leaned over to my chair and whispered wetly into my ear. "Do you want to go to a bar with me?"

I felt my body stiffen. "No thanks, I think I'm going to bed pretty soon."

He leaned in again, and I flinched. "I'm gay," he said, then sat back in his chair, swaying, watching me. His brother's song entered a thrumming, chord-heavy climax as Carlos watched me, a tortured expression on his face. "My family doesn't know."

The song ended. Carlos looked away and began a drunken cheer for his brother, who looked chuffed. A skinny white kid called Felix showed up with a drum kit and he, Eric and Ray began to jam.

"I gotta work in the morning," Carlos slurred. "Eight years at the goddamn Walmart." I watched him wobble off toward the house. Soon after, when Eric began falling out of his chair, his 14 year-old daughter appeared at his side. She took him by the hand and led him away into the dark.

I slept in a spare bed and in the morning found Ray sleeping upright on a couch, the floor around him now filled with mattresses dotted with irregular heaps of blankets, pillows and at least seven children. Stella seemed confused when she found me packing my panniers. "I assumed you were going to stick around for a few days," she said.

I hugged them all and began rolling south through the Central Valley's grid of rectangular orchards girded by straight, bumpy roads that met at right angles every few miles — North America's great produce market. Stretching more than 700 kilometers from north to south and a mere 100 kilometers across at its widest point, this basin the size of Denmark produces more than half the fruits, vegetables and nuts grown in the United States. Rivers of snowmelt are dammed and diverted into canals and irrigation ditches to feed seven million acres of farmland. Pomegranates, pistachios, grapes, olives, oranges, walnuts, lettuce — I passed them by the square kilometer. Towns speckled the valley seemingly at random, swelling around a supermarket or a school at some strategic intersection.

Late in the afternoon I rolled into the parking lot of a battered convenience store. I nodded at the group of men gathered in the shady corner of the parking lot, leaned Baxter against a wall, bought a packet of biscuits and then sat down beside the bike.

A shiny, late-model SUV pulled into the parking lot and a white man holding a clipboard and wearing a Budweiser-branded polo shirt walked into the store, glancing at me as he went. I leaned back and closed my eyes, chewing biscuits, listening to the men talking.

Some spoke with the irregular beat poet's cadence I'd come to associate with Mexican Spanish. Others spoke in rapid, unfamiliar accents that I found hard to understand. A handful talked among themselves in hissing, clicking languages transported north from the jungles that awaited me in Central America.

At intervals someone would appear — a man in boots and a cowboy hat driving a battered pickup, another in sweatpants and a grubby 49ers cap on an old BMX bike — and the others would raise their paper bags in greeting. Some stayed, others shook hands and moved on. A breeze moved up the road between the orchards, plucking dust and whirling it into the air. The asphalt was warm against my legs as I sat and ate.

"Looks like a fun trip," a voice said, and I looked up to see the Budweiser man standing by his car's open door. He was ticking boxes on a checklist fixed to his Budweiser-branded clipboard.

"Has been so far," I shrugged.

The man tipped his head towards the laborers sipping their afternoon beers and said, in a lowered voice, "don't stay anywhere near these towns at night." He doffed his cap and drove away.

The next day I pulled up beside a field of grape vines and asked a group of pickers for directions to Bakersfield. They were short, dark and wiry men and women wearing thread-bare t-shirts, faded hoodies and stained jeans. They wrapped rags around their heads to fend off the sun. Unsupervised by a manager, the pickers filtered out of the rows to consider my question. One offered a bag of supermarket-ready grapes as a sort of ruse to get a closer look at Baxter. Low whistles and raised eyebrows accompanied my exhibition of his panniers, racks and odometer.

"¿A dónde vas?" asked one.

"Argentina," I replied, which provoked murmurs. Suddenly, a fierce little man in a tattered yellow shirt offered his hand.

"Then you will pass through El Salvador," he said in gravelly Spanish.

"And Honduras," added another, nodding.

A portly man stepped forward. "And Ecuador!" he cried, and I spotted the Salvadoran rolling his eyes.

As I stuffed the grapes into my food pannier, a picker expertly unbuckled the pannier on the opposite side and added a second bag. He fastened it again and flashed a yellow smile.

"For balance," he explained.

While their grapes were tasty, the pickers' directions weren't fantastic. Too late, I discovered they'd sent me to Route 99, a pockmarked strip of multi-lane asphalt cutting through flat, gray country under a dun-colored sky. Though the shoulder was wide, it was littered with wheel rims, smashed bumpers, broken glass and twisted scraps of metal. I skirted wide around the shreds of rubber that had once been tires — the tiny steel ribs within were notorious puncture culprits — and spotted oil wells for the first time.

I had hoped to find a host in Bakersfield, but the connection fell through. Disgruntled at the prospect of an unexpected game of "Where Am I Sleeping Tonight?" in the midst of a large city, I succumbed to my urges and found an all-you-can-eat Chinese buffet. I paid my fare, took a plate and, through the next three hours, I let my Hunger guide me.

I demolished three plates piled high with every type of golden-fried chicken — honey chicken, orange chicken, fried chicken, General Tso's, chicken bites. Overwhelmed by poultry, I moved on. I ate stir fries, Mongolian beef, fried rice, and then soups, spring rolls, won tons, a second serve of cashew chicken. I was panting as I disappeared into the bathroom, praying that the plumbing was strong enough to withstand the coming onslaught.

I returned to the table. The restaurant was full of squirming kids with ice cream on their faces and families in Saturday polo shirts, all unaware of the ecstatic, compulsive struggle occurring in my booth, the addict taking a particularly heavy tumble off the wagon.

Messages arrived from my gut begging me to stop, but muscles all over my body were in ecstasy and countermanded the order, shrieking for more. I had turned my legs into machines built to turn pedals and now, ignoring my stretched stomach, they sent signals masquerading as a large, leaky vessel which I strove in vain to fill with food. After a particularly challenging pile of braised pork, I moved on to dessert and lingered, sweating, over a bowl of canned peaches and ice cream, the Hunger willing me onward.

I staggered outside, grease seeping from my skin and strange bubbles and pops emanating from my digestive system. I mounted Baxter and wobbled out of Bakersfield.

On the outskirts of town, I saw women chatting at plastic tables with the older children sitting politely nearby. The men crowded around smoky barbecues. Roosters patrolled the margins and dogs slunk between ankles, while weeds and corn stalks grew from scruffy gardens. Large speakers stood in the dust, blasting norteño ballads accompanied by overzealous snare drums. The city petered out into farm country again and, as night fell, I pushed Baxter up an embankment and into an orchard of olive trees. Bakersfield glimmered across the flats. An oil derrick wheezed and clunked in the center of the square orchard, a strange, rhythmic motion in the plantation's geometric gloom.

Cars going to and from parties passed a nearby intersection all night. The frantic horns of ranchero ballads ruffled the edges of the otherwise silent orchard long before the car arrived, the singer bellowed a few choice lines as the driver slowed at the stop sign, and then the horns faded to silence once more.

# CHAPTER 9

"Hey-hey-hey." It was Robbie's voice, electronic and tinny over the internet connection, but unmistakably him.

"Rob!"

"Hey buddy, where are ya?"

I was in Tehachapi, a small California town that sits astride the southern terminus of the Sierra Nevada, just before it dives under the Earth's crust. "I've been here a few days resting up, doing some planning."

"You're not thinking about going back to Berkeley to hang out with that girl you texted me about? Or convincing her to join you?"

I heard the smile in Rob's voice. Hailee and I had begun a correspondence of lengthy messages and links to music we enjoyed. In time, we would develop a routine of checking in on each other every few weeks. We would never directly address the romance we'd shared in the Bay Area, but her stories about senior year life and caches of music became a treat I looked forward to between my increasingly rare internet sessions.

"Na man, she's got to finish her degree. No female riding partners for me yet."

"Speaking of which…"

Aha. Here it was. "Hit me."

"When is your U.S. visa up?"

"Just before Christmas. I was looking at the map today and it's possible to do this big loop through Death Valley and Las Vegas to the Grand Canyon. I reckon I can do it and still be at the border by the time I'm supposed to be out."

"And about the trip into Mexico..."

"Yeah?" I'd been trying to avoid thinking about Mexico. Americans and Canadians alike had been telling me awful things about their southern neighbor, and I was starting to believe them.

"It looks like you're in this thing for the long haul and, well, I've just been daydreaming over here about quitting my job and joining you... if you'd have me?"

A wave of excitement and a little relief washed over me. "Shit yeah Rob, let's do this thing!"

I planned a 2,000-kilometer eastward loop that would take in Death Valley National Park, Las Vegas and the Grand Canyon before turning south and west toward the coast in time for a rendezvous with Robbie at San Diego. I had yearned for the desert since I'd arrived in this country. There was something about the idea of uninterrupted views for miles around, like proof of one's isolation, plus the romance I'd picked up from movies like *Butch Cassidy and the Sundance Kid* and *Vanishing Point*.

I rolled off the range and turned north, cycling in the shadow of the Sierra's abrupt eastern flank where dried-out peaks dropped onto smooth, wide valleys. On my right, lesser ranges lined up one after another to the horizon. This altitudinal drop-off was so dramatic that Death Valley's Badwater Basin, the lowest point in North America at 86 meters below sea level, lies only 136 kilometers south-east of Mount Whitney, the highest peak in the lower 48 states.

Nothing grew much taller than knee-height on this side of the range and as the agriculture disappeared, so did the vibrant Latino communities who picked and packed the crops. Inyokern, Ridgecrest and Trona were bleak, sun-bleached towns servicing vast military bases and mining facilities in the surrounding desert. I left Trona late in the afternoon of my second day out from Tehachapi and climbed a gently rising valley, playing "Where Am I Sleeping Tonight?"

I found a dry creek bed to pitch my tent a few miles up the road. Lights shimmered on down in the town. The salt lakes behind Trona glowed against the brown desert, ringed with mineral refineries silently spewing white smoke into a still-blue sky.

As I was building my tent, I spotted a woman in a black cap and tights on a loaded bike pedaling up the same way I'd come.

"Hey!" I shouted too loudly — I hadn't spoken to anyone all day — and sprinted through the creosote bushes to meet her. She dropped her bike in the road and walked towards me, but the wariness in her step reminded me that I'd just leapt out of the desert at her on an isolated road.

"I'm on a bike too," I explained, breathless.

Her name was Olga. She was wiry and strong. She didn't smile easily and she still seemed wary, both with me and with English.

"Where are you from?"

"E-spain," she said.

I tried my Spanish and she nodded in acknowledgement.

"My partner is on his way now."

Pablo rolled up a few minutes later, wild hair pulled into a ponytail and his sun-weathered face hidden behind a long, scraggly beard that tumbled over an old blue-and-white striped shirt. They accepted my invitation to share the campsite I'd found.

After several weeks of more or less lonesome camping, a bit of after-dinner chat — the Spaniards called it "la sobremesa," literally "the over-table" — was a joy, and we lingered in the detritus of stoves, crusty pots and vegetable ends under a glittering moonless sky. A small kit fox with large ears visited us during hot chocolate and returned at intervals to nibble a small pile of crackers and cheese Pablo had put out for him.

"He has a special relationship with foxes," Olga said cryptically as her partner crouched at the edge of our camp, holding a piece of cheese and purring into the starlit desert.

They had been cycling for two years, having left Spain and crossed Europe, Central Asia, Siberia, Mongolia and parts of China — all by bicycle. From Vladivostok, on Russia's Pacific coast, they'd flown to British Columbia and spent a season picking apples. Now they were headed for Patagonia. After that, they planned to fly to South Africa and ride back to Spain.

"Home again!" I cried.

"Well, the road is our home now," Olga replied, nodding in a way that encompassed the hissing stove, the tent, the bikes, the valley. "But yes, we will return to where we started."

We woke before the sun was too high and ground up towards a notch in the rim of hills ahead, stopping at the top to admire the deathly silent Panamint Valley at the edge of Death Valley National Park. Another range loomed on the far side, and from this height it was possible to spot several more stacked behind, alternately colored black, yellow or red, like a groundswell marching in from the ocean. These were stretchmarks in the earth's crust, ripples emanating from the mighty Sierra now far behind me that had begun to form some 17 million years ago.

The only signs of human civilization here were the highway, which cut a solitary, angular path through the creosote, and the remains of a gold rush-era settlement cowering in the skirts of the valley's eastern flank.

"Bueno," Olga said. "¿Vamos?"

"I feel like I could sit here for days," Pablo breathed. "But yes, let's go."

Though we were alone, they spoke in whispers.

Twenty minutes later we'd reached the valley's floor, where the only sound came from the steady hum of our wheels on the road.

"What do you think?" I asked Pablo once I'd started to bore of the silence.

"¡Hermoso!" he cried. *Beautiful!*

"How does it compare to other deserts you've seen?"

He pondered this for a moment. I flicked Baxter into a lower gear as the last of the angle went out of the road. "Nobody lives here anymore," he said eventually.

"It's a national park," I pointed out.

"That's right. They've set this land aside so that nobody would live here, and therefore it hasn't developed in a natural way."

"Surely it's more natural, keeping humans out."

"Humans are natural, too," he said. "In the Gobi and in Mongolia the roads were full of villages. People would come out and yell greetings. Children ran alongside us. Their animals stood in the road."

I dropped behind him as a car approached, the first of the day. Once it passed, I pushed on the pedals to catch up.

"Isn't it nice, though? To have no humans around for a change?" I asked.

"Yes, but look at the rest of the continent. They have filled it with people. If it wasn't for the national park, the valley would not be this way."

"But the rubbish? Development? It would ruin the ecosystem."

Pablo sighed. "Probably."

Olga was waiting at a junction half an hour later, where an older path cut straight up the eastern slope away from the main highway. This was the Wild Rose Canyon Road. It was officially closed, though the Spaniards had heard it was still passable by bicycle.

The road sought out a ravine in the higher craggy reaches of the range, where a flash flood had bitten off chunks of asphalt years before. In other places, drifts of rounded stones and sand covered the road — at some point, for a few strange days some years earlier, this fissure had become a river. The sun was properly hot now, magnified by the still air. The only sound I heard was my breathing, and the occasional wheeze of Baxter's gritty chain.

Olga and I rested in the shade of a low cliff to wait for Pablo, who had fallen behind.

"He was really tired out by the Sierras," she explained. "He became sick and weak." Last time I had spotted him over my shoulder, Pablo had been on foot and whistling as he pushed his bike.

"Is he okay?"

She was staring at the patch of dirt between her legs, using a twig to brush it into mounds of concentric circles. Her face formed a rare smile. "Si el lugar es bonito, no sufre mucho." *If the surroundings are pretty, he doesn't suffer much.*

We found water at the deserted Wild Rose Campground, then climbed on in a high lunar landscape. Clouds gathered through the afternoon and we were racing nightfall by the time we reached Emigrant Pass and began speeding down into Death Valley itself.

In the morning we descended through the tourist centers of Furnace Creek and Stovepipe Wells, where we filled our bags and bottles with water — the last source for the next 75 miles. Despite this scarcity, there was a golf course at Furnace Creek, one of the driest places on the continent. I laughed at the hubris of it — "pinches americanos," I shrugged, borrowing a bit of Mexican slang — but the Spaniards looked stunned. We followed Death Valley south toward Badwater Basin, a salty flat nestled against the eastern hills, the lowest point in North America. There was no traffic beyond it, and we kept riding as stars flickered on in the purpling sky.

After we made camp, a pack of coyotes visited. The green lights of their eyes betrayed them in the beam of a head torch. They kept a respectful distance, though the pairs of eye-lights bobbed and drifted, curious, in the moonless dark. Pablo and I had taken a few hits from a joint I'd been saving, and I turned to him as we and the coyotes contemplated one another.

"I have to admit: I'm a little stoned. Is this actually happening?" North American-grade THC had claimed me yet again.

Pablo chuckled through his beard, eyes on our visitors. "They're probably saying the same thing right now: 'Oye, primo! You seeing this shit?'

"'I am, but I just ate a massive brownie and I'm almost certainly seeing things…'"

We crested Salsbury Pass the next day and entered yet another wide, barren valley. We were riding three abreast when a flash of furry legs brought us skidding to a halt.

"Yo la cogo!" Pablo cried. Spaniards use the verb "coger" when they take something or pick it up. But on the American continent, "coger" means "to fuck." It took me a moment to realize Pablo wanted to grab the tarantula, not fuck it — which was only slightly less concerning.

He scuttled about the road for a moment, mimicking the spider's attempts to evade him.

"Ufff, está fuerte," he grimaced once he'd pinned it with his fingers, then picked it up. The tarantula waggled its legs in a ferocious display of displeasure and gnashed two pairs of black fangs arranged around a misshapen pink mouth.

Olga pointed out the fine hairs shedding into Pablo's hands which, she said, the tarantula flicks at enemies to irritate their skin. "It's not dangerous, just hurts a bit when they get in your eyes. Other than that, they're not venomous."

A rental campervan approached as Olga began to explain the tarantula's diet and mating habits, and I watched a girl in the passenger's seat look from us to our bikes. It must've looked bad: crouching cyclists, bikes strewn carelessly in the road, alone in the desert and miles from anywhere. The van stopped beside us.

"Are you guys okay?" the girl asked.

Pablo turned and thrust the spider up at her. "¡Mira la tarántula!" he shouted, beaming through his beard and sunglasses, and the girl shrieked. The van took off as the Spaniards launched into a discussion on the theoretical merits of eating roasted-on-a-stick tarantula versus baked-in-foil tarantula, and potential accompaniments for each.

We parted ways the next day — I had two more ranges to cross before I would reach Nevada, while the Spaniards rolled south toward Arizona and Mexico.

"Me and you again, Baxter," I said, and took comfort from the click of his chain finding a higher gear. I stuck to quiet roads, where I saw nothing but empty plains bordered by fences and distant ranges. I liked to think about how I might look to an observer on one of those nearby peaks — a lonesome blood cell inching along one of civilization's forgotten capillaries.

A headwind made for tough riding, though I crested the second pass in the late afternoon and found an unearthly sight sprawled across the desert far below, a shining gray expanse puddled around a series of toaster-shaped monuments: the casinos of the Las Vegas Strip.

It took a full day to ride across Las Vegas, including a lengthy stop at an In 'N' Out Burger and several blocks' worth of riding along the Strip itself, a sort of adult Disneyland that, from the street, hummed with the sound of traffic, air conditioners and Jon Bon Jovi. I left via the Boulder Highway, a desolate roadway that sloped up towards Railroad Pass south-east of town. Dingy casinos — Arizona Charlie's, the Longhorn, Jokers Wild — faded in the sun between rundown apartment blocks and dollar stores, and above it all lawyers smirked from billboards addressed to drunk drivers, wife beaters, divorcees and custody battlers.

My nerves jangled with stimulation as I crested the pass and left that particularly strange plain— until I spotted a peculiar figure backlit by the south-westering sun. I was astonished to realize that he was riding a penny farthing, one of those old-timey bicycles with a front wheel as tall as he was, and with a much smaller wheel in the rear. I had never seen a penny farthing in-person, let alone one that served as a long-distance touring machine — the bar that connected his seat to the rear wheel was laden with bags. He wore a pith helmet, the kind worn by British soldiers and explorers at the height of their empire. I waved and yelled above the highway noise. The figure turned and gave a dapper little salute, and then he was gone.

I crossed a high bridge over the Colorado River into Arizona the next day and looked down at the Hoover Dam corking the water on its way to Mexico. Although Highway 93 was a rushing river of traffic, I saw few people and felt alone. At Kingman I spent an afternoon at an all-you-can-eat buffet and then wobbled out on old Route 66.

A car pulled over in front of me one afternoon outside Hackberry, and I met Betty and Nadine. They were middle-aged ladies in flowery blouses, and they offered directions, food, shelter — "Anything we can do." When I said I was fine, they tried to give me five dollars.

"When you pass the cemetery at Valentine, you're entering Hualapai country — our ancestral land," Betty said.

"So if you could remember to say a little prayer when you go through, or just talk to yourself and let the spirits know who you are, and that you'll be passing by," Nadine added. "When you reach Nelson, you can tell them that you're leaving."

With the Spaniards far behind me, I was talking to Baxter plenty enough nowadays, so I didn't see any harm in adding some spirits to the conversation. We had a long, friendly chat as I climbed through a canyon toward Peach Springs the next day, though the spirits did not acknowledge my requests to turn off a vicious headwind.

# CHAPTER 10

A day later, out in yet another wide, windswept valley, I spotted a top-heavy silhouette balanced upon a pair of skinny wheels on the road up ahead — another cycle tourist. Once I had drawn within shouting distance, I hung back to take stock of him before announcing myself.

He was small, hunched in a woolen cap and a thick, mottled brown jacket. Worn bags hung from his racks and a great big blanket sat on top, a few bits of gear wrapped inside. A wilted star-spangled banner hung from a stick poking out of the load at an odd angle. Sitting on top of the pile was a small, scruffy-looking dog in a blue-and-purple sweater looking back at me with a sort of disdain. I pulled alongside them and said hello.

The cyclist's name was Leo, and he had the kind of southern accent I'd been yearning to hear ever since I'd entered this country.

"Betchoo neyver seen a dawg ridin' a bye-sickle befur," he laughed.

As we exchanged Where-To's and Where-From's, Leo suggested that he and his dog, whose name was Sassy Max, were on their way to New Mexico or even Texas.

"Somewhere warm," he said.

For Leo, the Where-From question was more complicated. Ten years earlier, on his 50th birthday, he had retired and taken off on an old bicycle from his Missouri home.

"Never been much'f a biker befur," he said. "Just seemed the cheapest way to git started, and I wanted to see if I could do it fer-a year."

"How was it?"

"I wadn't in very good shape. I was pushin' my bike and walkin' up

61

mountains. Yep." He leaned over and spat at the road's shoulder. A couple of globules caught in his tangled beard. "I wadn't doing so good."

Leo let the silence hang between us, eyes fixed on the road ahead as it climbed toward a notch in the low, bare mesas that fenced the horizon. Each new pass acted as a step up onto the immense plateau that covers northern Arizona. Over the last couple of days, the scraggly creosote bushes of the desert had turned to fields of brown grass studded with voluptuous pinyon pines.

"Then I met this young feller," Leo said. "He told me, 'You put yourself out here. Nobody else did it for yer. And if you got yerself all the way out here, then you can keep going." I saw him watching me behind his sunglasses. "Made sense to me."

"Sure," I answered. I thought about my own trip, and everything already behind me: the dry desert, the agricultural Central Valley, the Sierras, the wet Oregon coast, the mossy Cascades. I had gotten this far all by myself. No reason why I couldn't keep going.

After taking this advice to heart, Leo kept cycling and eventually spent an entire year on the road. After that, he decided to see if he could do another year, and then another, and ten years later here he was: inching his way across Arizona — and fairly sure he hadn't been on this particular patch of road before.

"I been in Arizona, that I know, but I think it was someplace else. Tucson maybe."

We compared notes on the joys of dewless desert camping, riding under the influence of marijuana and all-you-can-eat buffets.

"Best one I had was in Michigan," he said, "but I forgot the town so I cain't go back!"

Leo also confided his theory of West Coast Miles and East Coast Miles.

"I was ridin' across New York State last summer. Now that is a big state. You ride miles and miles and miles and you never get to the end! I was thinking, 'Surely I must be across it by now, look how many miles I rode,' but I was stilla long way 'way.

"That's when I realized: there's shorter miles on the east coast and longer ones out west."

"Wait, really?"

He spat again.

"Hell yer! I mean, you think about it. You go five miles in New York State and you'll run into a town, I guarantee it. 'Nuther three miles and you got another one. Then you see there's 15 miles until the next town and you're gathering supplies and gettin' ready 'cuz 15 miles is like a wilderness over there." He wheezed out a laugh.

"Out hurr-tho, you go 40, 50 miles sometimes and you don't see shee-it! You got all those goodfernuthin' miles in between and they ain't doing nuthin', so they made 'em longer. Less miles, same distance. 'Smore economical."

I waited for another wheeze or smile to betray him, like the Cheshire cat's grin that would split Uncle Kev's face whenever he couldn't bear my credulity any longer. But it never came.

Leo was riding slowly, and the day was getting late. I needed to reach the town of Seligman to fill up on water before nightfall and figure out "Where Am I Sleeping Tonight?"

Leo sensed my twitchy legs and claimed, "You know, in my ten years of biking yer the first person to ride along wid me and talk."

As I said goodbye and pulled away, Sassy Max shuffled on her perch and though the movement wobbled Leo's bike, he handled it well.

Two days later I reached the top of the plateau and turned north toward the Grand Canyon. Junipers had joined the pinyon pines to create a forest of low, colorless trees on plains of hibernating grass. The sky was clear, but a chill hung in the air and sapped all enthusiasm from my tired legs. I entered the national park and found a campground in a nondescript bit of forest, built my tent and sat around wondering what to do. This whole detour from the coast — weeks of riding — had been leading up to this moment of arrival but I felt no joy. There was no warmth in the sunshine, and my yawning Hunger was angrier than usual. I sat on a bench in my allocated campsite between van people and car campers, stewing over what I thought was an outrageous dollar-a-minute charge for hot showers.

I felt lethargic and underwhelmed, uninspired by the forest, but with nothing to occupy me but a smelly tent, what else did I have to do but keep moving? I rode a bagless Baxter to the supermarket — if I hadn't been so hungry, a sour piece of me might have grumbled about Americans building a supermarket at the Grand Canyon — and left with corn chips, salsa and several beers to see what all the fuss was about.

There is no overture or prelude as you approach the Grand Canyon, nothing to warn you of what's coming. One moment you're walking in a sparse, unremarkable forest and the next you're at the edge of an ochre abyss wide and deep enough to hold an ocean. It is filled with jutting sandstone temples of red and purple and bordered by cliffs stacked upon multi-colored cliffs, a geologic rainbow from deep violet to sandy yellow. Desert plains as wide as towns undulate between the vertical rock. The artist behind it all is the green Colorado River which, based on the few available glimpses from the rim, appears as a shy and slender creek running through a small crack in the canyon's floor. The effect of this sudden arrival is a bit like an orchestra breaking a deep silence with a single magnificent note: *Ta-daaaa!*

I was sitting on a quiet patch of the southern rim, drinking beer and smoking the last of a bud I'd been nursing since Yosemite when a young man appeared at my side. He wore a down vest, gel in his hair and white sneakers, like a college student-turned-office worker enjoying disposable income for the first time. He wore a pair of sunglasses in the sporty wrap-around style that Australians affectionately call "speed dealers."

"What beautiful pics," he muttered, awe in his voice and smartphone in his hand. When I offered to take photos, he took his time exhibiting a variety of poses: hands in pockets, casual style; hands on hips, staring away over his shoulder; hands clasped as he crouched on his haunches, like a tech entrepreneur in a sports team metaphor.

"You are traveling?" he asked in slightly stilted English as I handed his phone back.

"Yeah," I replied. "You?"

"I'm visiting Arizona for business, but I have always wanted to see the canyon."

We turned to consider the view together.

"Stunning, isn't it?" I said.

"Yes," he whispered.

A community of small wrens were darting and chirping merrily in some bushes nearby, oblivious to the humans in their midst. Suddenly, a burst of warning squeaks from a sentry sent them diving for cover. A tense silence followed, during which my new friend nudged me and pointed out a red-tailed hawk cruising overhead, head cocked and scanning the canyon's edge.

"So," I said after half a minute, once the hawk had disappeared and the wrens resumed their happy racket. "Where's your accent from?"

"Guadalajara," he replied, the name rattling like marbles in a jar. He lifted the purple-and-green reflective lenses from his eyes and offered his hand. "You know it?"

I had seen it on maps — a city hidden deep inside the invisible, enticing and slightly threatening presence that was Mexico, waiting over the southern horizon. The country had been haunting me for a while. For three months now, Americans and Canadians alike had warned that crossing into their southern neighbor meant almost certain death at the hands of gangs, cartels, bandits, police or some combination thereof. Many took apparent pleasure in these predictions of doom. Some were confident enough to predict my likely cause of death: decapitation.

Yes, decapitation. They were fascinated with the idea. And everyone who said it did so in the same way — the wording, the emphases, even the tone of voice were all identical.

I knew better than to believe them — Colombia had a similar reputation, after all, and I had lived there in relative safety for 12 months. I knew Mexico had its problems, but I also felt that my command of Spanish and general familiarity with Latino culture would help me navigate most hazards. But as I approached the frontier, any thought of Mexico was besieged by ranks of glassy-eyed Anglo-Americans and Canadians I'd met in highway diners, forested campgrounds and forlorn gas stations chanting as one: "Decapitation. Decapitation. Decapitation."

Now, I told my new friend about these warnings, and confessed my growing fear.

"I know I shouldn't believe them," I said, "but I keep hearing it again and again. It's in my head. So I have to ask: Will I be in danger down there?"

He watched me for a moment, then glanced up to Baxter propped against a nearby tree.

"You are going to be on small roads, in small towns and villages, yes?"

"I would think so, yeah," I said. "It's always better to avoid the big highways."

He nodded. "And you travel only with a bicycle? You carry everything in this way?"

"That's right."

There was a penetrative clarity to his eyes now. For most of the people I met each day, my life in a tent and on Baxter put me well outside the scope of daily reality. This created a small wall between us, and from behind it they could pretend I was crazy, delusional, adventurous, admirable, whatever they wanted. The result rendered me as little more than a caricature, a small projection of their own hopes, fears and biases.

But a precious few really understood. I watched it dawn across their faces that I was no lunatic or hero — just a regular person who'd hopped on a bike one day and hadn't turned back by bedtime. They briefly saw the world as I did and knew that with just a little preparation, they were equally capable of such a thing.

A small smile had now formed between his cheeks and I was sure I didn't imagine the weight behind his next words.

"I think you will really enjoy Mexico," he said. I had been waiting months for someone to say those words. I felt them wash the fear away.

We shook hands again to say goodbye, and I lingered by the canyon's rim to soak in the last of the sunset colors and the feeling he'd left behind. Robbie was coming. Mexico was nothing to be afraid of. It might even be fun. And Robbie was coming.

# CHAPTER 11

The next day I hiked a busy trail down into the canyon, where I was startled to find that the small crack at its bottom was actually a forbidding chasm in its own right, and that the slender creek was really a pulsing freshwater highway scraping and sawing deep into the plateau. I had my first wash in well over a week in the Colorado River (*Who needs a dollar-a-minute shower?* I thought smugly) and shared a campsite with a retired schoolteacher beside a little tributary creek.

"This all used to be seabed," she said, gesturing up at the black walls pinching a starlit sky. "Over time it rose and compressed to form the plateau and, well, then the river came."

In the morning I tramped back up through the folds in the terraced cliffs and watched the dust on my shoes turn from purple to orange to red to yellow. As I rested, I kicked my feet together and watched the specks drift away, failing to fathom the deep vaults of time through which they'd traveled to be here.

I reached the canyon's rim and wandered along to find a sheltered, sunny place to sit. When I let my gaze stray out over the canyon, I felt myself shrinking into my boots as the world grew strange and indifferent, just as it had atop the Yosemite Valley.

As silence settled, though, I heard chirruping and saw a group of wrens out socializing in a nearby bush. Beetles picked their way through the dirt and twigs around me. Overhead, California condors rode invisible thermals at the canyon's edge, their bald and shriveled heads scanning for a perch. The sun was still high enough to filter in and warm my tired bones.

I fixed my gaze back onto the wider canyon, letting the world grow large around me again. Now, however, with the wrens playing and the condors swooping and the beetles beetling, I felt an absence of fear. The aimlessness that came with an empty mind was still there — there was no child or spouse or career tugging at the edges of my attention — but the fear had gone.

The landscape and its creatures had primed me for this moment. By stepping out of normal life, the cycle tourist becomes a bystander at the nexus of human civilization and the wider world. They see it all: swarms of workers filling the big-city commercial hives, the creak of living timber in a storm, the immovable silence of the desert, the heavy clunk and shriek of industry on the move, the yips of coyotes in rural backyards, the conferences of tourists at the bucket list monuments, the rustle of plastic caught in barbed wire. To step out of civilization is to watch it all race away without you and remember that the Earth remains a very large place.

And yet, despite all this solitary talk of stepping away and looking on, I'd found places for myself everywhere. I'd fit in the easy company of Stella, Eric and Ray. Once I'd learned not to jump at every snapping twig, I felt at home as the nighttime creatures came and went around my tent. I felt at home in dry mountain passes with Olga and Pablo when we'd whispered to one another — even though we were the only people for miles — because the valleys below felt as sacred as a church. This feeling was strong in the impromptu communities of northern California's hiker-biker campsites, and it surged when Betty and Nadine offered a sort of supernatural meet-and-greet with the spiritual guardians of their land. I felt it in silent desert mountains, water-rent chasms and solemn forests where the trees recited histories in rhythmic languages I would never understand. I felt it in an apartment that wasn't mine, lying in the arms of a woman I'd only just met. And I felt it when a stranger's smile and words of assurance magically stripped darkness from the southern horizon. I would find this feeling down there, too.

I still had no real life to "go back to" in the conventional sense, and therefore no immediately practical application for this feeling of belonging in a wide and strange world. But from this vantage point, as one among billions of living things sharing a bikeable planet, the universe appeared to require very little: do right by the life forms around me, love the family that evolution had trained me to love and find ways to have fun along the way. I stood, walked to Baxter, prepared him for the long ride to the Robbie Rendezvous and went to bed warmed by feelings of brother- and sisterhood with all living things.

\* \* \*

In the morning I left Grand Canyon National Park and climbed over the icy San Francisco Peaks to Flagstaff, where I tried not to ogle college girls — it had been weeks since I'd spent any time with people my own age. I smoked cigars and got drunk alone celebrating my 5,000th kilometer in Oak Creek Canyon. I sent Hailee a postcard in Sedona.

In Prescott I spent a day in a buffet (pacing myself this time) and eavesdropping.

"One time I had to escort a truck full of bodies back to Saigon," said a man in the booth behind me. "And you know, it's a long trip. Where're you gonna sit?"

"Oh shoot, right on the casket huh?" his companion replied knowingly.

"You'd be so lucky," scoffed the first. "Nope, they was all in plastic bags, one of 'em a senator's boy, somebody said. They made an alright seat though, hard as they was."

I camped in a park on the outskirts of town and rose early, sensing the edge of the plateau now, and pushing on Baxter's high gears as I sped out of the ponderosa and into the pinyon, leaning into corners and crouching low on the straights, hollering along to Bruce Springsteen's *Dancing in the Dark*.

The road was a country all its own, and by now I navigated it like a native. I could spot a pothole from 100 meters at high speed and felt confident pushing wide into traffic to dodge shoddy road repairs, shredded truck tires and drifts of pebbles pried loose from the asphalt. The road became a rollercoaster past Yarnell on a gloomy afternoon, a final leap off the great tabletop as vast plains of creosote stretched from the ramparts' feet to a horizon lost in bluish haze. Large, jagged hills loomed like fragments cut adrift from a mothership. The highway cut a path between them, with long West Coast Miles between the bends. Down in the desert, citizens of Congress and Aguila built high fences around their homes and warned me about their neighbors.

I felt no desire to linger in this unlovely country. At night I hopped fences and watched airplanes file one-by-one toward Los Angeles, just a few minutes away for them but a world away from me, lying in the dirt beside my fire. Days passed where I spoke to no-one but the odd shopkeeper. The towns were rubbish-strewn yards and broken RVs, demountable homes hunkered together amid piles of scrap metal, all

69

doggedly flying the stars and stripes.

At Quartzite I stole McDonald's Wi-Fi to contact the world and found a message from Hailee. My postcard had "made her week." I read and reread her message, added the songs she'd sent to my mp3 player — Bedouin Soundclash, Fleet Foxes — and listened greedily to the lyrics for hidden meanings. There was also a message from Robbie: "One more week until I fly!"

I crossed the Colorado River and entered California again, hugging the white lines of crumbling highways. I crossed weird patches of Central Valley-style agriculture and grid towns where dollar store cashiers addressed me in Spanish. A cook in Brawley said I would find torta sandwiches just like hers south of the border. "None as good as mine, though," she winked.

It was a disorienting landscape — the road wound through sand dunes for an hour and then suddenly I was listening to the rat-a-tat of sprinklers and riding between canals and crops. Black helicopters swooped overhead and packs of green-and-white Border Patrol SUVs scurried about in the southern distance, flashing lights illuminating plumes of dust.

I left the artificially verdant Imperial Valley and re-entered the desert, pushing hard until I spotted a burst bag of trail mix in the road. It had evidently fallen out of a car, and ants had only just discovered the chocolate pieces. I dusted them away, gobbled it all down in the shade of an embankment and moved on, mumbling Leo's words: "You put yourself out here." I knew nothing about San Diego, but its name was magic with the promise of rest and a familiar face.

The Santa Ana Mountains now loomed ahead, gathering clouds, the final barrier before the coast. I camped at their feet and started under heavy skies, and soon a rainstorm swept in from the west, pushed by a headwind tugging at every loose fold and strap on Baxter and me. It took the whole morning to get over the first pass and down into Jacumba Hot Springs. The wind was so strong that it pulled me to a stop if I didn't pedal, even on the downhills.

I was struggling down Jacumba's empty main street when a voice reached me over the wind: "You just missed a guy on a big-wheel bike!"

I stopped and looked around. The speaker wore a flat brim hat and sat in an old white sedan. His smile offered encouragement.

"He's probably 15 miles ahead, so you'll catch him."

"Is he wearing a funny hat? Like a pith helmet?"

The man's grin widened. "You know Joff?"

"I think I saw him outside Vegas, but I didn't get to talk to him."

"Well, he only just left my place. He's moving slow, you'll catch him for sure."

"Honestly? I think I'm gonna crawl in my tent and sleep the rest of the day away."

"Oh," he sounded concerned. "I mean, I got an RV out front of my place. You should come crash there — Joff slept in it last night, it's nice and dry."

I followed the man — his name was Walker — back to his bungalow. Walker was in his mid-30's but dressed in the baggy pants and skater shoes of a kid half his age. He had a kind of rambling, semi-stoned energy and we instantly got along. He showed me Joff's video diaries, which were all over YouTube, and introduced me to his favorite Southern California surf punk-turned-reggae bands. Later, he took me down to the RV to stash my bags.

"I'm going through a divorce," he suddenly announced once we were inside. Then he added, "My kids are coming around soon. I thought you should know. It's still kind of weird."

The RV was old and slightly musty but the bed was comfortable, and the clouds outside were starting to look heavy again. As I unpacked, Walker sat in the swivel chairs up front.

"Are you and your family okay?" I asked. "I mean, how recent are we talking?"

"She left last weekend," Walker said. "She says she's not coming back."

"What happened?"

"I made a mistake," he said. He looked at his hands, curled in the lap of his jeans.

"Oh, man," I said lamely, then, "My parents broke up a few years back."

"Why?"

"The same reason," I said. "More or less."

"Did you forgive him?"

I hadn't, but I told Walker that I had.

"My grandfather was this old Mexican man," Walker said. "Never forgave me for not learning Spanish. But I been thinking about some advice he gave me when I was a kid. The first thing was: 'Look after your back. You'll need it when you're old.'"

"Sounds about right."

"The second one was this poem," and he fished his phone out of his hoodie pocket, started thumbing it. "You ever heard of *If*? Rudyard Kipling?"

He read it out, a Victorian fantasy of stoic masculinity. After, I left the silence untouched.

"It's really speaking to me right now," he whispered in the silence that followed.

Later, I met Walker's daughters, aged 11 and 13.

"Another cyclist?" The elder, named Brianna, looked at her dad.

"What did you think of Joff?" I said. "Pretty cool, huh?"

"He was stinky," the younger, Ashley, wrinkled her nose.

In the late afternoon, as Walker drove us into San Diego for an annual "buy a dozen, get a dozen free" deal at Krispy Kreme, I noticed how the girls were quickly learning a skill that white collar workers call "managing up." They reminded Walker to put gas in the car, for example, and I watched them gauge his behavior to figure out how much he'd been smoking that day.

When we found that the Krispy Kreme line was hours long, Walker drove us to a discount supermarket nearby called Grocery Outlet (thrifty cyclists call it "Gross Out") for cut-price pints of Ben and Jerry's pina colada flavor. We visited all his old haunts — his parents' favorite pizzeria, views into Mexico from the summit of Mount Helix, a suspension bridge across a hidden canyon in Banker's Hill, the scruffy surfer's suburb of Ocean Beach. Walker smoked a joint by the water and then, as we drove back up the hill to Jacumba, began slumping over the wheel and complaining of drowsiness.

"I'm just gonna pull us over here and take a quick nap before we get home," he said.

"Daaaad," the girls groaned from the back seat.

I offered to drive. I hadn't been behind the wheel in months, and never on the right-hand side of the road, but I too was looking forward to my bed. Brianna directed me home while her dad snoozed in the passenger's seat beside me.

* * *

I was warm and dry that night and fell into a deep sleep as the RV swayed and rattled under the onslaught of a storm. The sky had cleared by morning, but the previous day's headwind remained. I had two more peaks to cross before a 35-mile descent into San Diego.

I bid Brianna and Ashley goodbye, and once the girls had gone to school I tried to assure Walker that his family — in whatever new form it was taking — would be okay.

"Give them time, hold no grudges, always be there," I said. "It's all you can do."

The first big hill, up through Boulevard and Live Oak Springs, was devilishly steep and all the harder for the wind pushing me back toward the desert. After a short downhill holiday, I joined roaring Interstate 8 where the climb wasn't as steep as the first and the wind wasn't as strong. As I rounded a bend I saw the cars dipping up ahead and knew the top was close.

Things sometimes became weird on long climbs. Exhaustion evaporated, but it was more like my legs had found perpetual motion than a surge of energy. The cosmic synthesizers of *La Femme d'Argent* by Air drove me on. Sweat ran around my eyes and dripped from my nose. My head felt airy, my legs were light and powerful and I kept whispering a single syllable: "Yeeaaah."

I was sick of the cold, sick of monotonous desert riding, sick of feeling hungry all the time, but most of all I was sick of the silence. Sick of talking to Baxter, who never talked back. I thought about my family and Christmas without them. I thought about Brianna and Ashley, who were early to the realization we all end up having about our parents: that their dad wasn't a superhero, just some guy. I thought about the way Walker's voice had broken on the final line of Kipling's poem. I allowed myself to acknowledge the loneliness of the previous weeks, and the coming end of it all pulled my legs through each stroke of the pedals.

"Yeeeeeeaaaaaah."

The road leveled out beneath my wheels and suddenly I saw the city huddled in the distance by an ocean I'd last seen from Berkeley. I sat up in the saddle, hooting and pumping fists above my helmeted head, and some legend in a passing car offered a congratulatory beep and thumbs-up through her open window. I swore and I screamed and then my voice cracked and I was crying, then sobbing, and I didn't stop for a long time, tears drying on my face as Baxter rolled off the mountain towards the water.

# CHAPTER 12

"Holy shit," Robbie yelled over his shoulder, then pointed to a line of low hills up ahead. "Is that the border?"

We were riding into Border Field State Park, a rectangular zone of protected salt marsh wedged between the beach, Interstate 5 and the international frontier, marked by a high wall that followed the hills down onto the beach, then poked out beyond the breakers.

We had just left the highway, which punctured the frontier's concrete barrier to become the Carretera Transpeninsular, a thousand-mile stretch of asphalt that would carry us the dusty length of Baja California.

But that was tomorrow's problem — for now, Robbie and I focused on finding a comfortable place to pitch our tents and spend our first night on the road together, and our last night in the United States. We had planned to camp in Border Field because it was as close to the frontier as you could get. This would put us in a good position to cross first thing in the morning, escape Tijuana and make some progress toward Ensenada, where I had organized a Warmshowers host for a couple of days before Christmas.

Robbie and I had met as planned in San Diego, after he'd landed in Los Angeles and rode south over several days. Newly freed from his nine-to-five and having already stayed with a Warmshowers family and cycled the barren length of a military base, Robbie was buzzing. We had stopped for lunch at the waterfront in Coronado and spent a good hour examining one another's bikes. Robbie's ride was built on a battered red frame fitted with black steel racks, fenders and shining new wheels. Oscar — as the bike had been christened — was a bit smaller than

Baxter, which was strange because Rob stands a full head taller than me.

At two meters, Robbie was often the tallest of any group he found himself in, which meant others often looked instinctively to him to make decisions. He carried himself surprisingly gently for his size, made his way carefully through the world and spoke in soft, measured tones that hinted at his law education. His current excitement showed in his rapid speech and the way he would look from the bikes to me and back again with an almost maniacal grin shining out from his brown eyes.

"I can't believe I'm here," he said.

On a trail leading into the park we met a white-haired baby boomer walking his white-haired dog. He said we shouldn't have any trouble pitching our tents and spending the night on the marsh. We were almost in the shadow of the wall. Tijuana's boxy cinder block apartments squashed up against the far side, the loftier windows offering a peek into their northern neighbor's backyard.

"The beach is nice, but nobody comes here anymore," the dog-walker said. "Back in the eighties you could sit on the sand, walk into Mexico to buy a beer and a fish taco and then stroll back into America to eat it." He shrugged. "It's still nice and all, but I sorta miss the way it was."

Robbie and I followed a trail that wound between tall bushes, stands of hardy coastal grasses and claggy mud pits until our tires sank into the soil. Leaving our bikes, we wandered over the dunes and sat on the beach. We chattered incessantly. He filled me in with the latest news of mutual friends back home and then smiled through stories of my journey thus far — campsites, cyclists, Hailee — many of which he had already heard over the phone. While I talked, he collected shells, patterned pebbles, sun-bleached flecks of driftwood and shiny pieces of smelly kelp, handing each to me for inspection. When I handed a treasure back, he added it to a small mound on the sand between us.

"It's the Cool Pile," he explained. "It's where I keep the Cool Things." When the warmth of the dipping sun began to wane, we left the Cool Pile to find a campsite-worthy patch of grass between the low bushes of the marsh.

We laid our panniers on the grass and began to unpack. Having prepared for this trip in a hurry, Robbie was anxious to see if his tent and portable stove would be up to the rigors of Mexican cycle touring. He was, however, especially pleased with two particular pieces of his kit.

"My sleeping bag cost seven dollars," he grinned.

"But Rob, it's the middle of winter!"

"I got it at a supermarket," he went on. "It was a combo deal with woolly socks."

His other treasure was a spoon, long-handled for reaching into deep tins and cooking pots. It was light and strong like a weapon and unlike the sleeping bag, which worried me, was perfect for a scrappy life on the road.

"Made from the same gear they built the space shuttles with," Robbie claimed.

"What did they build the space shuttles with?"

"I don't know," he admitted. "But it must be good. The spoon cost more than the bag."

After building and comparing our tents, we started on dinner — pasta with fried veggies and a jar of sauce. I was offering unnecessary zucchini-chopping advice to Rob when he looked over his shoulder and then skyward, suddenly alert.

There was a pale, eerie light on his face. Now conscious of a machine's roar that had grown in volume over the last minute or so, I followed his gaze to find a helicopter hovering overhead, beaming a spotlight that bathed the grass, bushes and bags around us in a pale glow against the gathering twilight.

The helicopter was black. Yellow lettering announced that it belonged to the United States Border Patrol, the same kind that I'd often seen moving in packs above the desert weeks earlier. It hovered three or four stories above us and a little to the west. The brush around us shuddered in the draft cascading off its rotor blades. Robbie and I waved.

Then a stocky man in an olive-green jumpsuit and matching motorcycle helmet appeared from behind a nearby bush. He pushed his visor back and put his hands on his hips, displaying an official-looking insignia on his shoulder.

"What do you think you're doing here?" he demanded over the drone of the helicopter.

"Camping," Robbie replied, a lawyer's air of mildly irritated authority in his voice.

The officer's eyes widened. He huffed up his chest, thrust a thick finger at the wall on the hill and shouted: "You know that's Mek-see-koh over there?"

"That's right," Robbie agreed, nodding slowly as if he'd just realized he was speaking with a simpleton. He pointed to his chest, then to mine. "We're going there tomorrow."

The man let his arm drop and took a step back, his face reddening, eyes darting from us — a pair of skinny white boys in padded shorts — to the bicycles and gear strewn on the grass.

*At least we showered this morning*, I thought.

"Lemme see your passports," he ordered, hand out. We obliged, and then he walked to a quad bike parked behind the bush. He muttered into a radio, his back turned. Robbie looked at me. He raised his eyebrows.

"You can't stay here," the officer said as he returned. "This is a restricted area."

I'd had several encounters with American law enforcement over the last few months. Generally speaking, I had found them to be overbearing and — from the way they delivered their one-liners — convinced they were starring in a bad Hollywood movie.

However, I had also found them fairly open to simple reasoning. I knew that my pale Anglo face put me at a significant advantage in these situations, and I had noticed that subduing the Australian nasality of my accent and leaning on its British roots gave me an almost invincible combination of charm and authority to many American ears. Now it was my turn to swell up my chest, and I deployed both my whiteness and my accent to their full effect.

"Hold on a second," I began matter-of-factly. "'Restricted area?' This is a state park. I've been camping in state parks for months. Besides, you're not really going to send us back to the Interstate at this time of night, are you? Where are we going to sleep?"

The officer glanced towards the ocean, where the sun had already disappeared. Lights were coming on in Tijuana. San Diego suburbs shimmered in a line on the northern horizon.

"Give me a second," he replied at last, and stepped behind the bush again. The helicopter *thwopped* overhead and when Robbie looked at me now, his eyebrows had almost disappeared into his hairline. The officer returned.

"I'm going to speak with my superior," he said. "If I don't come back, you can stay — but I want you out of here at dawn. If you see my face again," he pointed at his meaty chin, and then at us, "it means you have to go."

He mounted his quad bike and buzzed away. The helicopter soon followed.

Robbie let silence reign in our darkening patch of marsh for almost half a minute before he spoke.

"So… was that unusual for you?" he said. "Or should I get used to searchlights and helicopters and angry armed men?"

We finished making dinner and ate it from the pot. As darkness fell, we spied sharp red lights fixed atop tall, thin antennae hidden among the bushes, virtually invisible during the day. Standing around five meters high, they were arranged in a grid at 30-meter intervals around us.

So this was more of a tactical buffer zone than a state park, a heavily-surveilled gauntlet for would-be migrants before they could reach the relative safety and anonymity of civilization. Robbie and I stretched out after dinner, imagining ourselves on infrared cameras in subterranean control rooms. We imitated evening briefings with our presence as a footnote:

"'Oh, and you'll notice two civilians in Sector 7G. They're Australian nationals and they're camping, apparently,'" Robbie said in a voice that was part-Valley Girl, part-ESPN announcer — accents were never his talent.

"'Try not to shoot them. Management would prefer to avoid a diplomatic incident,'" I barked in my best impersonation of Kilgore, a surfing military man from *Apocalypse Now*.

"Seriously though, what are those tower things?" Robbie wondered, peering at the nearest light. "Cameras? Microphones?"

"Only one way to find out," I said, then leaned back and whispered into the bushes. "The Australian named Robbie has a brick of cocaine stuffed inside his panniers. My nanna, Thelma Gaff, was the second JFK shooter in Dallas and she's been bragging about it at the Tamworth Country Women's Association for 50 years. Oh, and the United States Border Patrol drives oversized SUVs to compensate for their tiny, shriveled..."

"The views expressed here only represent the individual who said them," Robbie cut in, addressing the same bush. "Specifically, the shorter of the two — wearing the black hoodie and blue pants. The taller one loves America, loves the Border Patrol and, uh, hates communism?"

Though our breath turned to clouds in front of our faces and we dared not light a fire, we stayed up late, relishing our first night together on the road. Our only visitor was the helicopter, which returned three times over the next several hours. It flew much higher than its first visit and it never used the spotlight, but every time it centered its high, wide orbit on our little campsite.

# CHAPTER 13

With my visa up and winter chasing us into this last warm corner of the west, there was nowhere to go but south. After all the detours and side trips, the long, thin peninsula of Baja California would funnel us southward and help to claim a few quick degrees of latitude towards Patagonia.

In the morning, the concrete border complex swallowed us as we pushed our bikes up a ramp and entered a narrow tunnel. Bulky, white-skinned Border Patrol officers became skinny, brown-skinned kids in olive-green military uniforms, bowl-like helmets wobbling on their small heads. They loitered around while we filled out paperwork and paid the fee for a six-month tourist visa.

I'd managed to use up my U.S. visa to the day, but Robbie and I doubted we'd do the same in Mexico. We'd formed a rough schedule for the time we'd need to traverse its exotically named states: two, perhaps three weeks to reach Baja's southern port of La Paz, a boat ride across the Sea of Cortez to Mazatlán and a quick jaunt up to Mexico City. From the metropolis we would dash down into the narrowing isthmus of Central America.

Two months total, we decided. Three, tops.

The border crossing deposited us in the smoggy heart of Tijuana where the air was heavy with pollution and the smoke from carne asada barbecues, buzzing with heat reflecting off the concrete on this sunny southern side of the wall. The traffic was slow with a sort of halting rhythm that the assertive cyclist could easily slip into.

Robbie and I followed a busy coast road out of town, then pulled over at a likely looking taco stand. Benches surrounded an open-air kitchen as an ocean breeze whipped dust up the street. We ordered tacos de pescado and camarón — *fish* and *prawn* — to go with Pacífico beers. As we waited for our food, three men ambled over from three different pickup trucks and took their places at the bar, each with the weighty presence of a farmer. They tipped their large cowboy hats back in the shade, sipped appreciatively at their beers, nodded to one another and at us.

We weren't in the countryside yet — the highway down here was a commercial strip — but we were out of the city, and with glimpses of bare hills and ocean we were getting a feel for the landscape. I felt the familiar sights of the morning — ranks of late-model automobiles gleaming in vast parking lots, beige strip malls, friendly dogs on leashes, an exaggerated sense of California relaxation — fading behind me. Skinny dogs migrated between storefronts. Frantic horns and snare drums raced from loudspeakers. Kitchen smoke carried hints of spice on the bracing ocean air. The cars and trucks were all older down here, and in their age — dents and dings, replaced doors and bits of wire holding bumpers together — each became an individual.

Rob and I toasted a new country as the tacos arrived, fluffy batter hiding soft, meaty pieces of fish and prawn along with crunchy cabbage, onions, creamy mayo and the hot sauce of your choice. Most of the contents spilled back onto my plate before I'd finished — it would take a while to master the taco-eating technique.

"What's into you?" I asked Robbie, and he flashed his pearly whites my way.

"I can get used to this," he said.

As we pushed along the coast towards Ensenada over the next couple of days I felt a distinct absence of the uncertainty that had descended in the deserts of Arizona and California. There was no feeling one another out with Robbie. I already knew him well, and we quickly fell into the old roles we had assumed back in Colombia: I was the translator, making contacts and gathering information about potential campsites or points of interest, while Rob was the analytical thinker who compared that information with conflicting reports we'd heard earlier in the day. He also had an eye for comfort and camp wellbeing that I lacked — by the second day he had added powdered milk to morning oatmeal, fresh vegetables and canned beans to dinner and eliminated instant noodle packets from our diet altogether.

When I had been cycling with Miki, Pablo and Olga, I had often tuned out the landscape as we absorbed ourselves in get-to-know-you chatter. But cycling with Robbie was like having a second set of eyes and ears. Many of the towns and hamlets we passed looked identical to me — concrete streets and cinder block buildings sinking into the sand — but to Robbie, every town had a unique look and feel. It would be weeks before I would learn to see them in this way.

In Ensenada we stayed with Jorge, a beaming engineering student who lived with his parents and young brother. Jorge could do no wrong in his parents' eyes and so, with very little parental consultation, he announced that we were welcome to stay for Christmas. This invitation was also extended to Tommy, a tall and lean American who had taken several months to ride to Mexico from his home in Bellingham, Washington, way up by the Canadian border.

Tommy wore a goatee beard and his curly hair long, so that it cascaded in brown locks down his back. His bicycle was a lanky white relic with large, slender wheels — a light rig made for road riding. The most distinctive piece of Tommy's kit — aside from a pair of Spandex bike shorts bearing an apple-shaped patch on the bum embossed with the word "Bellinghome" — were a pair of tall buckets mounted on his front rack in place of panniers.

"They're mayonnaise buckets," he winked. "Got 'em from a Peruvian restaurant I was working at back home. They make good camping stools."

Tommy's ride down the west coast had been a leisurely affair. He described a large bicycle gang that generally rose at 10 a.m., spent several hours feeding itself on pancakes, then rode only as far as the next liquor store and its closest campground.

On Christmas Eve we joined Jorge's family at the house of his grandmother — "mi abuelita," he called her — a small apartment of floral wallpaper and airbrushed portraits of unsmiling relatives. The place filled to capacity until midnight, when we were bid to eat.

It tasted unlike any Christmas I'd had before. Jorge's father brought out a plate of smoky, mysterious romeritos — herbs, potatoes and mole sauce — which he said was a specialty of Mexico City, his hometown. There was a shredded turkey dish in a creamy sauce, a strange marshmallow and fruit salad soup, a second fruity salad, mashed potato, a warming drink made with cookie dough and a bracing soup like a Colombian caldo, full of fatty chunks of sheep's stomach. Everyone seemed to know about the legendary Hunger of Jorge's cyclists, and Robbie, Tommy and I were endlessly bid back to the table by uncles and cousins. Robbie was mystified by this — he had barely been on the road a week, and his Hunger had not yet developed — but he pushed his limited Spanish to start food-related conversations with Jorge's relatives, asking after recipes and offering comparisons with Australian Christmas dishes.

As we left, abuelita embraced each of the tall ciclistas and invited us back for what she called "una gran tradición mexicana: el recalentado." Literally translated as "the reheated," December 25th was a day for finishing leftovers.

"Oh, hell yeah," Tommy groaned when I translated, smacking his lips. Abuelita cackled with delight.

"That romeritos is mine," Robbie claimed, prompting a private smile from Jorge's father.

There was more family about the next morning and we spent most of the day in abuelita's lounge room, lazing, chatting and digesting. Occasionally new faces would appear, young couples and families from out of town doing their rounds from house to house. All were swiftly recruited for recalentado duties and sat at a table with a piled-high plate or three.

"Ay dios mío," they would moan. Then they would start shoveling it in, muttering obligatory compliments to the chef around mouthfuls.

It was at the family's kitchen table the next morning — slurping a beef stew called birria to swamp a hangover caused by a riotous night out with Jorge and his friends — that the landscape ahead began to take shape. Baja, we learned, had many beautiful beaches, but most were along the Sea of Cortez coast, facing the mainland and quite a distance down the peninsula. Before then we would see cardon cacti that grew up to 15 meters tall and a tree called a cirio, which nobody seemed able to describe. And then there was the mainland.

"People are different down there," Jorge's father said cryptically. "More hot-headed. But you're going to love it. Mexico is magic." We would hear this slogan often: "México es mágico." He told us about Mexico City, a megalopolis home to at least 21 million people — almost as much as the entire population of Australia.

"It's our New York City," Jorge gushed. "You walk the streets with millions of people, you see the guards at the presidential palace with their fancy uniforms, the giant flag over the square at Zócalo — you feel like you're at the center of the world."

Jorge's father made us promise to spend time in Chiapas, a southern state full of ancient pyramids poking through a canopy of thick jungle — visions which felt alien out here in this distant and dusty corner of the country. The horizon of unknown — which had seemed perilously close for weeks in Arizona and California — now drifted away as the country began to fill with features, cities and stories. I had bought a large Mexican roadmap in San Diego, and we began scribbling notes among the unfamiliar names of towns and cities.

"It's already late," Jorge said as we heaved panniers onto our steeds in the afternoon sun. "Do you want to stay another day?"

"This is what Mexico's going to be like," Robbie said. "We won't be allowed to leave anywhere."

# CHAPTER 14

The basin floor was cut here and there by vados, dried creek beds scoured out by floodwaters once every few years. There were no bridges — the road simply dipped in and then out of them — and most were deep enough to hide a semi-trailer from oncoming motorists.

We were in a long vado when Tommy called "sem-eye back" from the rear — at some point after we took the stage of an Ensenada karaoke bar to sing Backstreet Boys' *I Want It That Way* together, Tommy had joined up with Robbie and I.

Baja California's Transpeninsular Highway had quickly left civilization, and our bags were currently weighed down with enough food and water for three days of riding. Robbie also carried a little leftover rum from the previous night's New Year's Eve celebrations, which had occurred in a narrow valley under a giant cardon cactus.

At the same moment that Tommy warned of the approaching semi, a hatchback appeared at the far rim, coming towards us. The highway had no shoulder, and therefore was not wide enough for the hatchback, the truck and a cyclist to safely pass each other simultaneously.

"Don't you do it," I muttered at the unseen semi-trailer, adding to the curses I heard coming from Rob and Tommy. "Don't you do it don't you do it don'tyoudoityoumotherfucker..."

But the engine's roar shifted to a higher pitch as the trucker found a gear and stepped on the accelerator. I heard Rob yell as it passed him, and I glimpsed a pair of horrified middle-aged faces through the hatchback's windscreen as it hugged the far shoulder to make way, dust kicking from its outer wheels. I was hollering with a kind of impotent, incoherent fury now, and held Baxter to the road's slippery edge as a shockwave broke over me, a split second of pressure that sucked the sound from my ears like the moment before the pitching lip of a large wave cracks against the ocean's surface. Then came the thunder, a flash of red chassis and the trailer clattering within a meter of my shoulder and swallowing my screams and then it was gone, fishtailing like a kite behind the engine, and I slumped over the handlebars and pulled away into an old gravel pit. I crouched in the dust, squeezing my eyelids shut against the desert glare, hands shaking with the adrenaline reverberating through my system.

Rob pulled up, dismounted and rummaged in his bags for the leftover rum. We each took a long drink, shared a banana and a few scoops of peanut butter from the jar and after a while I stopped talking about going home.

"New Year's Day, man," Tommy shrugged, squinting at the empty road. "Everybody's hungover and it's bright as shit out here."

In these remote northern reaches, Highway One's most common sign of civilization was the abandoned building. Most had been stores or restaurants, now blackened and gutted. They were creepy, anonymous places where groups of men gathered at night to stand around fires, drink beer and shatter empties on the stony ground. They were also popular public bathrooms.

However, we were drawn to them like oases. The nights in Baja were much colder than any of us had expected ("I thought it was palm trees and warm water all the way to Cabo," Tommy grumbled), and the walls and occasional roof of an abandoned building provided some protection from night winds traveling unimpeded across the desert.

Demoralized by the near miss with the truck and a persistent headwind, we pulled in at the next one we saw. The building had been stripped, graphitized and quite abundantly shat in, and the broken glass mosaics and burned tires in the dust outside suggested it was now a popular drinking spot. Remains of a cactus garden grew between painted stones. We found a shit-free corner in a large front room below empty window frames, kicked the debris away and made beds on our groundsheets, head-to-toe along the walls.

We collected bits of dead cactus and climbed onto the roof to scavenge loose pieces of timber. Robbie found an old chipboard school desk and we stamped and kicked it into smaller sheets. The wind was icy despite the sunshine, and as darkness fell we pulled on every layer we had and lit our fire in the corner of a small, roofless concrete room out back that we designated the kitchen. The fire stained the adobe black as we huddled around the flames.

Dinner came from our provisions: a packet of tortillas, cans of refried bean paste, onions, a head of garlic, a battered jalapeno, a few bananas, a packet of rice, a small bottle of Tapatio hot sauce, oats for porridge, sugar, powdered milk, a loaf of crumbly Bimbo bread and peanut butter. While we would augment it with regional specialties now and then, this inventory would become our basic cycling diet for the rest of our time in Mexico. All of these came from the general stores universally known as an "abarrotes."

As we fried up veggies, boiled rice and heated tortillas, Tommy talked about a cyclist he'd met in Oregon who claimed to have made meals out of roadkill. He revealed a theory he'd been working on: that the longer a cyclist stays on the road, the further they move along a spectrum from "traveler" at one end toward "vagrant" at the other. When the conversation died away we stared at the fire, where a piece of the chipboard desk was flaming up. It smelled like burnt hair.

"I don't know about you two, but this is about as close to vagrancy as I've ever been," Rob announced, holding his fingerless-gloved hands up to the stinky flames. He hadn't showered since Jorge's house, and his clothes billowed dust when he shook them. Just a few weeks earlier he'd been dressing in slacks and button-up shirts each morning, walking to his office in leather dress shoes. And though his hunched shoulders and hollow eyes spoke of terrible cold, when he grinned I saw the light of the flames reflected in his teeth.

"You ever see those DVDs that make your TV look like a fireplace?" Tommy said. "They've always got those options for different kinds of fires, to set different moods. 'Blazing Oak,' 'Late Night Embers,' that sort of thing?" He sipped the rum. "Can't say I've ever seen 'Scavenged Door Frame And Dead Cactus In Abandoned Building.'"

# CHAPTER 15

The next evening, we rolled into Rancho Chapala, which consisted of a single farmhouse, some sheds, a couple of old RVs and some scrawny trees clumped at the edge of a large plain. A burly little señora and her brood of skinny sons and nephews ran the place, country boys in patterned leather boots and grimy jeans.

"It's going to be very cold tonight," she said when I asked about camping. "Better that you sleep in the trailer."

We met another cyclist, a Bavarian named Dominik who was staying in a second camper trailer nearby, and we compared notes with him over beers, bistek steaks, salad and papas fritas later that evening. His hair was as blonde as straw, and he wore it in a short back-and-sides cut. His chin was large and thick.

Dominik loved Mexico. This was his second trip. The first had been a mission to learn the local language and, like his English, Dominik's Spanish carried a heavy German accent. But his command of both languages' grammar and vocabulary was very good. When the señora came over to see if we were "todo bien" during dinner, he put his hand gently upon her shoulder and lavished poetic praise upon her simple farmhouse fare.

"Muy amable," the señora blushed.

Dominik was an enormous man — taller than the señora when he was sitting down. He was halfway through a six-month loop of Mexico, having followed the Gulf north from Cancún, then turned west across the arid border states and was now headed south along the Pacific coast.

"Wait, so you were in Chihuahua and Sonora?" I asked, referring to two northern border states with particularly unsavory reputations.

"Yes!" he shouted, causing one of the ranch boys — dozing on a frilly armchair in front of a telenovela — to jump. "In Chihuahua zer men approach me wearing jeans and t-shirts, wiz Colt pistols in their belts. They would say: 'Ten cuidado — te disparamos.'"

He beamed and returned momentarily to his dinner, working the miniature cutlery with his massive fingers while I translated for Rob and Tommy: "Take care, we might shoot you."

"As I get kloser and kloser to the border wiz Sonora, I realize it hass been more than one week since I see a policeman."

In each successive village, the locals became more and more hostile, until people actually started telling him to go away.

"I play zer dumb tourist," Dominik shrugged, and imitated himself speaking Spanish with the locals of some troubled Chihuahuan town: "Ohh, lots of work on zer bicycle today! Lots of heat! What I need is a kold beer!" and he rubbed his discus-sized palms together.

Eventually, in one particularly hostile village, a man took him into his home.

"He says to me: 'You arc in a lot of danger. The Chihuahua cartel controls this area. People are suspicious.'"

"'But,'" the new friend went on, "'your most dangerous day is tomorrow because you will cross the border into Sonora. The Sonora cartel will think you are a spy! There are snipers watching zer roads. If they see policeman, they shoot. I do not know what they do with you.'"

Robbie shook his head. "You think you're doing something impressive," he said to Tommy and me, "but there's always someone crazier than you."

"Yes, yes," Dominik nodded emphatically. "Probably one week ago I pass two men: one on zer... how you call zis? Zer big wheel bye-sickle?"

"A penny farthing!" I cried.

"Aha," Dominik nodded. "And the other one — he was riding a... a unicycle!"

"There's always someone crazier," Robbie repeated, grinning.

"Finish your story man," Tommy said to Dominik. "What happened with those snipers?"

"I vos very scared zer next day," Dominik said. "But I continue wiz mein journey. When I take a break from zer bye-sickle, I take two smokes and a Coke. It is like a treat. So zis day I am sinking, 'I need to face my fear. I need everyone to know I am here, and I am not afraid.'"

Another forkful of bistek disappeared between his teeth, but Robbie,

Tommy and I had now stopped eating to stare at him — no small thing for hungry cyclists.

"When I reach zer sign, zer one that says 'Bienvenido a Sonora,' I put my bye-sickle to one side, I take out my smokes and my Coke, and I sit down in zer mittel of zer road. I am enjoying zer sunshine, zer cigarettes, zer Coca-Cola, yes? But I am alzo showing zer snipers that I am not afraid. I haff nothing to hide."

"I didn't see anybody, but I'm sure zer snipers are watching. When I finished my break, I continued riding. People were suspicious, but I did not have any real problems in Sonora."

Robbie asked if this was his first bike tour and he nodded, eyes wide.

"But I do not like it," he said around a mouthful of fries.

"What don't you like?"

"Cycling. I never liked it, never ride such things in Germany. For me, cycling is not fun."

"So why do you keep going?" Robbie pressed the point.

Dominik shrugged. "I wanted to see Mexico, yes? And even though I don't care for it, zer bye-sickle is still zer best way to know a place."

Smiles of recognition filled the silence that followed this statement. We just had observed a cycle tourist's ritual: a small ceremony honoring the bicycle for imbuing our lives with something approaching real adventure and appreciation for our place in the wild world.

# CHAPTER 16

The road sign appeared in the distance, a green blip against the drab colors of the desert. From up ahead, Tommy read it aloud.

"La Paz," he shouted, "772 kilometers."

"That's where we get the ship across to the mainland, right?" I asked Rob, our head navigator. He nodded, concern etched on his face.

"I'm worried what the other side of that sign is going to tell us about how far we've come."

Sure enough, Tommy passed the sign, pulled off the side of the highway and planted a foot in the dust, looking back. By the time we pulled alongside, he was shaking his head.

*Tijuana*, the sign said. *699.*

"We're not even halfway down Baja, boys."

"Wasn't it only supposed to take us two weeks to do the whole thing?" Robbie said. "Three max?" We had been cycling in this desert for two weeks already. Despondent under a harsh midday sun, we pushed on across a barren flat and took the first turnoff we encountered. It led to a town called Guerrero Negro.

Among the sumptuous sights and exhilarating experiences of the Baja peninsula, skulking about the dusty, broken concrete streets of Guerrero Negro is possibly the least sumptuous of all. For tourists it is a base for whale watching, but we had no budget for such excursions. This left Guerrero Negro with one redeeming feature: it was an actual town with big, greasy torta sandwiches, Wi-Fi, Domino's pizzas and liter bottles of beer in abundance.

As we rolled into town, we spotted a row of eight loaded bicycles propped against the first café with Wi-Fi. Seven of their owners were

American — known up and down the Transpeninsular Highway as the "Seattle Seven" — and the eighth was Julian, a Colombian. And though we'd heard rumors of female cyclists further ahead of us, all of these cyclists were men.

Each of the Seattle Seven wore beards, varying from permanent five o'clock shadow to mountain man avalanches spilling down their chests. Some wore little cycling caps, others wore scarves, one wore a beret. All wore odd socks. They were two sets of three brothers. The seventh, Dylan, was actually from Los Angeles but had become an honorary seventh Seattleite somewhere along the way. A friend was waiting for them on the Caribbean island of Trinidad, where they would build an organic, sustainable farm. They were abandoning the sinking ship of capitalist society and going off-grid, they said. They'd been planning this trip for two years.

Puzzlingly, during two years of preparation the idea of actually learning Spanish — spoken almost exclusively in the nine nations between Trinidad and the U.S. — had never occurred to any of the six original expedition members. This was where Julian came in. The Colombian had crossed the United States from east to west by bicycle and was now riding home to Bogotá. He was like a newly arrived visitor to Earth, perpetually in awe of the smallest details in his surroundings and excited to commune with every living being that crossed his path. This suited the self-important Seattleites well, as did Julian's native command of the language they had neglected to learn themselves, and he dutifully translated every mundane thing that wafted into their heads:

"How old is that dog?"

"Ask him where he bought his hat."

"Why does this cafe have two copies of the same Alaska Airlines in-flight magazine?"

"Is the pozole gluten-free?"

In return for his services, the Colombian was allowed to be nice to everybody. He seemed quite happy with the arrangement.

Julian had done some reconnaissance of Guerrero Negro by the time we rolled in, and said the local police were cool with us sleeping in a soccer stadium by their station. This was how eleven cyclists took up residence in the stands or pitched tents on the soccer field itself and hung around for four days.

"I wonder if we've been brought up at city meetings yet," Tommy said under beige skies one morning, stirring his cream of wheat over the stove and watching the Seattleites awaken to thunderous, joyous cries of "¡El panadero tiene pan!" from a nearby baker's truck. On the field, power-walking women in brightly colored sweat suits threw stern looks our way.

We spent our days resting on street corners, and every now and then Robbie would disappear into a nearby abarrotes to find some new treat. He had a great eye for snacks but, in light of my constant scavenging, soon learned not to be too generous with his sugary treasures.

In the course of our people watching — kids playing, teenagers flirting, old timers sitting around doing more or less the same thing as us — we discovered the joys of dog watching. Though humans and dogs shared the town, street dog society operated on a totally different level, separate from and parallel to human society. Old friends greeted one another with a sniff and a yawn. A female in heat toyed with a lovesick male like a fisherwoman grappling with a tuna, reeling him in and easing him out at her pleasure. Companions trotted from storefront to storefront, politely inquiring about food scraps.

The only dogs that disturbed this small-town peace were the leashed pets — those inbred, airheaded aristocrats of the canine world — on their afternoon walks. The pets would whimper or explode with rage at the sight of a street dog, who observed these fits with puzzled interest.

Everybody had long dreamed of endless tortas and lazy rest, but after a couple of days a weird malaise seemed to take hold of Stadium City. Upon arrival into town, the cycle tourists underwent that joyful transformation from "Cyclist" back to "Human." We stuffed our faces in an attempt to get on top of our Hunger, we shrieked with joy in the showers and rejoiced in a torrent of overdue phone calls, emails, uploads and updates.

But once we had told our tales to our digital communities, vanquished our Hunger and forgotten what it was like to be so dirty, we didn't know what to do with ourselves. Our bodies kept telling us to eat, but without the daily exercise and endorphins of cycling we took little joy from the act. We sat for hours in Wi-Fi zones, staring at Facebook feeds, spending too much money on greasy food and sugary sweets. The cycle tourist, by definition a fun-loving and easy-going creature, became abrasive.

The Seattle Seven in particular were testing my patience. I couldn't understand how they had managed to get so far, and once Julian left them — he would eventually veer off to finish in Bogotá — I doubted they would make it to Trinidad without him.

The logistics involved in traveling with such a number were incredible. Every decision ("Where are we going to eat? And what about a vegan option for Mark?") required endless coordination and discussion, exacerbated by that uniquely American need for each individual to elaborate on their personal plans and motivations — often with long explanatory digressions and always in precise detail — before anything actually happened. Then the deliberations would begin on where to meet up afterward, and at what time, and what about Jeremy because Jeremy had felt a deep connection with the cashier at Domino's yesterday and he was going back to see if she was around and maybe he wouldn't make it back to meet up for dinner because this girl was different, she really was, not like Jenna — you remember Jenna? From the fire twirling class in Beacon Hill? — who had turned out to be quite needy, emotionally speaking. Anyway, even though they didn't speak the same language, Jeremy had felt something between himself and the cashier as she'd handed over his change for that grande Cuatro Quesos pizza. So approximately how long will everyone be staying at the gas station to get snacks? And how will Jeremy contact them if things work out with the Domino's girl?

"Startin' to get kinda antsy, boys," Tommy said one evening, and if the eternally serene Washingtonian was feeling it, we knew the time had come. We had to leave Guerrero Negro.

Morphing from Human back into a Cyclist again was always a slow business, as any bicycle maintenance you'd planned had inevitably been forgotten as soon as your feet left the pedals and you walked into the first taquería in town. So the morning was spent rolling up tents, checking tire pressure and lubricating chains, and it was late when we finally swung our legs over our seats and stood on the pedals, setting the bikes back into motion.

# CHAPTER 17

"That's not where I would've put the bathroom," Tommy said, "but the dead bird works really well as an accent piece in the dining hall."

We were reconnoitering a small concrete house that had apparently been abandoned midway through construction. We'd found it on a track half a mile or so down the coast from the gringo holiday and fishing village of San Bruno. Through the empty window frames, the Sea of Cortez glowed like a jewel in the late afternoon sun.

"Hey Quinten, you ever try Tillamook ice cream while you were in the States?" Tommy asked.

"I did. It was good stuff."

"I could do a pint of the Mudslide right now, I'm telling ya."

"Mudslide," Robbie drooled, resting his bike against an inside wall. "I don't know what it is, but I want it. With some warm caramel sauce on the side…"

"Hot cherry pie…"

"Alright boys, that's it," I snapped. "I can't take this anymore!"

"Brownies with walnuts…"

"No I'm serious, you're driving me crazy," I said. "We already checked the abarrotes, they've got none of that stuff. From now on, new rule: no talking about food that we can't have in our hands within a few hours."

"You ever have that Thai sticky rice? With coconut and mango…"

"Rob, I'm sorry we have limited options. But it's your birthday and I know you've been hanging out for that packet of churro mix Tommy found in Santa Rosalía. What's say we cook that for breakfast? We could get some flour and eggs and make some pancakes?"

And that was how we celebrated Robbie's 28th birthday, falling asleep under the stars on some abandoned concrete husk, watching the stars overhead.

We spent a few days rolling along the coast, looking for the beach we'd been promised, and found it in a paradisiacal stretch of sand called El Coyote. It sat between the long Bay of Conception and the spiny desert, with the highway running alongside.

We set up our camp among the cyclists and road trippers who had already staked out the beach, made introductions and plunged into the water before the sun dipped behind the hills and the afternoon became cold. Ray and John, a pair of cyclists from Toronto, hopped a bus and returned with a pile of chicken wings seasoned with spices while the rest of us gathered dead cactus for firewood and jugs of a concoction we called "mescalito" — too cheap to be real mescal at 15 pesos a bottle — from Señora Bertha's store across the road.

A little after 4 p.m., a chubby white-haired man ambled out onto the dock at the southern end of the beach, where a community of "Snowbirds" — mostly white retirees from frigid parts of Canada and the northern United States — had set up their RVs for the season. At the same time, a thinner white man walked onto a private dock running from his holiday home at the opposite end of the beach. At precisely 4:20, they blew on a pair of conch shells fashioned into horns, signaling the ritual smoking hour. As guests on El Coyote's sands, we had little choice but to obey.

That night, sitting around a fire under the stars and munching greedily on fire-cooked chicken wings, John pulled out a ukulele. He was a tall, bulky, sunburned Nova Scotian who sported a full Abraham Lincoln-style neck beard. "Tonight I want to play you the song of my people," he announced.

His cycling partner was Ray, a slight guy of Filipino background with wispy long black hair and a few stragglers decorating his upper lip. He had found a large fish skull on a beach and lashed it to his bike's steering column, the cyclist's equivalent of bullhorns on a truck. He produced a djembe to accompany his friend.

John taught us the chorus of a song called *Barrett's Privateers*, a Canadian sea shanty where a young man signs up to help plunder U.S. ships during the American Revolutionary War.

> *"God damn them all, I was told*
> *We'd search the seas for American gold.*
> *We'd fire no guns, shed no tears.*

*Now I'm a broken man on a Halifax pier,*
*The last of Barrett's privateers."*

I made a mental note to ask Hailee, my "History of the Americas" phone-a-friend, about these privateers next time I was in an internet cafe.

This motley group resided on the beach in a happy, inebriated coexistence until, on the third day, a van pulled up a little ways down from the piles of sandy bikes and gear which passed for our camp. Three young women emerged and proceeded to "ooh" and "aaah" over the white sand and the clear green water. They took selfies with arms around one another, stripped down to their swimsuits, then took turns posing for photos.

As this exhibition took place, we cyclists loitered on the sand and pretended to be busy with derailleurs and journals. El Coyote is a long way down the Baja peninsula. It was the middle of winter. And although Robbie, Tommy and I had often rolled out of some dusty nowhere town spouting verbose, often obscene soliloquies in honor of a local beauty, it had been a long time since we'd seen three women near our age in one place — and in swimsuits, no less.

The photo session dragged on. Tommy looked at the rest of us with a sheepish grin. Rob watched restlessly. John raised his eyebrows.

Tommy made the first move, and it was a strange one.

"Yup, think I need some exercise," he announced, eyes now fixed on the island plugging the bay. "Might try swimming it."

Rob and I didn't believe him. It had to be at least a kilometer out to the island, possibly two. But as the resident Australians, we could hardly let ourselves be out-swam by this lanky, long-haired Washingtonian. Rob and I resolved to go along and "keep an eye on him."

I lasted about 100 meters. I surfaced to find Rob had also given up a little way ahead. But Tommy's skinny brown arms were still pitching forward. Robbie and I exchanged glances that said "bugger this," and turned towards shore.

An El Coyote road tripper had a pair of binoculars, which we trained on Tommy's now-miniscule form. He was only visible at distant intervals now, when he crested a particularly large piece of wind chop.

In the meantime, the three women had taken their bikini tops off altogether and were now splashing about in the shallows. Robbie, as the tallest cyclist, was in charge of keeping an eye on Tommy but when he quietly admitted that the occasional "magnified boob" had begun to drift into view, I fought him for the binoculars.

"Is it me," I said as I wrenched my gaze from our new neighbors and back to Tommy, "or is he going to miss the island?"

Our young friend had drifted south and seemed to be stroking for open water. Then we lost sight of him completely and began to panic.

"He's from Washington State for fuck's sake — isn't it cold up there?" Robbie said. "We're going to get a call from his mom asking, 'How could you just let him go alone into the open ocean? He's from Bellingham — he's never swum before in his life!'"

In the midst of this crisis, I spied an opportunity and turned to Grant, a surfer from California.

"Grant, can I borrow your board?"

With a glance at the sirens, who were still play-fighting in the shallows, I ran theatrically at the water, leaped aboard and began paddling for the island.

Surfing requires a very specific type of fitness in the arms, and if you haven't been out in a while your body never waits long to remind you of this. By the time I judged myself to be about halfway, my hands felt like lead and I was barely lifting my arms out of the water. An onshore wind whipped spray into my eyes. Lying low enough to be wet but high enough to cop the wind set my teeth to chattering. I sat up a few times and looked for Tommy, but wondered how I'd ever spot him in an ocean that suddenly seemed much larger now that I was in it.

I eventually labored onto a small beach on the landward side of the island, flanked by a pair of stone monoliths standing in shallow water. I dropped the board, staggered up the sand and collapsed at Tommy's feet — for he was dry and sunning himself on a comfortable-looking rock.

"Oh hey," he said mildly. "Fancy seeing you here."

Cold to my core and shivering uncontrollably on the sand, I explained that I was here to rescue him. He watched me dig a feeble hole and curl up in it, out of the wind, and we sat like that in silence for about ten minutes.

"Think I'm gonna go back now," Tommy announced at last, and strode towards the water. I moaned a little, then stumbled after him, picking up Grant's board as I went.

"I was a little worried when I saw you just sitting on the beach," Rob said when we returned to the mainland. "I was watching through the binoculars, thought you'd had a fight or something. Then I was jealous because you two got to hang out and I was stuck here. Until..." and he nodded towards the southern end of the beach, where the three women had now shed their bikini bottoms as well and were contorting their naked bodies into yoga positions on the sand. If they'd noticed Tommy's daring feat and my brave rescue mission, they weren't showing it.

That night, the Naked Yogis (as they became known) donned their winter woolies and joined us around the nightly campfire. It was unclear if Katie, Lyndsay and Michelle from San Diego were aware of how long it had been since any of us had seen or spoken with a woman our own age. But once Lyndsay, who lived in the van full time, had spoken long and eloquently about the joys of "just hanging out naked in my van," we were putty in their hands.

However, it was their attempts to satisfy our collective Hunger that won our undying devotion. They lavished us with treasures fresh from the Californian grocery chain Trader Joe's: canned trout, banana chips and peanut butter-stuffed pretzels along with homemade rice pudding and fried eggs. They handed out cannabis-infused cookies and used a Dutch Oven to bake a red velvet cake in the fire. In the morning they brought coffee to soothe our mescalito hangovers — and then they went skinny dipping again.

Robbie was up early and got caught watching on multiple occasions. He turned red every time and pretended to be absorbed in his porridge while the women laughed, until I sat up in my sleeping bag and told him to get in the water with them.

Instead, he served me porridge.

"We can take consolation in the fact that we're their favorites," he confided.

"Whaddya mean?"

"You, me and Tommy," Rob said, nodding at the Naked Yogis. "We're their favorites."

It was easier — and a nicer thought — to believe him and leave it at that.

The Naked Yogis left that day, and in their absence the stationary cyclist's malaise began to set in. Silences became prickly. Cyclists stopped absorbing one another's road stories and began trying to outdo them. This wasn't helped by the fact that every Snowbird on the beach had apparently been watching us through binoculars during the Naked Yogis' stay.

"You mean to say, not one of you even got close to them?" said one white-haired fellow who came down to share a joint that evening. "What the hell were you doing?"

# CHAPTER 18

There were a lot of shrines on the long, straight road to Ciudad Insurgentes, in remembrance of the startling multitudes who had perished in car wrecks along its length. They usually bore fresh flowers, and could be anything from a steel cross stuck in the soil to a full mausoleum complete with statues of weeping Virgenes de Guadalupe. If I were to die on a Mexican roadside, I decided it should feature a flame that would not extinguish until I was raised from the dead.

"Who's keeping a flame going for that long?" Robbie wanted to know as we rode side-by-side.

"It shall be tended by 23 beautiful virgins — one for each year of my life," I said.

"Virgins?" Robbie frowned.

"I dunno, it just seems like any time you hear of shrines and temples and eternal flames, there are usually virgins involved."

"Virgins, gotcha. Men or women?"

"I suppose it doesn't matter, does it?" I shrugged. We were silent for a moment as another iron cross approached on the roadside. "You know what? Scratch the virgins. The flame'll do. But you have to visit every year on the anniversary of my death."

"What reason do I have to come back every year?" Robbie wanted to know. "I might be busy."

Robbie wanted a large tree for his own Mexican roadside death shrine, under which a sort of bike tourist spa would be built.

"Mechanics lube your chain and straighten your spokes while you hang in the hot tub," he said. I couldn't find any fault with that.

"Hey, Tommy," Robbie called over his shoulder, and we eased up on the pedaling to let the Washingtonian catch up. "Let's say you get hit by a truck."

"Smooshed," I added.

"Geeze fellas," Tommy winced.

"Good news is we're going to build you a shrine, like all these crosses and mini-churches out here. Only you get to choose what it is," Robbie went on.

"I've got an eternal flame, Rob's got a spa with bike mechanics on the side."

"It has to be on the road?"

"Yeah."

There was a silence as Tommy pondered this in the saddle.

"Okay, so my shrine is a sign giving directions to the nearest beach. When you get there, there's this big open palapa. Pool tables, darts, all that shit. Open bar, beach shacks for all my buddies. You guys can run it if you want. And, uh, the walls are decorated with pictures of me wearing Hawaiian shirts, Guy Fieri-style."

We made Ciudad Insurgentes in the late afternoon, and found it a sprawling, smoky city of compounds and dust about three quarters of the way down the peninsula. But the shadows were getting long, and it was about time to play "Where Are We Sleeping Tonight?"

Over the weeks that Tommy, Robbie and I had been traveling together, we had assumed assigned duties within the group. Robbie had proven himself the most talented Navigator of the trio, seeking side road adventures away from Highway One's traffic while simultaneously acknowledging its capacity to cover ground quickly. Robbie was also the most interested in the various problems and opportunities presented by camp cooking in rural Mexico and had taken the crucial role of Head Chef. Tommy, an eager and imaginative eater, supported him as a sort of Creative Consultant, while also offering astute suggestions when it came to bicycle mechanics.

Tommy was also the most sociable of the three. Robbie and I weren't the best minglers or small talkers, and often tended to recoil into one another's company among large groups of strangers. Tommy, however, could chat up the president of Kazakhstan underwater if he had to, and so he became our Envoy. As we spent more time around Snowbirds and other cyclists, Tommy would glide on in, smooth as butter, make some new friends and then return an hour or two later with an invitation to a party or some valuable piece of gossip or information.

Tommy's limitation was the Spanish language — in which he could ask politely for beer, tequila or certain types of tacos, but not much else — and that was where I came in. As the group's Translator, my role was to speak with and listen to locals. If a bike was leaning on someone's gate, I was the one to smooth things over. When locals asked questions like "Where did you start?" or "How much does the bike weigh?" or simply observed "You're getting a lot of exercise!" — a common conversation we'd started calling "the Interview" — I answered questions and attempted to keep pace with that most Mexican of pastimes: idle banter. And if we needed to find the local Western Union because Tommy had lost his credit card and his father had wired him a loan, I was the one who asked likely-looking locals for directions.

I wasn't shy. When someone spoke too quickly, or when they gave the directions in a confusing manner ("Go all the way to the right"), or when they pointed right when they said "left," I found a new person on every street corner, hoping they would all say the same thing. This tactic often resulted in confusion, but it was all we had. And when we played "Where Are We Sleeping Tonight?" I was the one who approached poker-faced ranchers, using as much conditional future tense as possible to ask if it might be possible to pitch a tent round the back of that shed over there.

Occasionally, Robbie would suck in his courage and have a go, but he usually came back with a variation on the following:

"Um, he's a very cheerful man. He has lots of beers, and they're twenty or thirty pesos each, and he's never been to Australia but he would like to try eating kangaroo. His son's name is Felipe and" — glancing over his shoulder — "we can or can't sleep in his backyard… but I'm not quite sure which."

Today, however, I forced Robbie to take up the Translator's mantle. We had spent a day and a half riding a taxing dirt road that followed — and often crossed — a shallow river running west out of the mountains dividing the peninsula, and I was dead tired. Concentrating on finding a rideable line through the soft sand had drained my brain and put me in a bad mood. I said I would find an internet café to send Warmshowers requests for La Paz — secretly, this also meant checking for new messages and music from Hailee — and left them to it.

I had set them a pretty tough task, especially for their first time. We were in the bustling center of a small city. As villages become towns and towns become cities, you reach a certain point where sleeping in a public space stops being a harmless novelty and starts becoming a homeless problem. So this round of "Where Are We Sleeping

Tonight?" involved lots of approaching and talking to total strangers in a language in which Robbie wasn't fully confident. On top of everything, non-Spanish-speaking Tommy had drunk a Tecate too many at our Celebratory Arrival Taquería, and his tipsy heckling did little to assist their quest.

But they did well under the circumstances, wrangling us a campsite on the grounds of a Baptist church in the care of a fussy man named Santiago and his timid, smiling family.

"Sometimes, when we're on a boring stretch of road," Robbie confided while Tommy was giving himself a sink shower later that evening, "I like to play an imagination game called 'Tommy's Baja Trip If He'd Never Met Us.'"

Santiago and his wife Yessica served coffee and bread in the morning before they departed with a portable fruit stand. They were from Oaxaca, a state in Mexico's deep south that retains a heavy influence from pre-Columbian cultures. But as uninspiring as Ciudad Insurgentes was, they were grateful to be there.

"We escaped the violence, thanks be to God," Yessica said of their journey to Baja California. She didn't elaborate. When they disappeared into the street, we took oranges from a tree in the yard and wound our way through the city's waking bustle — brooms and buckets of water, newly optimistic street dogs and children in miniature uniforms hauling oversized school bags — back to the main road out of town.

The sun hid behind colorless clouds all day, and a nasty headwind kept trying to send us back to Insurgentes. We took turns slipstreaming behind one another right up until Oscar's front wheel tapped Baxter's rear (or vice versa — this would become a contentious debate) and I glanced back in time to see the last of Robbie's death wobbles. The bike then appeared to crumple beneath his falling body as he hit the pavement at speed. His bags exploded gear across the road, and an approaching car swerved into the oncoming lane to avoid him.

Robbie's hands were shaking as I took him by the arm off the highway and sat him against a fence in the shade of some bushes. We all flinched when Oscar's front tire belatedly exploded with a bang. Rob had skin off of his palms, elbows and hip and while Tommy dripped disinfectant on the wounds, I changed out Oscar's blown tube.

The fall had rattled Robbie and added a new sense of desperation to finish with Baja once and for all. The city of La Paz signified the end of a long cycling tour for Tommy and the last cold desert riding Robbie and I would encounter until Chile and Bolivia's Atacama, halfway down a continent that had never felt further away. Robbie complained of a pain in his chest that suggested a broken rib, and even when we mustered the enthusiasm to crack jokes Rob begged us to keep quiet, as laughing only brought more pain.

He became a quiet and melancholy presence among Tommy and I's increasingly forced attempts at light-hearted banter. His eyes bored into the desert floor when we rested, his consciousness lost deep inside his own head, and my attempts to coax him out ("So now's probably a good time to plan out that bike spa shrine of yours?") had little effect.

The landscape lost all color beneath low clouds and the headwind strengthened. Robbie now refused to ride in anyone's slipstream, meaning Tommy and I pedaled behind one another, or became separated out along the highway, struggling alone. The traffic was heavy and unfriendly. During a climb out of a particularly deep vado, Tommy swerved to avoid a pothole and "tacoed" his wheel around a roadside boulder. I held his bike as he smacked the bent rim on the concrete, gritting his teeth. I'd never seen him so mad.

"I don't want to hitch the last 50 kilometers goddamn it," he grimaced.

I grunted in sympathy, and he looked up at me.

"Any idea what's up with Robbie?" Tommy asked.

"I guess he's just really sore and a bit rattled."

Tommy shrugged. "Maybe. He almost seems depressed to me."

After Tommy had whacked his wheel back into shape, we caught up to Rob and sheltered from the wind in abandoned buildings, passing time by throwing stones at blackened turds to see if they were still soft.

"Interesting life we lead," Robbie said.

At last, we limped into a military checkpoint on the outskirts of La Paz.

"¿Drogas?" asked a bored lieutenant. *Drugs?*

"No."

"¿Armas?" *Weapons?*

"No."

"Adelante." *Go ahead.*

Later, once his rib had healed, Robbie told me that it was here that he felt his first wave of real pride in himself. La Paz was his first milestone, a geographic endpoint, and from now on he could point to Baja California on a map and know that he'd spent six weeks — not two or three, as we'd originally thought — riding a bicycle from end to end.

# CHAPTER 19

As we followed the directions to our Warmshowers host in La Paz, we spotted magic words: El Bufet Gran China — The Great China Buffet. We made a note of its location — a strip mall on the outskirts of town — as well as the sign that promised a 20-peso price drop after 6 p.m.

We returned the next day at 5:40, our host's advice to "be careful" quickly forgotten at the promise of unlimited food to quell our Hunger. Tommy had produced a hunk of old turmeric infused with hash oil from his mayonnaise buckets, and we ate a little piece each in the street outside the buffet, reasoning that this would enhance the experience of the meal.

We entered, paid our fee and quickly realized that the post-six o'clock discount only applied because the buffet food had been sitting under heat lamps since midday. We weren't deterred — we had been living on tortillas, canned beans, old vegetables and warm beer for weeks. Our bodies commanded us to eat.

As veterans of several buffet tours of duty each, Tommy and I knew the drill. We knew to pace ourselves, to mix in vegetables with the meat and take regular breaks. We knew the value of tactical bathroom interludes.

But while Robbie was by now a veteran of the road, he was still a first-time buffet eater and rushed in with the zeal of a seminary-fresh missionary cut loose among pagans. So in the time it took Tommy and I to chomp through two moderately-sized piles of fried chicken, steamed and sautéed greens and fried rice, Robbie had inhaled four plates piled high, and consisting exclusively of animal flesh.

Bewilderment marked his face as he returned with a fifth helping. "You guys are soft," he mumbled around a hunk of chicken. "Why is there green on your plates?"

The hash soon began to take effect, and after the brief honeymoon of giggles came and went Robbie disappeared into the bathroom. Tommy and I continued our assault for quite some time, advising one another on the condition of this dish or that, before the Washingtonian remembered our friend.

"I think he's been in there a while, man. Should we check on him?"

I shrugged at my food. "I'm sure he'll be fine."

When Rob finally returned, he did so with small, somewhat delicate steps. Tommy and I watched, eyebrows raised in expectation as he sat and apologized for what he was about to say.

"I had to walk out of there," he explained. "If I didn't just stand up and walk out, I don't believe it ever would have stopped. I kept looking into the bowl expecting to see undigested chicken." With that, he rested his head on the table, occasionally summoning the strength to feed himself another spoonful of the saucy matter cooling on his plate.

Later, I returned from a bathroom break to find Robbie propped against the dessert buffet, face scrunched in apparent pain as Tommy leaned over and scooped ice cream into a bowl.

"Robbie," Tommy was saying in a schoolteacher's tone, "if your belly's so full that you can't physically bend over to scoop your own ice cream, it means your body is trying to tell you something."

He looked up over his glasses at Rob, who was shaking his head at the ceiling and mouthing the word "no."

"Robbie, buddy," Tommy added slowly. "It means you should probably stop."

"No no," Robbie whispered to the fluorescent lights overhead. "Just give it to me. Please. Just do this for me, Tommy."

Rob took the bowl and sat down, contemplated the ice cream (Tommy had drawn the line at sprinkles), then dashed outside. Five minutes later, he returned shaking his head.

"The chef was outside smoking a cigarette," he winced. "I couldn't spew in front of him."

We told him to sit, to ride it out, that the pain would soon subside. But it didn't, and when Tommy and I couldn't hold our giggles in on the walk home, Rob crossed to the other side of the street. He leaned back as he walked, pushing his distended belly out in front of him.

"You can never, ever let him forget this," Tommy murmured with a grin.

Our Warmshowers host in La Paz was a middle-aged woman named Tuly, and she offered a calm, easy-going hospitality. She lived in a modern home with her daughter, Bertha, who was in her final year of high school. Two other daughters — a medical student named Geysa who lived in Cabo San Lucas and Génesis, a chef who lived in Ensenada — were also home for the winter holidays.

This saintly family took us in as easy as siblings. Bertha moved into Geysa's room and we cyclists crammed in to share her vacated bed and the floor. Génesis took our insatiable bellies as a challenge, trying new recipes and old favorites and relishing our rapturous reviews. After a week we became spoiled and, to Génesis' delight, began submitting requests. Once we cooked them dinner to say "thank-you" and though they made lots of appreciative noises about our mac 'n' cheese, it's possible they were ready for Génesis to take over the kitchen again.

In the evenings we sipped beers and frozen margaritas and talked. This was slow, as the girls didn't speak English, but there was something effortless about their company. In Robbie and Tommy, Génesis found undying devotion and a culinary enthusiasm that almost rivaled her own. They spent hours comparing recipes.

Meanwhile, Geysa talked us through a dilemma — would she stay in Baja after her studies, or leave for the distant lights of Mexico City? And Bertha, who was rapidly approaching the end of high school, wanted to know what Australia and the United States were like. We came and went as we pleased, and when a week had passed and I told Tuly we would hopefully be out of her hair soon, she seemed confused.

"I assumed you were going to be here for a few weeks, at least," she shrugged. "Don't feel rushed. We like having you here." And so we stayed.

While Tommy contemplated a ride to Cabo San Lucas and the true tip of the Baja peninsula, Robbie and I weighed our options for reaching the mainland. There a container ship which sailed for Mazatlán, Sinaloa several nights a week, which we could ride for USD$100 each. Alternatively, it was said that private yachts regularly dropped into the La Paz marina on their way to the mainland, and some would offer rides to travelers in return for crew work.

So we began hanging around the marina, where we found other cyclists trying to do the same. We did our best to schmooze with the boat people and subtly inquire about the possibility of a ride. Robbie and I printed flyers and turned up for the morning radio announcements, inserting our petition among detailed discussions of weather, tide and where to rent kayaks.

The hunt centered around a fish taco restaurant near the marina. The food was subpar and nobody ate there but the Snowbirds and boaties, who were determined to speak Spanish at every opportunity — even when they were being served by a Frenchman:

"So, what can I get for you guys?"

"Dose tacos de peskahdo para mi, y dose de camer-own para ella."

"Okay, take a seat and I'll let you know when they're ready."

"Grass-ee-ass. Oh, y… y… what's the Wi-Fi password?"

Robbie and I soon grew tired of trying to chat up wealthy American sailors, and with more and more cyclists showing up each day — including many of the friends we'd made at El Coyote — we had competition. And yet without even trying, Tommy had soon set us up with a South African woman named Julia, who offered to take us over to Mazatlán on her trimaran if we could "make sure the thing doesn't sink" while she slept.

We spent a day helping ready the ship — which mainly involved moving stuff whenever she changed her mind — but when we returned at the appointed time that night after a farewell dinner with Tuly and her daughters, we found the boat gone and our bags piled on the dock.

"Easy come, easy go," said sage Rob, and we went back to Tuly's.

In the morning Tommy, Robbie and I rode down to the Malecón, a sundrenched boulevard of bars and restaurants, teenagers clutching at one another in discrete corners, promenading families and Snowbirds loudly observing that "it's happy hour somewhere."

Following Tuly's recommendation, we asked for a bloke named Hector. Hector introduced us to Luis, who was 21, and his assistant, Germán, who was 16. We hopped in a lancha together and Luis steered us out of the bay and around the spit of land they called "Mogote."

Eventually Luis pointed to a dark shape on the port side, about four meters long and moving apace with the idling boat. We pulled on snorkels and flippers. Then Luis was shouting, "salta salta salta!" with his eyes fixed on an indeterminate point in the water, and we flipped over the edge. Through the mask I peered around, seeing nothing but sand about six meters below me. My breathing was shallow, and I was about to surface when, from my left, an enormous head appeared, cruising impossibly close across my field of vision. I reared back and water sloshed down the snorkel.

I watched it drift by, the angular tail snapping right by head as it propelled the whale shark through the water. From behind, the array of fins on its back and sides looked exactly like some Discovery Channel vision of a monstrous shark. From the front, however, its small, wide-set eyes and gaping mouth betrayed the whale shark's docile nature. But I couldn't stay near its face. My breathing became forced and shallow, and I knew I'd become scared again.

For its part, the whale shark endured our thrashing and the nuzzling of smaller remora fish with an admirable dignity and grace. I noted that if I was a whale shark, I'd probably go out of my way to chew on a human every now and then to make sure they left me alone.

"It was awesome?" Luis said as we surfaced, spluttering expletives. He sounded bored.

While I had been losing my mind underwater, Rob and Tommy had been studying the shark intently. They compared notes on the distribution of its spots, the different types of fish swimming under its fins or in its wake and the gentle way it propelled itself through the water. I just sat with my head in my hands, trying to wrap my feeble brain around what had just occurred.

We repeated the process three more times. We swam alongside each whale shark until it outswam us or dived out of sight. The last one was seven or eight meters long, and I felt the fear again as I flapped my flippers alongside. I popped up, gasping.

Ten meters on, Robbie noticed I had disappeared and surfaced.

"You okay?"

"I'm fine. I'm done," I panted and, later, he told me I'd had a wild smile on my face.

We re-enacted our goodbyes in the morning, lingering in Tuly's motherly embrace.

"Good luck, and come back some day," she said. Tommy, too, was leaving our girls. He'd heard of a commune in the hills near Cabo. So we pedaled south out of town together, bought our tickets and hugged him goodbye. We had been together for six weeks.

Rob and I squeezed through the gates and rode our bicycles along the mammoth docks at Pichilingue, darting between rumbling trucks into the iron bowels of a huge ship filled exclusively with semi-trailers. The lounge rooms were dens of drunk truckers, smelly air conditioning and violent movies so we found an isolated corner of the deck, high above the ocean. A gray whale was making its way into the bay as we motored out of the harbor, flapping its tail while the sinking sun ignited the few clouds and the fingers of dry land reaching at the wine-dark Sea of Cortez. We rolled out our beds as if we were cowboys camping in an arroyo, and slept there.

# CHAPTER 20

The mainland air was sticky and sweet on my tongue. Movement felt labored, like walking on the floor of a warm ocean. From the ship the coast appeared as a lumpy green mass under a haze of humidity and smog, with broad-leaved plant life leaping out of the earth.

Robbie and I camped on the roof of a Mazatlán backpacker's hostel, swam in the bath-warm sea and strolled by the hotel where Joaquín "El Chapo" Guzmán was first captured by police during a rendezvous with his wife, now a local landmark. By night we tried and mostly failed to impress our fellow hostel guests with our "rugged explorer" act.

"Still shaking Baja dust out of my shoes," Robbie said, leaning back with his hands behind his head as we sat around a patio table one evening.

"It's a long way back to Tijuana," I added, affecting a faraway gaze. "But we only showered a handful of times in six weeks."

The pretty young Russians and Kiwis nearby merely wrinkled their noses at us.

We had one success in the hostel though: we met Joff, the Englishman I'd seen from the highway outside Las Vegas, and who had stayed in Walker's RV near San Diego the night before I had arrived. Joff was a celebrity in every village he'd passed, and most cyclists who followed in his wake had heard stories of the Englishman on his penny farthing. We'd heard that he was on his second lap of the planet, which made him cycling royalty as far as Robbie and I were concerned, and we were awestruck in his somewhat goofy presence. I practically tripped over myself talking about the first time I'd seen him.

"I wondered how you'd found that lovely bike path when I was stuck on that bloody freeway," he said.

In the several days we spent with him, Joff exclusively wore a sort of uniform of black sandals, black three-quarter length pants and a black long-sleeve shirt over his lean frame, for it was all he had room for in his bags. For cycling, he added sunglasses, a backpack to supplement his limited carrying capacity and — the finishing touch — that imperial-era pith helmet. Eager to see this setup in action, Robbie and I offered to accompany him on the ride out of town.

Mounting his giant bicycle involved standing on a step by the smaller rear wheel, pushing off like a skateboard to gain momentum, then quickly scaling another step and hoisting oneself into the saddle. He did so in front of the hostel's transient family, who turned out to see us off — well, mostly him — and the spectacle precipitated an ongoing and often chaotic commotion that began the moment we left the hostel and didn't stop until we'd left the city limits.

People stopped dead at the sight of him, faces splitting into wide smiles. Some whipped out their phones for photos, others yelled at friends and total strangers to "Come look!"

Joff spoke no Spanish and responded with jaunty waves and the odd "Hallo!" Mostly, he kept chatting with Robbie and I, who flanked him like cops in a motorcade. Before long we'd picked up a harassed-looking reporter who tried to interview the disinterested Joff through the window of his car as he followed along.

"It's like this everywhere?" I asked.

"Oh, yes. You get used to it," Joff said breezily.

"Have you ever felt threatened by all the attention?" Robbie wondered later, while we rested on a picnic table on the outskirts of town.

"One time, in China, I had this peasant bloke following me on a dirt road in some mountains," Joff said. "He would ride his motorbike in front of me and brake hard, so that I would either have to stop, hop off and start again — or else plunge over the edge of a cliff. He found it terribly funny.

"I had this whip under my saddle that I used to scare off dogs, and after the third or fourth time — it's not easy to get the penny going on a sloping dirt road — I was pretty fed up, to the point where I actually pulled out the whip and had a go at him. Not the best look, obviously: an Englishman in this hat whipping a Chinese peasant from on high. Of course, he became quite angry after that, yelled at me for a little while

110

and then raced on ahead. I sort of wondered what might be waiting for me in the next village, but I never saw him again."

Robbie turned to me, eyes wide, and repeated a line he'd once said back in Baja: "There's always someone crazier, eh?"

"Oh no," Joff said, shaking his head. "There's no point in comparisons like that. As I always say: 'Everyone's on their own adventure.'"

There was silence around the table as Robbie and I absorbed this comment. Coming from Joff — the guy who had ridden around the world one-and-a-half times on a flipping penny farthing — it felt profound.

"Everyone's on their own adventure," I repeated.

It reminded me of Leo, way up near the Grand Canyon: "If you got yourself all the way out here, then you can keep going."

*We're all on our own*, I thought, watching cars drone past on the highway nearby. *Each and every one of us on our own adventure.* Patagonia was a long way away — but so was Vancouver. And if I'd come this far, there was nothing to say I couldn't make it. I thought of everyone in my life — my parents, my sisters, all my friends — all of them capable of doing amazing things.

As I zoned back in on the conversation at the picnic table, Joff was talking about a man named Thomas Stevens, an Englishman who had set out from San Francisco on a penny farthing in 1884 and, with the occasional help of steam ships, eventually became the first person to complete a circumnavigation of the globe by bicycle.

"Apparently his presence started riots in China," Joff said. "Though he didn't carry a whip for protection — he had a revolver in the spare raincoat he was using for a tent.

"He's actually buried not far from where I live," he went on. "When I left for the first time, I visited his grave and found a small piece of his headstone that had been chipped off. I took it with me, then returned it when I came back."

He'd done the same thing this time around. "I like to think of it as old Mr. Stevens continuing his travels around the world on a penny," Joff said.

When we at last mounted the bikes, the country began to undulate softly beneath the asphalt as we left the city and entered a wide, sun-drenched motorway. Joff slowed almost to a standstill on these gentle climbs because his only gear was the penny's gigantic front wheel. Often, he said, he had to walk his bike up over mountain passes.

Descents were another matter altogether. As he gathered speed the pedals — which were fixed to the wheel — would spin so fast that his legs were unable to keep up, and the most comfortable thing to do was lift them up and hang them over the handlebars. He would careen off mountains seated six feet in the air with his legs dangling out in front. Of course, he couldn't apply too much pressure on his one and only brake because doing so would cause the bike to tip forward and pitch him head-first into the pavement. This catastrophe happened "with surprising regularity," he said. In an age of high-speed rail, cheap buses, luxury automobiles and budget airlines, this was how Joff had chosen to see the world.

While he understandably planned to stick with Mexico's relatively flat Pacific coast, Robbie and I had other plans. We said goodbye at a turnoff, wished him luck and watched him go, leaning into his pedal strokes high above the road.

# CHAPTER 21

Back in La Paz, Robbie and I had pored over our road map of wider Mexico with a mixture of excitement and trepidation. Baja California was a laid-back, sparsely populated corridor, with a single paved artery to follow southward. Sure, there had been long distances between settlements and water sources, and the cold nights had caught us off guard. But the weather had stayed dry, navigation was relatively simple and the open desert made for easy camping and car-free cycling.

Compared to Baja's empty white spaces, the mainland map was a squiggly mess of roads — "That means mountains," Robbie said excitedly — and jumbled piles of strangely named states, towns and cities crammed up against one another. Looking at it on the map, I felt like we were standing at the edge of a dense and raucous labyrinth.

We chose a route that would take us directly into the heart of the maze, on a road known as El Espinazo del Diablo — *The Devil's Spine*. The road would take us northeast — further away from Patagonia — up the central Mexican plateau to the high desert city of Durango. From there, we could ride wherever we liked — south-east to Mexico City, east toward the Gulf or south along the central highlands. As we left Joff and pedaled away from the roaring coastal highway, the first foothills were a green wall glowing in the late afternoon sunshine.

Geographically speaking, Mexico encompasses the transitory landmass that condenses North American plains into Central America's knobbly isthmus. A high plateau spills out of the southwestern United States flanked by a pair of coastal ranges, each called the Sierra Madre, each a tempestuous borderland where plateau refuses to make an orderly transition to coastal flat and must therefore be subdued by erosion and the wet weight of the tropics grappling at its edge. Here and there a high holdout rises, cut off from the mothership, beset on all sides by rivers and valleys, doomed to succumb to the jungle yet still tall and triumphant.

The Devil's Spine traverses one such holdout, a long, narrow rampart trailing off the plateau's edge. Thick, broad-leaved forests clamber the slopes while indomitable communities of pine and oak hold high flats and survey the roiling country below. Hidden in the folds and crevices of the range, small villages eke out an existence within the slow-motion battleground around them. In 2013, the federal government completed a USD$2.2 billion project which bored a freeway straight through the mountains and canyons of the Sierra Madre. It was said to be easier for cyclists — less climbing, and not as steep — but it also diverted most motorized traffic away from the narrow old road. We were excited by the prospect of riding over the Devil's Spine (not through it), so we opted for the higher, quieter, older route.

Away from the sea breezes and oven-like concrete streets of the coast, the forest air took on a sweet viscosity, like syrup. It condensed in beads under my helmet and formed rivers down my face and arms. Over time, persistent drips from my nose and chin would eat holes in Baxter's paintwork. It took most of the first day to climb the first range, soaked in the pitiless heat until we reached an altitude where pine trees grew, rolled over the top and sped down the other side, reaching the foot of an even larger sierra behind. On the third day we found the peak of the spine and followed the road along its length, skirting the tops of bare granite cliffs or scooting below, climbing out onto stony promontories and speeding back to the mountain's breast, where wicked curves awaited to send us laboring outward and upward all over again.

At a bend in the Spine, the hamlet of Los Ángeles nestled into a notch in the sierra. Five families inhabited the clutch of houses there, according to one man who seemed old enough to know. He invited us to follow him out onto the flat concrete roof of someone's house. From the edge, we had a view of the sharp Sinaloan peaks stretching away to the northwest, falling to distant valley floors and villages that, from this vantage point, fit inside my thumbnail.

A dirt track left the road beside the house and disappeared into a fold of the mountain.

"That track is the only way to reach those villages," he said.

As evening set in we carried our bikes and bags up a slope and camped on the flat top of the range, the tropical lowland forests and their evening mists visible through gaps in the pine. We spotted headlights from our campfire after dark, which turned out to be semi-trailers grumbling for the coast. Over 20 minutes we watched them twinkle towards us, gingerly making their way along the range until they roared beneath our campsite and the noise ebbed away.

On the fourth day the road at last mounted the plateau. The cliffs curved away into the distance on either side. The first community of consequence was the logging town of La Ciudad, a place of mills and old trucks piled high with timber from the low hills fringing the town. We camped behind a restaurant outside the cold, compact city of El Salto where the owner's dog — a Labrador named Candy — forgot who we were every few hours and barked hysterically until Rob or I ventured out of our tents to offer a pet and remind her that we were friends.

On the fifth day we reached Durango, a pretty brownstone colonial center ringed with crumbling suburbs that cowered behind walls and barbed wire — a city where few ventured outside after dark.

The Espinazo del Diablo had well and truly whetted our appetite for more central Mexican cycling. "I'm keen to get my wheels on the road once more and get stuck into some more mountains," I wrote to Hailee from Durango.

The city and its surrounding countryside was a film hub during the 1960's and 70's, and many classic Westerns — both American and Mexican versions of the genre — were filmed here. During our stay I downloaded a 1967 picture called *The War Wagon* — starring John Wayne — onto my little laptop after learning that several scenes had been filmed at the Sierra de Órganos, a small national park on the road south to Zacatecas. We decided to have a movie night in the national park where it had been filmed.

First, though, we pulled off the highway to the town of San Vicente de Chupaderos. The town rested in a valley ringed with low, dry hills, spires of rock poking from the hillsides here and there. Chupaderos resembled any other Mexican town until we found the Main Street movie set, a wide avenue flanked with wooden facades impersonating a hotel, an old-timey bank, a saloon, a general store and other businesses you might find in an Old West town. Gallows loomed at the center of it all, right outside the faux-adobe church.

The place was eerily deserted. When I asked a señora selling beer out of the fake doorway of the saloon, she said everyone had gone to "los gallos." *Roosters.*

"Why don't you go, too?"

She wrinkled her nose and shook her head. "A mi no me gusta," she said.

Sunday is cockfighting day in Mexico. The crowing of many roosters guided us through dusty outer streets until we found a vacant plot of land, outside of which hundreds of battered pick-up trucks were parked.

The Chupaderos fights were held in a walled-off lot of scrappy grass, a third of which was taken up by a building that was either abandoned or never completed. It served as a makeshift urinal for the Sunday punters.

We peered over the heads of men clustered around a ring of weatherboards — called a palenque — about ten meters across, the fence reaching as high as my hip. Sprinkled water held down the scratched dirt inside. Feathers gathered at the edges.

Men in leather boots, large hats and jeans ornamented with the biggest belt buckles I'd ever seen stood around small cages, sipping cans of beer while their kids scampered and munched on snacks. There was laughter and easy weekend banter, and above it all the bellows of 40 or 50 roosters bristling in cages or the hands of their owners.

Two men showed their fighters to the crowd, and wagers flew around the ring. A drunk shouted, "oye güero," and tried to make a bet against Rob or I, but I was busy watching the men inside the palenque as they placed their champions in the dirt and held their tail feathers, provoking them to run on the spot. A man in a grubby baseball cap brought a third, smaller rooster in, and the two fighters were invited to peck at it, thus completing the warmup. Both had a steel blade attached to one leg, curved and glinting.

At a word from a referee, the owners let go and the birds charged one another, melding into a flurry of feathers and talons moving too fast for the human eye, a blurry ball of motion bouncing around the ring to the staccato beat of the roosters' wings.

A white-crested fighter looked dominant and before long the other — sporting a brown crest — had collapsed, panting. A timeout was called and the owners grabbed their animals. I spotted blood for the first time, running from the talons of both roosters. The flow was heavier from Brownie. His owner sucked blood from a wound in his back and spat it into the ring with an ugly squirting sound. In a bizarre moment, both owners made as if to French kiss their roosters, but instead put the birds' entire heads into their mouths, sucking them clean of blood, then spat mouthfuls of water and beer into their faces to stir them up again.

A word from the referee sent them back to the ring, circling each other slowly, conserving energy and watching for an opening or a moment of weakness.

Though both were now bleeding and panting, Brownie looked far weaker. After several flurries of action — in which he appeared to receive fresh wounds — he lay on his back, feet in the air, chest heaving as he watched his opponent and waited for the final blow. But Whitey hung back, seemingly content to strut and prolong the bout. The referee allowed the trainers to attend to their fighters with beer sprays and head sucks, then sent them in again.

Brownie lurched away under a fresh attack, but the crowd rallied behind him as he retaliated and went after Whitey in a frantic, slashing wave of energy.

This became a pattern of attack and retreat that went on for some time, until Brownie could barely hold his feet. Meanwhile, red patches had appeared among Whitey's plumage, and his sides heaved. Brownie fell onto his back again, but Whitey couldn't summon the energy to finish him and tottered about in the middle of the ring. The referee summoned the trainers and had them place the fighters face-to-face. The crowd rumbled. There was money riding on this. A draw or withdrawal was not an option. All afternoon, from proud cowboys in high-heeled boots and drunks sipping plastic bottles, I heard the words: "Hasta la muerte" — *Until death.*

The birds were so weak by now that both trainers were holding their fighters' heads aloft. At the very moment that Brownie's trainer took his hands from beneath the gladiator's throat, the rooster's sides went still. His head tipped forward in theatrical slow motion, beak-first into the dust. The crowd jeered, and most were exchanging cash before the owners had carried their fighters from the ring, one swinging limply by his feet, the other cradled in his owner's arms.

"A nice gesture by Brownie, dying like that so Whitey didn't have to finish him off," I said, but my voice sounded hollow. Robbie had turned a few shades whiter since the fight began.

"I'm not sure what I expected, but it wasn't that," he said. He took a fortifying gulp from his beer and then stared into the sudsy dregs with a leaden face.

A new fight was starting, so we retreated from the ring — Rob to the bar and I to the back of the lot where I struck up a conversation with Ramiro, a serious-looking man with a black mustache and a big black hat. His boots and belt buckle weren't as flashy as those of his companions, though he exuded a quiet confidence. The clean, practical clothing that he, his wife and his son wore spoke of understated wealth. Ramiro didn't speak often — and when he did it was in a half-mumble — but the helpers around him hung on every word.

"We've got ten roosters, but only two fight today. One already played," he said.

"How'd it go?"

"Ya ganó," Ramiro replied dryly. *It won.* His face was unreadable. "Now we're looking for another rooster that weighs 2.5 kilograms, the same as this one here, so they can play."

He pointed to a white-feathered bird strutting and crowing arrogantly in a nearby cage.

"I feel confident with this one," he said. "It has already won six times here."

"How long do you keep them fighting?" I wondered aloud, thinking that surely a six-time champion in such a perilous sport had earned a nice retirement.

Ramiro was matter-of-fact. "Pelean hasta la muerte," he said.

"Yes I understand that, but you've never had a rooster that kept winning and, no sé, retired from the sport because it became too old?"

A boy ran up, breathless, to save me from the ensuing silence and inform Ramiro that a suitable opponent had been found. The rancher nodded and the boy scurried off.

Ramiro had been fighting roosters for ten years, but the Chupaderos bouts were for fun and pocket money. He earned his living selling cattle from his ranch, called La Morena.

"How do you train the roosters for the fights?"

"You just hold the tail feathers, and make them run on the spot," he said. "That's all you have to do to build their muscles. It's natural that they fight one another. You just have to put them in the ring and they go for it."

I was tempted to point out that fixing steel razor blades onto comparatively benign talons wasn't exactly natural, but this didn't seem like the time or place to challenge the ethics of cockfighting. Instead, I asked him to explain his birds' pre-fight routine. It involved meals full of vitamins the night before, and Ramiro always made sure they were well-rested. Afterwards, the victorious rooster had his wounds stitched up. Within two weeks, he would be ready for the ring.

"Just two weeks?" I ask.

He nodded. "They're strong animals. It doesn't take them long to recover."

Ramiro was well-known in Chupaderos, and he spent the next half-hour peering over the crowds to watch bits of various bouts, shaking hands, talking to friends and, finally, spending a quiet moment with his rooster, carefully fixing the blade to its left ankle.

As Ramiro and his opposite number entered the ring, I sensed that this was a big-ticket fight. Both Ramiro and the other owner had brought their own secondary birds to warm up their fighter, rather than a ring-in rooster chosen at random. They waited a lot longer than usual for the bets and wagers to die down, letting the stakes rise until both were satisfied.

Ramiro's bird looked far stronger from the outset, slashing away with confidence and flaring his plumage as he leaped into the fray like the frightful battledress of some ancient tribe. But within two minutes, the weaker rooster managed a lucky strike at Ramiro's bird's face. The six-time champion staggered and his opponent threw everything at the opening, landing several more punishing blows from beak and blade, and in no time at all Ramiro's bird lay lifeless in the dirt. When the rancher picked him up by the feet, a stream of blood poured from the white rooster's beak and hacked-out eyes, like a tap that had been left on.

"A lucky day for the other guy," Ramiro shrugged when I offered my commiseration, the dead bird dangling uselessly from his hand. He offered a firm handshake and a rare smile, and his family wished me a pleasant afternoon.

# CHAPTER 22

Our next destination was the Sierra de Órganos, where we had planned the cowboy movie night. The country had thickened with agricultural towns and villages once we'd reached the plateau, making it easier to find spare power outlets in restaurants or the odd café. A fully charged battery in my hardy little laptop would last long enough to play one movie. If we were camping alone, I could plug in the portable speaker to enhance the cinematic experience. Headphone splitters and ear buds sufficed when we didn't want to disturb hosts or neighbors.

The Sierra de Órganos was a small range of mesa-like hills walled with tubular rock formations, rising from a flat landscape coated in pine trees and red dirt paddocks. We pitched our tents in a shady picnic area and spent an afternoon climbing up and around the orange columns of sandstone shaped like pipe organs, which give the place its name.

Returning to the picnic area, we found fifteen or so men and three women gathered around a van parked by a picnic table. All were dressed entirely in white, including trucker hats bejeweled with glittering plastic beads arranged to say "Jesús Te Ama" — *Jesus Loves You* — or crosses and hearts framed with angel's wings. A middle-aged fellow invited us over, and I noticed that his white clothes, white sneakers and browned skin were all spotlessly clean except for a black smudge on his forehead.

"You like it here?" he asked.

"It's very pretty," I said, eyeing their sound system — which was currently pumping banda hits — with concern. If they planned to stick around, those speakers would almost certainly disturb our sleep. "Very, ah, peaceful. What did you think of the Órganos?"

"Some of the most beautiful mountains we have seen so far," he replied.

"Where have you come from?"

"We're all from el D.F." Mexico City is also known as the Federal District — Distrito Federal — which is usually shortened to "the D.F." In Spanish the anagram comes out as "de effe," in much the same way as Americans call their capital city "dee see."

"And where are you headed?"

"We are walking to Mazatlán. It's a religious pilgrimage," he said, and I realized the mark on his forehead was a cross drawn in ash. They all had one.

Mazatlán was 1,300 kilometers from Mexico City. They had been walking for six weeks, completing one of the many Catholic pilgrim routes crisscrossing the country. They offered food: a bitter soup of pickles, radishes and so many chilies that we could barely stomach it in polite fashion. But they were friendly, so we stuck around.

We chatted about the roads north and south of there, and once dinner was finished — the women did not speak, but they did most of the work — one of the pilgrims produced a large mason jar. Packed inside were the largest, stickiest nuggets of marijuana I had ever seen. Jumbo-sized rolling papers appeared, and a pilgrim of at least sixty began shredding buds into a small mountain of odorous greenery. Another took up rolling duties, skilfully connecting three or four papers together at a time and before long, no less than four blunts the size of carrots were making their way from pilgrim to pilgrim. A younger traveler of 16 or 17 replaced the banda with throbbing techno beats and pumped his fists.

"We walk in the day and party at night," a pilgrim grinned, offering me a smoky blunt.

I glanced at Robbie — the afternoon had taken quite a turn.

All of a sudden, a pilgrim abruptly sprinted away and disappeared into the forest at the feet of the nearby range. Before long, his fellows began guffawing and pointing at the nearest outcrop of Órganos. The forested valley floor rose at an angle before the bare rock broke through, sheer until the sierra's flat table top some fifty meters above. At the very base of the cliff, the white linen shirt and pants of the pilgrim were visible against the red rock.

"Le gusta escalar," the pilgrims explained. *He likes to climb.*

"Does he have any ropes?" I asked lamely and got giggles in response.

The climber had impressive form, and quickly scooted upward. Then he paused. He was standing straight upright on a ledge, clinging to the rock face. He reached up with his right arm, searching for a hold, and found nothing. There was nothing to his left, either. Rob caught my eye from across the party while the hilarity around us reached new heights.

The pilgrim began searching for a way down, but whatever route he had taken up was evidently not suitable for a descent. He didn't move for five minutes or so. Then he started waving at the others who, by now, were actually rolling on the ground in insane fits of laughter.

"No way up and no way down!" wailed one.

"¡Se va a caer, güey!" another guffawed. *He's going to fall, bro!*

The oldest among them was chuckling merrily but, unlike the others, had managed to keep his feet beneath him.

"Is your compañero going to be okay?" I asked him quietly. "Does this happen often?"

The man let out a stream of Spanish that, while too fast and slang-heavy for Robbie and I to catch, seemed to strike an optimistic tone. I glanced back at Rob, who looked satisfied and tilted his head ever so slightly toward our campsite.

"Geez, is that what I was missing at Christian Youth Group all those years?" I wondered as we power-walked back to our tents. "Don't get me wrong, I hope that kid's okay — I just don't want any part of it."

"Mate, if that lot has made it this far from Mexico City, Jesus really must be looking out for them," Robbie said then added: "He certainly looked after us." He showed me a fistful of buds, passed to him by a generous pilgrim.

*The War Wagon* was mindless good fun with John Wayne and Kirk Douglas leading a band of scruffy outlaws in a wagon heist, but it was also quite racist. As an uninitiated John Wayne viewer, I was particularly shocked by one slapstick scene where hooting Native Americans fight over a bottle of whiskey. At one point, Wayne and Douglas — a pair of white men — are seeking a gang headed by a man named Calita. Wayne approaches two Mexican peasants in ponchos and sombreros to ask for "some información" in clunky gringo Spanish.

"Dahnde es el campo de Calita," he says, and the peasants shake their heads. Wayne shrugs and offers them a drink from a bottle of liquor.

"Un trago," one smiles gratefully — every non-white character in the movie seems obsessed with acquiring alcohol.

Meanwhile, Douglas approaches a young Mexican woman. She offers him tequila, they whisper in one another's ears and he drops a few coins down her low-cut top. After theatrically leaping aboard his horse, he surprises Wayne with directions to Calita's hideout.

"You have to appeal to their intellect," he explains, smirking. Gross.

But this was still Hollywood's heyday of sprawling location shoots, and the Sierra de Órganos played a starring role. In several aerial shots, we could actually see the place where our tents were currently pitched.

Our days soon developed a rhythm as we pedaled south along this industrious plateau. We rose, gobbled porridge and pedaled until lunchtime, when we could generally count on some pretty little colonial town or village to appear amid the gentle brown hills around the highway. After a quick grocery stop at an abarrotes we'd make for the central plaza, surrounded by storefronts and a church or cathedral, and shaded by trees painted white against insect attack.

Every town and village had a plaza, but the look and feel would vary from town to town. Cuquío had piped-in music and an abundance of elderly ladies in colorful summer dresses. Sain Alto was chock-full of children. The sole line of business in Villa Hidalgo appeared to be clothing retailers — we struggled to find a supermarket amid all the tailors. Once we had located one (a small, understocked abarrotes — what did the people of Villa Hidalgo eat?), we sat in the plaza and watched a procession pass. A small boy led the group holding an airbrushed portrait of a woman in her fifties, while six men sporting her distinctively flattened nose carried a casket. The plaza old timers stopped muttering and held their hats to their chests, parents quieted their children, teenagers slunk off to canoodle elsewhere.

So we made our picnics in the squares and then, while one of us stayed with the bikes and sat for Interviews with curious passersby — "Where did you start?" and "How much does it all weigh?" — the other ventured off in search of the nearest Michoacana.

Michoacana is the main purveyor of aguas frescas in Mexico, and though the garish pink décor and faded posters of eighties-era fruit spreads remain more or less the same across the country, the flavors and the quality of the aguas themselves vary with local tastes. Aguas frescas are made, as far as I could tell, by combining water, the juice of whatever fruit or flower the flavor was named for and copious amounts of sugar in a large Styrofoam cup.

Here in the central northern part of the country, the milky cinnamon horchata was in its prime. Robbie often experimented with the various fruity flavors — Jamaica (*hibiscus*), coco (*coconut*), maracuya (*passionfruit*), sandía (*watermelon*) and naranja (*orange*), among others — but these, we later learned, were but shallow imitations of what they would become in the tropical south.

"I probably look quite poor right now," Robbie announced one afternoon, having slurped the dregs from his limón con chía (*lemonade with chia seeds*), "but I feel very rich." We were sitting on the cobblestones of a plaza in Sombrerete and leaning against a raised garden bed — the shady benches having already been claimed by this town's peculiar abundance of elderly men in gigantic cowboy hats.

And so we waited out the hottest parts of the early afternoons, which were becoming hotter as we rolled southward and February turned to March. We rose early to beat the sun and replaced our cycling helmets with broad-brimmed straw hats, which flipped off our heads on fast descents and tugged at our throats from makeshift chinstraps fashioned from old shoelaces.

One morning, we were sweating up a breezeless stretch of road that cut narrowly through a hillside. Robbie's map assured us that a town called Teocaltiche would appear soon, and lunch with it. There was little traffic, and the accompanying silence allowed us to hear individual cars as they approached from behind. I was now able to determine the size and velocity of the approaching vehicle by its sound alone. As this engine droned up from behind, there was something in the unyielding pressure the driver exerted on the accelerator, the directness of the noise, that said it was pointed straight at us.

I guessed everything correctly except the color of the truck (dual-cab late-1990's Chevy, but it was silver, not red), including the size of the gap between my elbow and its side mirror as it blazed by. I was hot and cranky and I gave the truck's diminishing rear an impotent middle finger.

The brake lights flashed immediately. The truck gurgled in the road, waiting. I pulled over, leaned Baxter against the inner wall of that gouged hill and peed in the gutter. Rob labored up toward me. The car had not moved.

"I think I've gotten us into a bit of trouble," I began.

"You got yourself in trouble," Robbie puffed and pushed on without looking back.

Abandoned to my fate, I pulled Baxter upright and pedaled the few strokes to draw alongside the driver's window. An entire family was inside: three gawking daughters in the back, a mother with greasy flyaways in the passenger's seat and a grumpy father in a black cap to match his mustache.

"¿Qué?" he snarled, turning his palm over at me through the open window.

"Señor, you passed very close, you scared me," I stammered, careful to address him in the respectful third person, averting my eyes. The driver looked me up and down, put the truck in gear.

"Puta madre," he growled. He lifted the clutch and his family lurched as one as the truck pulled away.

Later, we found shady grass behind a bus stop above little Apulco. Before long, a kid of nine or ten named Santiago sat down for a chat. Robbie was giving me a haircut at the time, but Santiago didn't appear to notice for he was in the midst of possibly the greatest adventure of his life thus far.

He had been attending his cousin's seventh birthday over in Teocaltiche when his mother — for some reason or another, we never heard the full story — realized she needed cash. As the eldest son, Santiago had been instructed on the whereabouts of a piggy bank in the family's Apulco home, entrusted with a handful of coins for the bus and sent to retrieve it. He now had the money squirreled away in a small backpack decorated with images of the kid's cartoon character Ben 10, and was waiting for a bus to take him back to the party.

When asked what awaited him back at his cousin's house, Santiago's eyes began to swim dreamily. They had cakes there, he said, a big pink one — not his absolute favorite color, mind, just when it came to cakes — and a jumping castle and loads of balloons. There had been murmurs among the older kids about the possibility of a clown, though Santiago wasn't sure if his sources could be trusted. Los dulces, however — *the sweets* — were calling his name.

Santiago became so caught up in fresh memories of chili-coated treats that the bus to Teocaltiche was a cloud of receding exhaust before he'd registered what had happened.

Now our little friend was in trouble. His mother was expecting him. He bent double as he sat beside Oscar and groaned.

"¡Ay! ¿Saben si viene otro bus?" he asked desperately.

We didn't know if another bus would come, and he trotted off to ask a group of ladies nearby — sitting in the shade of the bus shelter, but with no apparent intention of actually hailing a ride — to ask them the same question. He then became so absorbed in this conversation that he failed to notice the next bus as it growled over the rise, the word "Teocaltiche" prominent in the windscreen. Robbie and I yelled and waved, the bus thudded over the dusty kerb, and it was only when the door opened and the driver glared at Robbie and I that Santiago noticed it.

"Mi salvación!" he squeaked, and leapt aboard.

A day later, we awoke in a park outside a town with the wonderful name of Yahualica de González Gallo. On the invitation of a teenager we'd befriended the night before, we went into town to look for Gorditas Antonia Martínez, his mother's gordita stand. The town center was a packed-in jumble of large, century-old multi-story buildings. A mercado took up a whole city block adjacent to the central plaza. Inside, the various types of restaurants — gorditas, taquerías, loncherías, birrieras — vied for attention along with the butchers, fruit and vegetable vendors and leatherworks.

We found the gordita stand on a corner outside the market, the small tables and sprawling open-air kitchen jostling for space amid the snack stands and juice vendors. Antonia Martínez herself was away but her daughter, who had taken over as head chef, smiled and said she'd been expecting us.

A gordita — which translates to "little fatty" — is a corn tortilla that has been fried, slit open and then stuffed like a pita bread with whatever concoctions the chef has cooked up. There were thirteen terracotta pots arranged on a large hotplate, full of various pieces of pig and cow including tripa, lengua — or tongue — and corazón del puerco alongside nopal cactus and fried potato. The heart was stringy, almost gamey, and I preferred the greasy chicharrón.

A man sat next to me at a communal table and introduced himself as Sebastián. He had lived for some time in the United States and spoke English with a New York movie gangster's accent.

"This yoosed to be a dangerous town faahve o' six years ago," he said.

"Why not anymore? What happened?" I asked.

"It was war, man," he said, loud enough to make me uncomfortable. "One side won, one side lost." He shrugged and refused to say any more.

I looked around at this community serenely going about its mid-morning routine — trucks full of laborers and farm hands rolling over the cobblestones on their way to hardware stores across town, aproned women industriously stirring at frying pans on their wheeled kitchen carts, folks taking time to stop and chat with one another. I wanted to know more — what war? Who was fighting and why? — but, as guests of Antonia Martínez's family, I preferred to avoid asking impolite questions and stirring up bad memories.

The younger Señorita Martínez refused to let us pay, as did her kitchen hands. As a last resort, I tried to leave a paltry 50 pesos as "propina," but even this was politely handed back.

Midday heat had settled in a stillness over the countryside as we climbed out of town, and at the top of a large hill, on a road lined with sooty mechanic workshops, Robbie's odometer clicked over to 3,000 kilometers. We never failed to observe our usual thousand-kilometer ritual, and by the time I'd returned with beers Robbie had found a seat at a bus stop, sheltered from the sun by a broken concrete roof. He sat next to an old man in a red shirt, a blue vest, jeans and a hat. The man's skin was deep brown, and he wore a bushy white mustache. His name was Jesús, he said, and he was 82 years old.

Jesús had seen it all, apparently, and two gringos on bicicletas cargadas didn't elicit any surprise — just an opportunity to tell his life's story. He entered the world in Yahualica de González Gallo, grew up there, then left in 1951. He said he'd traveled up through Baja California when the Transpeninsular Highway was little more than a donkey track.

"Tijuana was just two streets," he wheezed. "Los Ángeles era un pueblito, nada mas." *Los Angeles was no more than a little town.*

He hopped a train to the Bay Area, where he settled in Oakland.

"I lived in Oakland all my life," he said, swallowing Oakland's "d." "I have five children, thirteen grandchildren."

"Todos viven ahí en Oakland?"

"Sí."

"¿Entonces hablas inglés?" I wondered, eager to hear his English.

"Pues," he smiled. "Unas palabras. Train. Bus. Dollar. Please. Tank-you."

"Don't you miss your family?" I asked, switching back to Spanish.

"Yes. I do. I visit them often. But in the end, we return to where we were born."

It wasn't until we'd crested the hill and Baxter's weight began to carry him forward again that I understood what Jesús had said: "Siempre regresamos a donde nacimos." After building a life far away, Jesús had returned to be buried in the soil that had raised him.

# CHAPTER 23

We were following a small creek at the feet of some low hills beside a wide plain of empty fields. Old haciendas decomposed into the forest, while stores and houses with boarded-up windows stooped at the roadside. Robbie pointed at a patch of bushes by a bend in the creek.

"I think we've found it for tonight," he said.

But I was impatient to make a dent in the remaining kilometers to the city of Guanajuato, still a day away, and there were at least a couple of hours of sunlight left in the afternoon.

"I think we can keep going."

"Sure?" Rob said. "We're not gonna do better for privacy. Plus: there's running water."

It was tempting. We'd been on the road for almost a week without a shower since the city of Guadalajara, and running water meant washing off. But I felt frisky on the pedals and I was sure we'd find an even nicer spot further along.

We pedaled on into the plain as the road curved away from the creek. Stone walls marked farmers' fields right up to the road, and there were no stands of trees or patches of public land to hide in. I entered a shaken looking abarrotes where, apart from the ubiquitous American soft drinks, there wasn't much on the dusty shelves besides a handful of sad carrots, some old sweets by the counter and a few mismatched cans. I felt the other customers watching me from the corners of the room, eyes flicking back to the shelves when I turned to wish them a "buenas tardes." When I asked about a place to camp, the cashier kept his gaze on the till as he shook his head.

Eventually we found a sloping field with an open gate. We camped in a corner under a small clutch of trees. There was a homestead much further up, but we saw no-one. Mud from the field clogged up the wheels of the bikes. It started to rain.

We cooked and ate dinner sitting in my small tent. Rain thrummed on the fly. We said nothing. Rob grabbed the washing up, stood to leave, then forced his eyes to mine.

"Next time, we stop at the fucking creek," he said.

"Yeah," I whispered. "Shit, sorry."

In the morning I woke to a stern "Buenos días." I poked my head out to find a farmer wearing dark jeans and a button-up shirt of black and blue checks. He wore gumboots to guard his feet from the mud on this chilly highland morning. He stood a respectful distance away from our camp, but his mustache bristled with a quiet anger.

"We saw your lights," he said coldly, nodding at his house further up the hillside. "Thought you were here to steal our cattle." He spoke slow and clear, careful to make himself understood. "We were up worrying all night. We thought maybe you had weapons."

Silence emanated from Robbie's tent, but I knew he was listening.

"In future, I advise you to take care," the farmer continued. "There are people here who are not as kindly as us. You can get hurt, entering land that isn't yours."

"That happens?" I asked. "The cattle rustling, I mean. It's just that we've camped like this in many other places and never had any trouble."

"Here it does," he said, then "have a good trip." And he stumped away.

"I know, I know," I said to Robbie's still-silent tent. "Next time, the fucking creek."

The tent's fly zipped open.

"Always nice to have visitors in the morning," he smiled.

Around midday we stopped to wait out more rain in a town called Romita, where the plaza's defining feature was a border of trees with canopies trimmed into thick, identical trapezoids. I left Robbie shivering under a shelter by the bikes to seek out an internet café and when I found one, sent a flurry of Couchsurfing requests to hosts in Guanajuato and resisted the urge to head straight to my Facebook messages. I was expecting a message from Hailee.

In her last text she'd mentioned her travel plans for India and Southeast Asia in June and July, but now her companion for the Indian leg had accepted a job and pulled out. Having recounted this turn of events, she mentioned that "if I could go to one place in Mexico right now it would be Chiapas, I would so like to learn more about the Zapatistas."

Despite our regular exchange of messages every few weeks, Hailee and I had never broached the nature of our relationship, or what had happened between us in Berkeley. But now she was flagging — semaphoring, really — that it was time to make good on the invitation I'd suggested when we last saw each other, when I'd said she was welcome to join me in Central America after her graduation.

*You've kind of been stuck in my head since I left San Francisco,* I wrote, *and, well, I'm not sure that's really happened to me before. We've talked a little about this but in all seriousness, I'd love to see you again and doing so among the beaches and jungles and pyramids down south would be very cool. So consider this an invitation: if you have the time, the resources (and I completely understand if you don't) and most of all, "las ganas" to tack a little Central American leg onto your SE Asia trip you should go ahead and do it. You're more than welcome. You mentioned Chiapas. Well, it's possible I'll be in Chiapas in around two months and if you're going to be there, I can make sure I am too.*

I'd sent this message just before we left Guadalajara, then spent hours of collective saddle time actively pushing her away when she wandered into my mind, refusing to indulge the fantasy. Small-town internet cafes had tempted me with the promise of a reply all the way across the central highlands, but I resisted until I had a plausible reason to enter — like the need to send Couchsurfing requests. Now, in a Romita cybercafe, I ignored Facebook's gaggle of irrelevant notifications and — heart thumping in my chest — headed for the messaging section of the site.

*Let me start by saying yes, absolutely yes, to a rendezvous in Central America. Because, well, you've kind of been stuck in my head too. So let's do it!*

There were logistics to figure out and parents to notify, but she sounded excited and so was I, reading and rereading her message amid the usual internet cafe crowds of young boys shrieking over the shoulders of their zombie-slaying friends, or furtively ignoring the stern, crucifix-bearing signs forbidding internet pornography within this particular establishment. She'd also sent music: Mac DeMarco, The Districts, James Brown. I hurried out and positively floated through the rain back to Robbie — cold, hungry, I'd been gone far too long — to tell him the news. His jaw was vibrating with cold, but he grinned, shook his head and slapped me on the back.

In the afternoon the highway skirted a gray city called Silao, where the traffic thickened and then clogged a waterlogged ring road. We threaded our wheels around puddles and potholes, slipped between sooty trucks, smoking buses and the resigned faces of commuters in fogged windows. At a bend in the road, a line of auto stores and mechanics sat back across an expanse of scarred bitumen. The lightly crunched body of a bus kneeled on a broken wheel against the façade of one, and a truck stuck out into traffic, blocking several lanes. The truck's red cabin was mangled like a scrunched piece of paper and a door hung like a half-severed ear. There were police cars and squat officers in jack boots chatting into radios. Lying off to the side amid mangled bits of metal, rancid puddles and drifts of shattered glass, a pair of bodies drew the commuters' eyes. Somebody had thrown old blankets over them, but grazed hands, mussed hair and scrubbed trainers were visible at the edges.

"You okay?" Robbie asked later, once we'd stopped for a rest outside town.

"Yeah." I was looking at the asphalt between my feet. "I'd never seen a body before, though. Guess I still haven't, really — just those blankets. How're you doing?"

"I'm okay," he said, voice drooping. "Just thinking that no matter how bad your day is, there's always someone out there who's got it worse."

We entered Guanajuato city to find my Couchsurfing requests had gone unanswered, and the few hostels and hotels all too expensive. It was raining and dark, the city was hilly and its streets were cobblestoned. Lights glowed in high windows, cathedral bells echoed in the adobe alleys twisting up the valley walls, cobbles slicked in lamplight. We stole Wi-Fi and sheltered in the doorway of a hotel, taking turns to warm our hands or scan Couchsurfing with Robbie's phone. At the last moment, a student named Alejandra gave us her address.

Alejandra — Ale to her friends — lived in an angular apartment wedged into the base of one of the steep valley walls cradling the city. Later, once her friends had cleared out and her housemates had gone to bed, I lay back on the fold-out couch, plugged in my headphones, called up her latest batch of music on my phone and at last allowed myself to dream of Hailee.

## CHAPTER 24

As a car-free city of cobblestones, plazas and charmed alleyways, Guanajuato was an urban paradise. The city was packed with students, centuries-old cantinas and street dogs whose names everyone knew. Students and storytellers endlessly congregated in Ale's apartment. Several days went by before Rob and I had avoided a drink of mescal or a hit from Ale's house marijuana pipe — named Ashanti — long enough to check a calendar and realize we had better leave now, or we might never do so at all.

Our Australian cycling duo was due to double in size in two weeks' time. Robbie's university friend Jamie would be the first to arrive, followed by his older brother Simon.

So we had something of a schedule, and had planned an expedition for the weeks in between to an area known as La Huasteca. The name refers to the Huastecs, a pre-Columbian people who occupy the eastern edge of the Mexican plateau at the intersection of the modern states of San Luis Potosí, Querétaro and Hidalgo. This section of our road map was now completely covered with an unusual concentration of notes in varied handwriting, including a cryptic sentence: "Tierra de montañas y selvas." *Land of mountains and jungles.* A Couchsurfing host in Aguascalientes had underlined it twice.

So we scooted east across the dry plateau, crossed a dust-wreathed freeway and followed a scrappy road strewn with rubbish and tumbleweeds into San Luis de la Paz. We stayed with a former competitive cyclist named Luis, who we met at a bike store on the way out of town.

"I think of cyclists as vagabonds," he said. "That's how I feel on my bike — I come and go, often alone. When I was younger, I used to be up at four in the morning to train, and out on the roads around here you'd be completely alone. Maybe you'd pass a car or a truck every hour or so. I loved it. Whenever I had a few hours to spare, I'd be off on my bike."

"Luis gets it," Robbie said later, once the wiry old man had shuffled off to bed and we were brushing our teeth over his kitchen sink.

In the morning, the road led us into hills ringing the eastern edge of a sparse and scrubby plain. Rain had started the night before with a theatrical booming of thunder and continued into the morning, but we figured such a storm would soon peter out in dry country like this.

It was still raining around 9 a.m. when Robbie and I pulled into a gravel pit and hastily drained cans of Modelo to celebrate my 9,000th kilometer. Then we left the highway and began pushing up steep hills, finding and then skirting the high edge of a craggy ridge. It kept raining. We stopped at the pass and entered a smoky hut of salvaged timber, tin and sheets of plastic. Inside, a woman in a white cardigan and starched pink gown fried gorditas in a pan over an oil drum fire. The hem of her gown was soaked in mud. A daughter sat in silence, ready with a Coke bottle filled with grease.

We ate. My feet were cold and heavy in sodden shoes, and a hole in the roof dripped down my neck if I leaned against the tin wall. The gordita woman stared out at the rain in silence. Robbie caught my eye and cocked his head in the direction of the bikes. I took a deep breath and nodded. We murmured our thanks to the silent cook and her daughter, and walked back into the rain.

We climbed into the clouds and the world outside our patch of road faded to silhouettes of mountain spines floating above and below us, disconnected from any discernible horizon or earthly landscape. In time these were replaced with a tall, dripping pine forest ringed with mist. A group of men raised large caguama bottles of beer and cheered from a ruined abarrotes.

"Chequeá los frenos porque viene la bajada!" one hollered. *Check your brakes because the descent is coming!*

And down we went, incinerating brake pads to maintain purchase on the wild road as it wound and bucked off the plateau's edge. Landslides covered the road in patches. My hands ached from pulling on the brake levers and rain stung my eyes. Dark sierras appeared across the gray abyss, looming like a rising swell as we hurtled down into this first fold of the country's tumultuous descent into the Gulf of Mexico.

We waited out the rain for two days and nights at Xichú —
pronounced like a sneeze — in the canyon's narrow floor. We followed
a river on a dirt track out of town, promptly lost our bearings and only
rarely recovered them over the next two weeks. Constantly twisting
mountain roads mocked the "inner compass" we thought we'd been
nurturing and humid, omnipresent cloud cover meant we didn't see the
sun for several days. We navigated based on Robbie's offline maps app,
the name of a town and the word of villagers who confirmed that our
current route might take us there.

We climbed a series of muddy switchbacks away from the river and
into the low sky, only to emerge completely disoriented at the bottom
of a misty valley. We spent the second and third day bumping along a
stony dirt road with mist, sloping meadows and happy cattle on either
side. We paused two or three times a day to let a pickup truck pass,
camped early on the flat patches when we could find them. There were
few people to speak with, and we seldom found any reason to speak to
one another.

One night, I played the Beat Connection song *Silver Screen* — a
Hailee recommendation — as we cooked dinner in an early, misty
twilight. I hoped the upbeat synths would chase away the gloom.

"Can't say it's my favorite," Robbie said as the last notes died away.

On the fourth day the clouds lifted to reveal that we'd actually been
perched on a high ridgeline the whole time, and then we zoomed down
into a sunny valley to a paved road and a clear river. When we looked
back, the Sierra Gorda was dark with clouds again, and our memories
of that place faded almost without trace.

# CHAPTER 25

As we ventured deeper into the Huasteca, the edges of reality turned increasingly fuzzy. The scrubby foliage of the plateau became a jungle that steamed by day and screamed at night. The skin of our legs became a jumbled mess of insect bites, but we soon became desensitized to the itching. We peeled clothes from the musty mess in our panniers, discovering that a shirt we'd sweated into days before had never dried.

At night, the mountainous countryside dissolved into a starless, moonless dark. Speckled constellations of village lights ranged high and low around us, as if we were floating in outer space.

We stopped in at the Sótano de las Golondrinas, following a recommendation that had been scribbled onto my road map. We found it on an obscure hillside, hidden down a track in the seething jungle: an immense cave bored vertically into the limestone, a 370-meter hole. We lay on our stomachs, heads peeking over the edge, swearing loudly. At dusk, thousands of sparrows flurried out, hovering at the edges, billowing and swirling as one like steam from a volcano.

Next, we pedaled up a narrow canyon, then scaled a bluff carrying the town of Xilitla. Just outside town, we found mossy concrete structures sinking beneath the soggy weight of the jungle: twisting staircases that led nowhere, elaborate columns, arches and delicate facades blending into the foliage, mimicking the irregular shapes of the trees and vines. A series of stones and mossy concrete ramps funneled water from a waterfall to a series of pools through the steep jungle.

This was the surrealist garden of Edward James, a trust fund Brit who'd spent his youth hobnobbing with the likes of Dalí and Magritte back in Europe, and dabbled in his own writing and sculpture through the first half of the 20th century.

Then, in the early 1940s, James traveled to Los Angeles to build his own little garden of surrealist Eden. Finding southern California much too crowded and overrun, he ventured south and ended up in the steamy jungles of the Huasteca. He chose well — as the French artist Andre Breton reportedly said during his own visit in 1938, Mexico is "the most surrealist country."

With the help of hundreds of local artisans and laborers, James built innumerable sculptures between 1949 and 1984, when he died. All construction was halted upon his death, though unfinished staircases and dead-end alleyways were all part of the aesthetic anyway.

The place gave off a kind of dreadful whimsy, like stumbling through Rivendell long after the elves have disappeared and taken their civilizing enchantments with them. We drank mescal, swam in the pools and got lost in its twisting paths and deceitful passageways.

We left town and rode south on Route 85, the only toll-free highway linking Mexico City directly to the United States, a rumbling corridor of commerce ferrying goods between the high volcanic capital and the desert outpost of Nuevo Laredo. Mechanics, no-frills restaurants and little houses surrounded by hogs, turkeys and stands of banana trees, sugar cane and corn flanked this stretch of road, along with the sad little clutches of crosses and miniature chapels for the Virgen de Guadalupe. Among them, shrines now appeared dedicated to Santa Muerte — "Saint Death." In these, the familiar figure of the Virgin had a skull for a face. She was typically surrounded by half-smoked joints and cigarettes, bottles of cheap mescal with a sip or two left in the bottom and prayers petitioning punishment for one's enemies — a blend of Catholic and pre-Columbian belief that would surely scandalize the frocked bureaucrats in Rome. Kamikaze buses barreled into dusty kerbs and deployed teenage salesmen to shout city names at travelers. Truckers gathered around cook fires and liquor stores, waiting for their geriatric engines to cool.

The people here— gum-booted men bearing machetes, laborers sitting atop overstuffed pickup trucks, women in floral dresses working with water, tubs and sopping cloth in open-air laundries, stirring a pot or frying tortillas — were more reserved than elsewhere in Mexico. We had more conversations about weather and agriculture than Interviews about where we'd come from and how much our bicycles weighed, and for this we grew to like the Huastecs.

Cacti and agave reappeared as the highway climbed into dry country. Not long after crossing into the state of Hidalgo, we passed a turnoff marked with a sign saying it led to the "Cerro de la Cruz" — the *Hill of the Cross*.

"What is this hill of the cross?" I asked a mechanic in a nearby workshop.

"Pues…" he began, rubbing his hands on a rag. "It's a hill… with a cross."

The oversized crucifix stood on a hilltop balcony above the small town of Jacala, with the usual Huastec disorder of fog-wreathed mountains beyond. We stayed the night, then rolled off the hill into town to stock up on provisions the next morning. Robbie had plotted a route toward Mexico City via a series of small, ominously squiggly roads.

"Cycling-wise, it looks terrible," Robbie grinned. "Up for an adventure?"

We followed a gravel road down a steep-sided valley. Ancient haciendas lurked within stands of oak that had outlasted them, and masses of butterflies flurried around our wheels. We turned off at a junction and climbed a road that was little more than a slip of loose stones switchbacking its way up to the wonderfully named village of Chichicaxtla, then on past three granite pillars overlooking the slanted main street. At the top we crossed a small, chilly basin full of happy goats, then rolled over a small pass and down into a gigantic canyon. Ahead and across from us, a humongous granite wall reminiscent of Yosemite's Half Dome reared up, seeming to draw a black wall of cloud from the southern horizon, beyond which the metropolis lay in wait.

We made our camp among the goats on a grassy balcony overlooking the dome and the valley, watching lightning ripple through the sky as we ate dinner. The booms and cracks of the thunder grew, and by the end of the meal we were racing the storm, scoffing down the last of our dinner as the first rain drops began thwacking into the grass around us. We threw bags and cooking gear into the tents as hail began to ricochet off our arms and legs. I never saw Rob, just dived in and zipped the fly home. In the light of my head torch, I found my tent a sodden mess. Thunder boomed and rattled as if the gods were out for a night of bowling overhead.

I hoped Rob was dry and warm, but there was no way to communicate over the din of the rain. Dustings of moisture were filtering through my tent's aging fly, the wet outside world seeping into my dry bubble.

In the morning we descended to a river, then climbed up to the junction where steep canyon walls turned to vertical cliff face at the foot of the Half Dome impersonator. This was the Grutas Tolantongo, the third and final stop on this little Huastec tour.

Las Grutas Tolantongo is a complex of gardens, rooms and a restaurant arranged around concrete pools. These pools catch thermally heated water leaching out from the base of the granite wall. The water is laden with all sorts of strange minerals, and a series of gutters funnels it between bathing pools until it escapes the system and cascades into the river far below. Throughout this journey, the water deposits tiny pieces of calcium as it brims over a rim, or tumbles down a wall, or even as it drips on a branch, so that rocks, concrete and plant matter alike became covered in weird brain-like bulbs or concentric circles built like tiny steps, all in an opaque white material the color and texture of teeth.

Once we had set up our tents, I dug in my panniers for two tiny pieces of blotter paper. Tommy had left them with us as a farewell gift way back in La Paz. We arranged our campsite as if we were preparing for the arrival of children, making sure our head torches and stoves were stored in obvious places, stowing any fragile or easily lost items. We then ate the papers and settled into a nearby pool.

This was our first experience with LSD, and the chemicals focused — or distracted — our minds like never before. Robbie spent the first hour or three laying on his back in the water, playing with the effect it had on his hearing and exploring the ribbed walls of his little domain with his fingertips. I was following the progress of various ants as they roamed the geometric terrain, careful to avoid the ripples cascading over the miniature terraces.

Giggling and chattering, we followed the water downhill to a tunnel bored into the canyon wall, exposed by some kind of landslide. It was pitch black inside, and even darker in the many holes and crevices that fanned out from the main chamber. Hot water poured from cracks in the ceiling, and at the end of the tunnel we found a deep, hot pool. Our fear subsided when we discovered three families soaking there, so we joined them for quite a while and let our eyes adjust to the dark.

"Time for some sunshine?" I asked after a while.

"Sunshine time," Robbie agreed, and off we went. At the mouth of the tunnel, the cascading water turned into a brilliant shower of sunlight as it caught the afternoon rays. Without warning, Robbie sprinted for the exit, and I watched the big man burst into the open, throw back his head and begin to yell.

"It's raining!" he screamed and followed it up with a wild animal howl which lasted long after I arrived puffing at his side.

Señoras and waiters and children in floaties were peering down from the pools at the shrieking gringo in their midst. It wasn't raining — just the waterfall — but I felt the same unreasonable joy at being in the sunshine again. This center of attention was no place to linger, however, and I took Rob by the arm and led him away.

As the afternoon wore on, clouds gathered above the canyon's rim. We had tried flips into the deeper pools, picked at lunch in the restaurant and climbed up through the pools, seeking hotter water closer to the source. A joint venture to the bathroom — neither of us felt confident enough to be alone at this point — led to a long and introspective period of inspecting our sunburned, stubbly faces in a mirror. This was a rare treat for cycle tourists, but one that unsettled us in our current state. We returned to the warm upper pools and watched the skies overhead darken and rumble, throwing shadows over the canyon. Leafless tree limbs above us seemed cartoonishly menacing against the leaden sky. We dashed undercover as thunder began to boom directly overhead, and took seats to drink beer, nibble food and watch the storm come in.

Six or seven old timers in their swimsuits were playing Lotería at a table nearby. It had been many hours since we'd eaten the LSD, and a kind of melancholy had replaced the afternoon's dizzying chemical rush. We sat in silence, listening to the thunder and an elderly woman at the next table rhythmically calling the cards as her fellows scrutinized their boards: "El mundo. La sirena. El catrín. La rana."

"I'd much rather be an old person in Mexico," Robbie said quietly.

"Hmm?"

"Wherever your family goes, they take you with them," he explained. "Look at all these wrinkly people — their families packed them up, brought them along on holiday. How many families do you know that take their grandparents and great grandparents on holiday with them?"

"Not many," I admitted.

"Where we come from, you get hidden away in some retirement home," Robbie went on. There was a rare hint of bitterness in his voice. "You're a thing to be *visited*, treated with increasing condescension until you die and everyone can finally go back to their lives."

"'Everyone's on their own adventure,'" I said, thinking of Joff.

"Yeah, I know," Robbie sighed, plucking at the plastic tabletop with his fingernail. I followed his gaze back to the Lotería table, where an elderly woman was clapping her hands, celebrating a win. One of her competitors dandled a tiny baby on his lap. Parents were feeding plain tortillas to squirming toddlers, and grown children were spooning pozole into the mouths of ancient grandparents.

"You'd never have convinced me to stay in the town where I grew up, surrounded by family," Robbie said. "But all these people seem to be on their adventures together. And I envy them."

# CHAPTER 26

Mexico City pools in the high Valle de México, lapping at the surrounding mountains like a dam whose sudden disappearance would send a flood of concrete and traffic spilling onto the wide plains and steaming jungles below. The megalopolis is a citadel staffed with the nation's most ambitious and most desperate, petrocrats and refugees, street urchins and the trust-fund teenagers known as "fresas" (*strawberries*), corporate thieves and pickpockets. The lakes, canals, temples and markets of the watery Aztec capital of Tenochtitlan — a city five times larger than London at the time of the Spanish invasion — have long since been drained, demolished and replaced with dour Catholic monuments, highways, skyscrapers and teeming layers of brick and concrete.

It is a labyrinth of rooms buried under rooms and barriers upon barriers: high walls, shutters, electrified wires, broken glass lodged in concrete slops, and all of it stained with a smog that crowds the thin, high-altitude air. The traffic is so bad that it calcifies into eternal, unmoving parking lots. Many drivers who found a parking spot in the 1970's have left their vehicles on the street to rot, which is evidently preferable to actually driving somewhere and therefore having to find another space. Pollution hides the mountains ringing the city and, in doing so, erases one's daily reminder of the wider world. The idea of this faraway capital lodged in the country's cultural and geographic heart had thrilled me ever since we entered through Tijuana's remote back door, and I couldn't wait to see it up close.

We approached from the north, watching the multiplying traffic and increasingly polluted farmland warn of the metropolis ahead. Robbie navigated us to the very tip of one of the metro system's many tentacles and we rolled in right on time ahead of rush hour, but a jackbooted security señora shook her head as we wheeled the bikes into the station.

"No," she said, waggling a finger. "No, no, no. No se permite la bicicleta."

"You're going to throw us back into those crazy streets?" I pleaded.

"Sí," she replied, and walked away.

"Just this once?" I asked the empty station. Robbie shrugged.

"Welcome to the big city, I suppose," he said, and patiently began plotting a route into the center of the labyrinth.

We plunged back into the streets. It was Friday afternoon and, all at once, tens of millions of office workers and laborers were squeezing into their cars and crowding the kerbs in search of a bus. The sun went down, it began to rain. It was hours before we reached our destination. City folk hid their faces against the dim beams of streetlights. Headlights lit exhaust fumes and falling rain. Whole intersections submerged under a foot of water in the downpour. These evening thunderstorms would descend almost every afternoon during our two weeks in the city, and bewildered chilangos — slang for a Mexico City local — kept telling us that this was supposed to be the dry season, that they'd never seen anything like it.

Our host in Mexico City was Alejandra, an experienced cycle tourist who lived in the upmarket central neighborhood of Nápoles. She had pale skin, freckles, a frizzy shock of dark hair and the same deliberate movements as Robbie. She was little — her bicycle was small enough for a child — and she worked in an underpaid office job that she hated. She had a dry sense of humor and a rare, toothy smile whose appearance was only assured when the conversation turned to bicycles — the alley cat races she officiated and competed in around the city, her first tour in Guatemala, a recent ride across Britain. When she was finished, she would lace her fingers in front of her and sigh dreamily. She was a big advocate of the Brompton-branded folding bicycles, having used one on her British tour several years earlier.

"You fold it up, carry it like a suitcase and hop on the train," she said. "You two should be on Bromptons — then they would've let you on the metro."

"Ale, I don't mean any offense by this, but I'm about three times larger than you," Robbie said gently. "I love the idea, but I don't think they'd be suitable for us."

Alejandra shrugged. "Your loss. I'm a city-sized person." She looked Robbie up and down — he was almost literally three times her size. "You're much too big to survive here."

Rob's friend Jamie soon arrived and added his bags to my untidy piles of gear and Robbie's neatly packed panniers and folded clothes.

"Really looking forward to getting on the road with you blokes and riding this country's graceful southern arc," he said one day, one of his many grandiose pronouncements about the coming adventure. Jamie was as tall as Robbie, though he carried slightly more weight. His curly hair was a brownish red, and a feather earring dangled from an ear. "It's just hard to imagine there's a whole world out there beyond this city." He was smoking a cigarette, staring pensively out the window and wearing nothing but a pair of underpants. It was one o'clock in the afternoon. Then he grunted, clutched his belly and lurched off toward Ale's suffering toilet. He had thrown himself into the city's raucous nightlife with abandon during his first few days in the city, and the constant partying conspired with thin mountain air and cheap cigarettes to bring him to his knees. From there, an explosive bout with gastroenteritis had smacked him down for the count.

Jamie's plan was to ride with Robbie and I for three months and then pack up his bicycle, fly to Brussels and ride from there to Vienna where, inevitably, there was a girl. She was reputed to be beautiful and an avid cycle tourist, and Jamie had fallen in love with her several years before on a ride through Europe. Any passing acquaintance of Jamie's — and there were many, for he is an extremely sociable fellow — had heard the Steffi Story, and often more than once.

"What will you do when you get there?" Robbie wanted to know.

"Sweep her off her feet, mate," Jamie replied with a wink. "Or not, I suppose. Either way, I'm getting closure on this thing. And if I'm a little skinnier and a little browner from riding along Mexican beaches, that can't hurt."

Jamie's amorous intentions gave me a sympathetic ear to talk about my own love life, where things seemed to be progressing — Hailee had bought a ticket to Cancún and, somewhat surprisingly, planned to stay for an entire month. Speculation about where our respective romantic rendezvous might lead often morphed into long discussions on love, from which Robbie generally removed himself. Jamie had a sort of General Theory of Romance:

"Men meet a woman and if they like her, suddenly nothing else in their lives matter," he said. "Forget jobs, family, friends — nothing takes precedence over her. They'll do anything, even change themselves to please her.

"Women, meanwhile, hold out as a form of protection against getting hurt. But the man is so enamored and working so hard, and perhaps he's successful. She decides that yes, she really does like him. So she falls for him just as he has for her, and all is well.

"The thing is, all the effort the man has put into getting to this point has exhausted him. He can't keep up the image of being this perfect guy, and maybe he wants to start hanging out with his friends again. So now you have a power shift, where the woman has finally decided that she really likes the guy. But, having achieved what he was after the whole time, the guy is now exhausted. The thrill of the chase is gone. He's spent."

I tried to remember my time in the Bay Area and if I had acted like myself around Hailee or somebody else entirely, and found that I could recall little more than unconnected snippets of conversation. What on Earth had we talked about for almost a week? And did my inability to remember mean I had spent the whole time putting on an act? Perhaps I had fallen into the masculine trap of merely using a woman as a mirror to look back at myself, focusing on whether she had laughed at my jokes or found my stories interesting rather than actually getting to know her. That feeling from the night I had left San Francisco — what was it? Like we were old friends or lovers from past lives exchanging notes on our latest reincarnation? The memory of it had dimmed. Perhaps I'd made it all up? Now that she was coming — and for a full month, no less — these thoughts nibbled at the edge of quiet moments.

Robbie's brother Simon arrived several days after Jamie, positively vibrating with pent-up energy after another month staring at monitors in the Papuan mine he called "jail." He worked as an electrical engineer, and his work arrangement was the month-on, month-off system common among Australian mining companies. His first act in Mexico was to reinstall Tinder on his phone and spend an entire day swiping. "I haven't seen a woman in a month," he explained when he heard Robbie muttering.

Simon was shorter than his brother, with pale skin from working indoors and short, slightly receding dark hair. He had a big, winning grin that he called his "American smile," and he was full of the kind of blokey turns of phrase that endear Australians to all lovers of the English language. "Busier'n a one-armed cabbie with crabs," and "flat out like a lizard drinking," and so on.

So the bike gang was assembled, and we inaugurated our journey with long nights delving as far into the city's sordid nightlife as stamina and Simon's stack of mining boom pesos would take us. Cheap tobacco and generous new friends soon had Simon, Jamie and Robbie sucking down piles of cigarettes each day and, as often happens with smokers, our few daylight outings often dissolved into maddening searches for more cigarettes and places to smoke them. Thankfully, Alejandra didn't seem to mind us constantly rolling like thunder into her living room as sunlight filtered into the waking street.

One afternoon, after a particularly bad day at work, Big Al (as we came to call her) announced that she had requested time off starting in several weeks' time.

"I'll take a bus and meet you in Oaxaca," she said. "I'll bring my bike and ride with you for a while." That night, over mescal in some steaming bar, the bike gang agreed that we liked Alejandra a lot. She never asked our permission to join — she'd simply decided that she was coming, and that was that.

I was excited that our cycling duo had become a fully-fledged bike gang, and while Robbie was also chatty with the novelty of seeing his friend and brother in this strange new place, I sensed nervousness. Simon had no gear, just a small backpack. He would share Rob's tent and we had stoves and pots to feed him, but he would have to find a suitable bicycle before we took the road. This would be difficult in a city with few options beyond the snooty hipster fixed-wheel scene and the mercado ranks of cheap mountain bikes. I offered to accompany the brothers on their daily bike searches, but Robbie waved me off.

"He's my brother," Robbie said. "You and Jamie go have fun."

After three days, Simon found his steed. When we pressed him for a name, he decided to call the bike "Sex on Toast."

"I'm Sex, the bike is Toast," he explained. His Tinder adventures had not been successful.

For Simon, who was joining a crew of cyclists with enough room in our tents and pots to house and feed an extra member, finding a bicycle was the only real barrier to entry. Cycling exerts very little strain on the body — none of us had done any physical training before setting off — and the further you go, the more efficient your body becomes.

The morning of our departure was filled with the sort of last-minute adjustments and racing upstairs to retrieve forgotten toothbrushes that characterize the beginning of all great expeditions. A small crowd of Alejandra's neighbors turned out to wish us well, and Simon gave them ample reason to worry by attempting a celebratory wheelie as we rode out — and falling flat on his back.

# CHAPTER 27

I had been sitting under the pedestrian bridge for half an hour without sight of the bike gang. From up here on its mountainous ramparts, the city was a noisy, smoky plain. Volcanoes and sierras floated above the smog. Barrios spilled down the hillside beneath me into the Valle de México. I read my book, trying to absorb myself in John Steinbeck and his poodle Charley's road trip through 1960's America. Another half hour passed. I shut the book, mounted Baxter and rolled down the way I had come, irritated that I would have to climb this hill again.

At a bend overlooking the city, I found the bike gang in disarray. Simon sat in a restaurant icing a knee with a glass bottle of cola, indicating that Sex evidently needed to adjust Toast's saddle and handlebars. Robbie was rolling Jamie's bike, Stephen, into the shade of a tree. Jamie sprawled carelessly in the dust. Rob saw me coming and raised his eyebrows.

"My body has mutinied," Jamie gasped. "I have been shitting and spewing all the way up the hill." He waved a hand in the air. "Pass us a durrie, Rob."

He put the cigarette to his lips and then paused, rolled, struggled to his feet and lurched into the bush. Rob raised his eyebrows again.

"Which end?" I asked when Jamie returned. He didn't reply, just wedged the cigarette back between his lips and held a hand out for a lighter. We coaxed him back onto his bike and divided his bags between the rest of us. We struggled along and spied a patch of relatively flat grass on a rise behind a clutch of huts built from salvaged timber and corrugated iron. We were on the outer edge of Santa Ana, one of the latest villages to be swallowed by the metropolis.

A short, broad-shouldered man emerged and introduced himself as Agustín. He lived in one of the huts with his wife and daughter. Most of his extended family lived nearby and despite their modest homes, they had one of the best views in the capital. The hillside dropped steeply below the road, and beyond it Mexico City sprawled throughout the wide valley, ringed with a jagged line of mountains. As night fell, the metropolis became a terrestrial galaxy of lights.

We pitched our tents in the field above his home, among rows of corn and nopales.

"We need to be as far away from the house as possible, without being impolite," Rob explained to the newbies, keeping a suspicious eye on a rooster harassing some hens. Agustín and his wife brought tea and home-baked bread.

The maize and nopales were Agustín's, but his farm hadn't made a profit for some time. "There are dry years when it doesn't rain, or it freezes and kills the plants, and we make no money," he said, looking out over the smoking city. "The government doesn't help us, and there are no jobs." He shrugged and changed the subject. "Where in the United States are you from?"

"We're from Australia," Robbie replied.

"Oh, I thought you were Americans." He used the word estadounidense — literally "United Statesian" — instead of gringo, a rare sign of restraint in a country living under the long shadow of its bellicose northern neighbor. "I ask because I lived there some years ago."

"You did? Where?"

"En Chicago. Sin papeles," he added with a small smile. He'd lived there illegally.

The tale began in the late 1990's, after a couple of years of particularly difficult drought. Agustín's sister was the first to decide that she would seek better opportunities in the United States. Though more Mexicans are now migrating home than into the U.S., it is rare to meet someone in the country who doesn't have a friend or relative who has ventured "p'al norte". The country is full of stories, truth mixed with fantasy, of fortunes made north of the border.

"She encouraged us all to go," Agustín said of his sister. "This was in 2000. We needed the hand of God — without money, without any knowledge, how were we going to make it?" He had a wife and a three year-old daughter to support, and between his failing crops, the stories of American riches and his sister's enthusiasm, he decided to join her on the journey.

"We borrowed 25,000 pesos and off we went, on a bit of an adventure."

Under the instructions of a smuggler they'd contacted, Agustín and his sister traveled to Agua Prieta, a desert city squished against the border between Sonora and Arizona. Immediately opposite Agua Prieta lies the American town of Douglas — Agustín pronounced it "Doo-glass." Agustín and his sister were taken to a house and stayed for three days before their first attempt.

"No tuvimos suerte," he remembered with a wry smile. *We had no luck.* "There was a lot of border patrol, and it was very guarded. We walked for a day and weren't able to find a way." The guide returned them to the house in Agua Prieta, and they tried again the next evening.

"This time, the border patrol detained us. After a few hours, they sent us back."

In Agua Prieta, the coyotes charged a steep daily fee for the accommodation and food they provided, and as night after night passed without success, Agustín began to despair. "Se estaba acabando la plata," he said. *The money was disappearing.* He was also missing his family and beginning to question the wisdom of his choice to leave and put himself in so much debt. On the third night they tried again, with a different strategy.

"We had to run 500 meters towards a Walmart. There was one group on the left, one on the right, and our group was in the middle. Three groups of twelve. The border patrol managed to stop the two other groups, but we made it through," he explained. "We were free."

Again he smiled that wry, rueful smile. "The thing was, I did not have so much luck. I got lost in a small forest and became separated from the group. I was alone. I couldn't make it. Eventually they found me. They took me to a building, recorded my name, my fingerprints. My compañeros had made it through, and I had been detained again. You can imagine how I felt."

He said he was caught at 8 p.m., and it was 4 a.m. before the authorities left him at the gates to Agua Prieta. His sister had been in the same group and when he returned to the house, he was told she was safe in an apartment in Douglas. They had made it, and he had not.

Agustín was despondent. He would have to pay interest on his loan, and his funds were dwindling with each passing day. He called his wife and decided he was better off going home.

"But that same evening, the man I was staying with mentioned that the migra had released the chamacos" — a slang term for "kids" —

"that he had working for him. The chamacos are like guides. They cross the desert on foot."

These child guides had been detained in the U.S. for human trafficking, but were being released that same day.

"So if you'd like to try one more time," Agustín's host said, "you can go with them. If you can't get through and you want to leave, that's fine. You can go back. Just try once more."

Agustín gathered his resolve and decided to give it one more crack.

"On the other attempts I had walked with adults and we never had any luck. But when I met the chamacos I was astonished to find they were just kids. Twelve, ten and seven years old respectively. That way, when the migra caught them, they had to release them right away."

"The next day they gave us water and some burritos for the journey. They drove us out of town and left us, and off we went into the desert. We walked all day, all afternoon, stopping only for five or six minutes at a time to drink water, and then we walked again."

They ended up walking for two days and nights, and by the second night they were inside the United States. Soon, they found a road. Cars arrived periodically and carried four passengers at a time until the whole group of twelve, plus the guides, had been whisked away.

Agustín had smiled often during his story, but now he watched the dirt between his knees.

"I met many people on my journey who later died or disappeared in the desert, who were even killed by criminals on the Mexican side or by border patrol on the American side. It happened several times when I was detained and sent back across the border. There are always people who take advantage of the power they have in that moment."

"On the Mexican side, too, there are bad people — just like everywhere else, I believe. Many times we were robbed of any money or valuables we carried."

Most migrants carried only a few of their most treasured possessions.

"You're very vulnerable, and there are always people looking to take advantage," he said.

\* \* \*

At last, Agustín had made it to the United States, but he was still a long way from the promised riches of the stories. He was taken with the rest of the group to a mobile home, parked in an isolated patch of desert. He and his eleven companions were left to wait for two days.

"The mobile home became an inferno during the day," he said. "Such terrible heat. They only gave us one meal a day, no more than a hamburger, a handful of fries and a small soda."

Dirty, hungry, dehydrated, sweltering and separated from his family, Agustín's resolve faltered again. He decided that if no-one showed up by the end of the third day, he would leave. He knew he'd be caught and sent back to the same dismal job prospects — now 25,000 pesos out of pocket, plus interest. But he was fed up with the journey, and he missed his wife and child.

But a car did arrive on the third day, and while the chamacos disappeared back into the desert Agustín was taken to an apartment in the city of Phoenix, where his conditions improved.

"We could bathe, they gave us a little more food, we could wash our clothes, and once more we waited to see what would happen."

Again, Agustín's face turned solemn. "In the group with whom we went to Phoenix, there were three young muchachitas, the same age as my daughter is now." He paused for a moment. His daughter — no older than 18 — sat under a tree listening to Robbie and her mother chatting. "The men who took us to Phoenix had treated us well. But when we arrived at the apartment, they took the three girls into a room" — Agustín took a deep breath — "and raped them."

We sat in silence for a while, and Agustín shook his head, as if to dislodge the memory.

"It was horrible. So, so horrible," he whispered at last.

"As a man, they can assault and rob you, perhaps kill you. But women can suffer abuse far worse than that. This is one reason why I don't recommend migrating like I did."

Agustín was able to call his sister from Phoenix. She was safe and well in the northern city of Chicago. Agustín would be sent there along with three others.

Agustín's costs in the United States were covered by a USD$1,500 fee that he had paid to the coyotes back in Agua Prieta. He and his three companions were sent to Chicago on a series of buses, and Agustín remembered feeling awe at the new world he saw outside the windows.

"The coolest place that we saw — the coolest place we could've seen at the time — was Las Vegas," he smiled. "But they only gave us $20 spending money. So we just ate bread, drank bottled water, and sat on buses for four days."

They had been told to find a payphone and call a number upon their arrival in Chicago. They were to ask for "La Reina del Sur," the Queen of the South. "This would verify who we were," he chuckled at the reference to a popular telenovela. They waited until a van pulled up, and Agustín was taken to a house where his sister waited.

Having made it into the United States through a shadowy, complex network, Agustín now had to find work.

"My sister would drop me off at McDonald's or someplace, and I would wait with others to see if anyone would come by to give us work. The main jobs were in roofing, changing the tiles on houses. But usually nobody came, and I had to walk for two hours to get home."

I asked about his interactions with the locals.

"I saw Mexican Americans driving past as I walked home, and they would say ugly things to me. I think they believe that people like me, who come without the proper visas, give all Mexicans a bad name. The only ones who ever gave me a ride were American people.

"Obviously I couldn't speak much English. I could only understand 'ride,' 'yes' and 'no.' They would ask questions, but I only knew how to write down my address. It was very difficult."

Agustín made it to Chicago in April 2000 and stayed until December 2001, a period of almost two years. By his second year, he had paid off his debts to the smugglers and was living comfortably enough. He sent most of his wages back to his family in Santa Ana. He found steady work in a factory that made safes, where the manager taught him and other migrant workers how to weld, paint and laminate the metals involved in their construction. He was paid USD$6.50 per hour, plus overtime — this was one of his few English words — and lived in a "decent house."

But his undocumented presence in the country posed daily challenges. Having been pulled over for minor traffic infringements with no driver's license, many of his friends left police stations to find immigration authorities waiting outside to send them back to Mexico.

Furthermore, the promised riches were being eaten up by America's higher cost of living. Rent, electricity, gas and phone bills had all been left out of the stories he'd heard back home.

"You just think, 'I'm going to make a lot of money,'" he said. "In Mexico City, six dollars an hour will make you rich."

But most of all, Agustín missed his family. Even though their finances were in better shape than ever before, he was pained to hear that his daughter was growing up without him.

"Many of my friends up there told me to 'Send the money and save a little for yourself. Enjoy it!'" he remembered. "But I concluded that I'd prefer to enjoy being with my daughter. She's growing up and I'm not there. Before I know it, she'll be married and I won't be there."

So he returned, to the delight of his wife and parents.

"After two years and all the trouble I went through to get there, it only took four hours in a plane to return to Mexico City," he said. "It all happened very quickly."

Apart from the relief of seeing his family again, Agustín found his return difficult.

"Living in a city like this — ugly, dirty, people have no respect — it overwhelms you," he said, watching the capital pump smoke and noise into the sky. "It was very sad to be confronted with how we live, compared with up there. It's completely different." He shrugged.

He mentioned the cleanliness of the Chicago suburb he'd lived in, the lack of noise. He especially appreciated the way drivers would pull over at the sound of sirens to allow the passage of the police, a fire engine or an ambulance. "They got out of the way so that someone could get the help they needed," he said. "I had never seen this before."

"Drivers respect the road rules and it isn't necessary, like here, to put speed bumps all over the roads. Here, we're full of speed bumps and rubbish."

The speed bumps — known as topes — were among my least-favorite features of cycle touring in Mexico. It was common to find ten or more in a row in highway towns, the only way to slow drivers to a safe speed. We commiserated over our hatred of topes for quite a while.

Agustín now worked as a firefighter, earning just 70 pesos per day — less than he'd made in an hour building safes in Chicago almost two decades before. But he didn't regret his decision.

"The way I saw it, I had the choice between economic stability, or being here with my family," he concluded. "I chose my family. I think it was the right decision."

# CHAPTER 28

"Let's say Godzilla comes out of the ocean in Oaxaca," Jamie said. "How long does it take him to walk to Mexico City?"

We were cycling fast through an agricultural valley of brown fields. A narrow, foul-smelling creek trickled parallel to the road. Tendrils of smog occasionally drifted down the valley from the city, and a smouldering volcano towered over the valley adding more smoke to the air, but otherwise the cleaner air was returning sharpness and color to the world as the city receded behind and above us.

"How tall do you think he is?"

"Godzilla? About as tall as a medium-sized skyscraper, wouldn't you say?"

"I mean, we can't really know until we make it to the coast ourselves. And it's uphill for him — he'd be scrambling up all these giant ledges."

Ten minutes later, we reached the edge of one such ledge, where the volcanic valley spilled between highland peaks onto the wide flatlands of Puebla and northern Morelos. While these ledges would make annoying obstacles for a giant sea lizard dreaming of trampling a major metropolis, they were a source of incredible joy for four tiny cyclists headed in the opposite direction.

Jamie sped away with the force and purpose of an Olympic ski jumper, crouched low and leaning over his flimsy bike. Simon took every opportunity to let go of his ungainly handlebars — which weren't helping his knee trouble — and leaned back, hands resting behind his head. I alternated between hanging back with Robbie, whose policy was to wring as much leisurely saddle time as possible from these "free" downhill kilometers, and leaning into the turns in a hopeless quest to catch Jamie.

The big man was waiting for us where the descent bottomed out at the edge of a wide, populated plain. The creek we'd been following up above had swollen into a frothing river. Jamie gestured toward the river.

"*River's Revival*," he said with a satisfied smirk. He'd been coming up with fictional U2 song names since our departure from Mexico City — either puns on existing songs or phrases that, to him, sounded "U2-esque." *Breath of the Boy* and *Where The Avenidas Have No Nombre* were his favorites so far.

Robbie took the newbies on a Mexican cycle touring crash course, with lessons on the merits of each flavor of agua fresca, the prevalence of topes in highway towns and warnings against attempting to conquer a hill in high gear. He talked them through the menus at open-air taco stands, explained the rules of "Where Are We Sleeping Tonight?" and steered them carefully away from the bacon-wrapped hot dogs on sale at Oxxo convenience stores. When Jamie discovered his first flat tire, Robbie was absurdly enthusiastic about fixing it for him.

"I've only had one puncture so far," he explained as we watched from the shade.

Meanwhile, I had a new audience for my stories — though it wasn't long before Jamie was turning to me at choice moments to ask: "Does this also remind you of the time you were in Death Valley?"

We continued dropping out of the highlands level-by-level through cane fields and forests until we entered the state of Puebla and with it a wide, brown, trackless country. The earth was dry and coated in a fuzz of low trees, bushes and cacti, mostly useless for the purposes of a sweaty cyclist who only wanted a shady place to rest. It was here that my odometer clicked into five digits, indicating 10,000 kilometers since Vancouver, and we celebrated in the scrub with caguamas of beer and cheap cigars.

Across Puebla we pedaled, and for days we saw little beyond low hills cut by twisting gullies — a burned, barren country. One evening we climbed out of the plain and camped beneath a small oak, the only tree on a high bluff overlooking a deep valley, with a high range of hills facing us across the abyss. We woke hungry in the morning — a planning snafu the day before had left us without our traditional oatmeal breakfast, and rumbling bellies gave an added air of desperation to the laborious morning routine. Robbie's scientific packing method arranged items in a way that would place stoves, head torches, jackets, gloves and tools at hand exactly when and where he needed them. Jamie sat at the opposite end of the organization spectrum, simply stuffing things into panniers when and where they fit. After an eternity of packing panniers and strapping items to our racks, we mounted the bikes and took the road.

"Fuck."

It was Jamie. I turned back to see him dismounting. He opened his bags and began tossing pots and old shirts into the dirt. "Fuck," he muttered again.

"I just realized I haven't seen my passport in a week," he grunted. We rested our bikes against the oak tree and sat, looking out over the clouds that had filled the valley below. Apart from Jamie rummaging, ants wandering through the cold dirt and our breath fogging in our faces, the Earth was still.

"Dunno about you, but I'm hungry enough to eat the arse out of a low-flying duck," Simon grunted.

Sunlight bounced off the clouds and into our eyes, warming our faces.

"Where did you see it last?" Robbie said.

"I remember I had it out at the campground in Cuautla," Jamie said, and we all winced. It'd been three or four days since we'd left Cuautla.

"This bloke couldn't arrange a root in a brothel with a fistful of fifties," Simon said to himself. Silence descended once more. Robbie closed his eyes against the sun. Simon rummaged in the dirt with a twig. I cracked open my book.

After a few minutes, a tinkling sound of bells drifted up out of the valley. A herd of goats emerged from the mist, a jaunty spring in their step as they mounted the bluff. We sat in silence as they milled around us with heads down, lips sifting the dirt for a scrap of foliage. A single high-pitched bleat broke the spell, and we started to giggle.

"Hallo boys and girls," Simon said, holding his hand out to a brown-and-white goat that ignored him, investigating a stone we'd used to hammer in our tent pegs the night before.

A boy of about 14 or 15 dressed in soiled jeans, a patchy jacket and overlarge boots appeared among the goats. His hair was greasy and unwashed, his hands calloused, but he had the soft, open face of a child. He seemed unsurprised to see us.

"You slept here last night?" he asked Robbie. As the tallest in the group, strangers often subconsciously looked to him as the bike gang's authority figure.

"It's a good spot. Great view," Robbie said. "Where are you headed?"

The boy shrugged, leaning on a weathered tree limb he carried for a walking stick. "Looking for pasture. Pretty picked over around here, but I think I know a place." And with that, he bid us goodbye and crossed the road, climbing the small hill on the far side and whistling as he went. In fits and starts, his herd followed.

"Found it," Jamie sighed. He was sitting back from the pile of disinterred clothes and gear lying on the ground beside his bike, holding up a grubby passport.

"Where was it?" I could tell Robbie dreaded the answer.

"I stashed it in a sock," Jamie said. "Thought it was a safe place."

Once we'd hit the road, Robbie and I stopped every ten kilometers or so in the shade of a concrete abarrotes or, preferably, in the shade of a large tree known locally as the parota or the árbol de lluvia — the "rain tree," so-named because the air beneath it always felt ten degrees cooler, like stepping into a cold shower. It shed large brown seed pods and bloomed with purple flowers, and we always joined the chorus of birds and insects in singing its praises.

Robbie was leaning back against the sinuous curve of a parota trunk one afternoon, legs stretched out, eyes closed. "When you build my cycling spa shrine…" he began.

"…I should fill it with these trees?" I finished.

Eyes still closed, Rob lifted a fist and then waggled his index finger up and down, a gesture Mexicans use to say "sí."

Eventually, Simon and then Jamie would trickle in and flop in the shade, asking for cigarettes and what was good in any nearby stores. We would sit, panting and shocked by the heat, sweat rolling freely off our bodies until our clothes brimmed with it. We sucked down road-heated water from our bottles and cold, sugary drinks from the store. And then we'd set off again into the orange afternoon, the part of the day Simon called the "Gringo Barbecue."

One evening we camped near a lonely abarrotes on an isolated stretch of Pueblan highway. When Jamie, Robbie and I ventured inside we met another former migrant, though she had returned against her will. Like Agustín, Mariana thought we were American at first.

"If we were gringos, where would you say we come from?" I asked.

"You'd be from Tennessee," she began at once — I was wearing the corduroy shirt I kept clean for evenings after we'd washed in a creek or stream. Next she considered Robbie, whose glasses were tugging at the neckline of an old t-shirt. "He'd be from Colorado someplace," Mariana mused. "He looks like one of those outdoorsy types."

"And him?" I pointed at Jamie, who wore boxy, seventies-style glasses, beads on his wrist and a feather earring dangling from one ear.

"Oh, he'd be from Hollywood," Mariana said at once, giggling.

She had spent years working as a nurse in an Oregon retirement home.

"Some of the viejitos I cared for had nothing nice to say about Mexicans, so it took time for them to warm up to me," she laughed. "But I loved my job, and my life in Portland. My son is still there. He's a citizen, he'll turn 18 in two years. He is my hope — through him, I can sort out my papers and join him there again."

On the afternoon that we finally crossed into the state of Oaxaca, we stopped in for supplies at a little abarrotes set up a dusty slope from the scorching road. A rusty red pickup rolled in playing old corridos. Three men were squished inside: two squarish middle-aged guys with thick mustaches and trucker caps and a flimsy old timer sandwiched between them under an expansive cowboy hat. The two friends had been out all day checking fence lines on a nearby ranch, and one of them had evidently brought his father along for the ride. The old fellow moved slowly and deliberately, like a praying mantis, and didn't appear to completely understand the slow, loud sentences his chaperones tossed his way. But he was out and about, and seemed wonderfully happy. We drank a beer together under a parota tree, and there was much shaking of hands and slapping of backs as we mounted up and rode away.

Back on the road, Robbie seemed especially sunny under his straw hat.

"You thinking about being a Mexican pensioner again?" I said.

"I'm telling you, old people here have got it made. I can't wait to be that age and have my kids take me out on little excursions like that."

When the truck whizzed by minutes later with a shout of "¡Échale, güero!" Rob laughed and laughed. He was buzzing all afternoon.

That evening, we made our camp on a creek bed outside a small village, a popular picnic spot complete with a palapa and muscular stream-fed trees. Robbie strung up a hammock between two of the palapa's supporting posts while Simon, Jamie and I laid out our sleeping bags side-by-side under its roof. Unbeknownst to us, however, scraps of food left by picnicking villagers supported a colony of red ants that were small and light enough to climb unnoticed on human skin. Using this stealth to their advantage, they massed at strategic points until, at some sign, they all bit as one. My entire body erupted with pain all at once, and within seconds Jamie and Simon were also thrashing in their beds.

The resulting frenzy sent Jamie, Simon and I screeching and swatting out of our sleeping bags. We de-anted our bodies and sleeping gear and then moved further along the creek to remake our beds in neutral territory, leaving Robbie alone and antless in his hammock under the palapa. Simon, Jamie and I lay chattering under the stars until sleep took us one-by-one.

When I rolled out of my sleeping bag the next morning I found Robbie alone by his stove, boiling water for porridge. His face was pale, and he didn't look up when I sat on a nearby log.

"How'd you sleep?" I asked.

"I didn't," he replied.

He kept to himself all day. It reminded me of the aftermath of his crash outside Ciudad Insurgentes, back in Baja California. By the late afternoon, even Jamie was worried.

"I've only ever known Optimistic Rob," he confided.

We made our camp by another creek that evening. While Simon and Jamie were in town foraging for supplies Robbie took me aside, sucked in a deep breath and began to talk.

"I know it's silly — you had to move because of the ants," he began. "But I was listening to you guys chatting and laughing and having a great time, and I was in my hammock all alone. And then I asked myself why I felt this way — why resent my friends for something so small? — and this just sent me down a rabbit hole."

I was puzzled by his logic but kept it to myself. He seemed himself again and kept talking. He was excited about the adventures that would inevitably flow from traveling alone with Jamie after Simon and I left, but Responsible Rob also worried about the logistics of such an expedition.

"I'm excited for you that Hailee's coming to Mexico," he said. "I'm also a little jealous, to be honest. I wish I had something like that to look forward to. I'm not sure where all this is going for me. Every time I hop online I see everyone getting married, making career moves, buying houses, pumping out children. I don't want to go all the way to Patagonia, but I came halfway around the world to be here, after all. What the hell else am I gonna do?"

The question hung in the air for a moment as I searched for encouraging words.

"I dunno man," I said. "But I know you'll be fine, wherever you end up. Something will come along. And in the meantime, you've already proven to yourself that you can keep cycling for as long as you like — as long as it's necessary, even."

"It's not a satisfying answer," he said. "But I guess I'm getting used to that."

That night, lying awake and sweating into my sleeping pad, I tried to remember the feeling of clean sheets on a cool morning, and the warmth of Hailee's face nestled in beside mine. The memory's potency had worn away as it receded in time. And just as Baxter's handlebar grips had morphed and eroded to fit my hands, I suspected that the memory in its current form bore little resemblance to the original. But as I drifted off to sleep, the contentment that I associated with waking beside Hailee was flecked with fresh grains of anticipation.

At Huehuepan we turned south toward the famed Oaxacan coast, though we were still a long way from realizing our dreams of warm Pacific beaches. It was never "pure downhill all the way to the coast" as eager-to-please locals relentlessly claimed, but with each successive drop the country began to change again. The flowers were brighter and the leaves broader, as if the vegetation was gaining courage until we crested one particularly large wall and found a jungle seething at us from the roadside. One night we camped on a basketball court in the town of Unión Nacional, which crowned a small hill overlooking corn fields and, a little way on, the cool Río Copala.

The heat had acquired a viscous quality in this tropical valley, and we lay panting on the concrete after dinner — bean tacos, delicious as usual, but hot and heavy in the belly.

"How do you know if you're in love?" Simon asked as we lay on the rough concrete.

Jamie, of course, had a theory. "Say there are 10,000 people in the world who you could fall in love with, who would make you a better person and who you'd be happy spending your life with. Well, your chances of encountering one of those is roughly…" and so on.

Was Steffi, the woman he would eventually be leaving Mexico to meet in Austria, one of those 10,000?

"Gonna find out, I suppose," Jamie shrugged, blowing cigarette smoke at the starlit sky.

"True love, honest fucken true love," Simon decided, "is rarer than rocking horse shit."

An old man appeared in the dim light from a nearby home. He offered refrigerated bottles of water and whispered "bienvenidos a México" when we told him our names as they were pronounced in Spanish: Simón, Roberto, Haiymeh, Kintín. His name was Pedro and, when Simon offered a cigarette, he sat with us on the concrete. Pedro wore baggy slacks, scuffed shoes, a short-sleeved button-up shirt and a faded cap over his spare gray hairs. He lived on a small farm nearby, which he owned. He drew deep lungfuls of smoke and seemed content to sit in the silence that had muffled our debate.

"Ask Pedro about love," Simon said.

So Pedro told us about his seven living children, and the two others who had died at the ages of three and two respectively. "One of them was named Simón," he said, nodding to our Simon, who looked at me for a translation. Pedro had been with his wife for 46 years, and once they reached 50 he planned to marry her all over again.

"What's the secret?" I asked. "How did you stay happy together for so long?"

He thought about this for a while. We waited. "Puesss," he began at last. "First of all, you need to have a house. You need to be about 18 or 20 years old, and you need to meet a girl. You need to like her, and it probably helps if she likes you." We chuckled companionably at this.

"So you have to be novios for a while, go on dates, this sort of thing. Then, after some time, you can hacer un poco de fiesta, if you know what I mean." He winked. "After that, you get married before the child is born! And once you've been married for 50 years, you get married all over again — and make the children pay for it."

He settled back on his elbows and took a drag on the cigarette.

"That's all?" I asked, once I had translated his answer for the group. "Doesn't it get difficult at times? Don't you grow apart? Think about other women? Don't you fight?"

Pedro shrugged. "Sure, there are difficult times in life," he said. "Sometimes the rains come late, sometimes it doesn't rain at all. Crops die. Animals, too. Other times, the river floods and washes everything away, all at once." He traced the path of the nearby Río Copala in the air with the cigarette, then returned it to his lips.

"Things are always changing," I said, and Pedro exhaled thoughtfully.

"Sometimes, I can't decide if things are always changing, or if they are forever locked in place within some larger pattern," he said. He stubbed out his cigarette and shook each of our hands to say goodbye.

"So no wisdom from the old man, then," Simon yawned after Pedro had shuffled away.

"What'd you expect?" Robbie said. "Ask a farmer for philosophy, you're bound to end up talking about the weather."

# CHAPTER 29

And then, finally, it really was downhill all the way to the coast. It happened a few days after Unión Nacional, once we'd turned off busy Highway 200 in the late afternoon to a town called Cerro Hermoso — *Beautiful Hill*. Robbie, Simon and I rode together as we crested a rise and spotted the wide Pacific bouncing the late sun's tangerine rays in the distance. We stopped for celebratory hooting and back-slapping.

When Jamie arrived, the big man didn't stop — just rolled by without a word, fist in the air.

Simon left us after a few long nights among hedonistic Australians in the surfer's tourist trap of Puerto Escondido, taking his charm and ocker observations with him. The weeks that followed were a slow and, by cyclists' standards, luxurious tour of one of the more scenic sections of Oaxacan coast.

The first stop of note was Zipolite, a nudist colony a short ride down the road from Puerto Escondido. When we arrived, late sunlight was glowing neon over the beach's western headland. The water caught the light in fat globules that morphed and twisted before my eyes, and ran silky and clean over the fissures of my body when I dived, whitewash thundering overhead like a freight train while I waited in the frothy dark, listening.

I came up and turned to see Rob striding through swirling molten gold, a shadow against the sun. Jamie saw it too and began to howl and slap at the water. We hooted like maniacs, swum beyond the breakers and then let the waves toss us back to shore.

We took a second-floor room at a beachfront establishment slapped together from what appeared to be salvaged timber. There was space for our bags, a fan and a bed with room for two. We took turns sharing the bed and sleeping outside on the narrow balcony. We spent our days making pilgrimages into the rough ocean, wandering into town for cecina steaks, smoking on our small balcony and watching the routines of our fellow guests.

Most of our idle attention went to the photogenic family who arrived in an old Volkswagen van, which they had driven all the way up from their native Argentina. He had dark skin and curly dark hair, she was red-haired and pregnant. Occasionally they would force their squirming toddler into a pair of shorts but minutes later he would burst onto the beach, naked again and screaming in delight.

"I know the feeling," Robbie said.

"Off you go then," muttered Jamie, who was leaning against a post and hadn't worn a thread of clothing all day.

Then there was a squat señora living in a tent immediately below us. We never saw her without a large bottle of water, and she would stomp about in the shallows, industriously splashing seawater on her face and up into her armpits.

Beside her were a pair of French retirees who'd shipped their camper van to Canada and were driving the length of the American continent. She wore her hair in a beehive and would sit in a hammock in the shade, reading a paperback or stroking a tablet. Her husband — who we called "Big Dick" when he wasn't around — appeared to be regaining his shape after a lifetime in office cubicles, legs wrapped in new layers of hair and muscle. Big Dick would stand in the sun with his hands on his hips, squinting at the world in nothing but his reading glasses.

Jamie produced an old ukulele from his haphazard bags and began to exercise his falsetto croon. He chose George Ezra and Coldplay covers to win over women from Finland and Mexico City that we met in beach bars by night. We always smoked, and the days passed in a surreal haze weighed down by the heat.

When we finally left it took two days of riding to reach the next beach, a wide yellow bay called Playa San Agustín. It backed onto a swamp, with a necklace of islands protecting it from the mountains of whitewater traveling across the horizon. The town was a row of palapas and makeshift restaurants and bars, plus a resort of some kind at the far end.

We drank beers and smoked joints with Jose, a lanky bartender who hated the heat.

"I miss the cold in Wisconsin," he said with a grin. Like Mariana back in Puebla, he'd been abruptly kicked out of his adopted country after setting up a new life north of the border. "I'm saving up to buy a ticket so my son can come down and visit me. He's 13 now. I haven't seen him for three years."

"Would you go back?" I asked.

He looked around at the holidaying families, the islands, the palms and palapas and shallow green water. "It's pretty here, I admit," he said. "But my heart is with my son. This isn't home anymore."

Our next stop on the Oaxacan beach tour was La Crucecita, a complex of resorts and golf courses that served as the jumping-off point for the famous Bahías de Huatulco National Park. One of the nearby bays, named Cacaluta, appears as a deserted beach paradise in the 2001 road movie *Y Tu Mamá También* and, as budding experts in the nuances of Pacific coast beach appreciation, it clearly required our attention. We found a road out of La Crucecita's fairway country and down a steep slope, where we followed a track cutting through sand dunes and thick vegetation to the beach.

By this point we had become coastal connoisseurs, discerning critics who would discuss and evaluate the merits of each individual beach. Cacaluta boasted a tall island less than 100 meters off its sandy shore and though footprints and collapsed sandcastles belied the presence of humans earlier in the day, we were alone.

"The headlands really frame the island quite nicely," Robbie said, stroking his chin.

"How good's the sand!" yelled Jamie. He had already stripped off and was dismissing grains from his skin with a brush of his hand. "It's chunky, must be geologically young. Wait... *Young Sand*! That's our next U2 song!"

He dived for the ukulele, strummed furiously and shouted his best Bono impersonation.

"I will beeeee with you again... on the young sand!"

"It's almost a bummer that we have to leave to meet Alejandra tomorrow," Robbie mused, watching Jamie striding naked along the sand, strumming his uke. "Then again, it will be good to get some feminine energy into this bike gang."

After another evening of swimming, reading, smoking, eating and stargazing, I woke in the cool predawn gloom. It was my 24th birthday. I stole away from camp, dived into the water and swam the short distance out to the island. The ocean dropped me onto a shore of stones and boulders, and I scrambled up a rock face as high as my modest climbing skills would take me.

Though I was only a short distance offshore, I looked back on the mainland as if I were taking stock of the entire continent and my progress thus far. Vancouver was more than 10,000 kilometers of riding away, off to my left somewhere. Patagonia was vaguely to my right, much further off than Vancouver. My 24th year had been consumed with the preparation and execution of this cycling trip, but on a map I wasn't even halfway yet.

An early seabird caught my eye as it flew overhead and settled on the ocean — the same ocean that murmured against midnight Australian shores half a world away. My birthday had already come and gone for Mom, Dad and my sisters. Birthday messages would be waiting next time I found an internet cafe. I threw a stone into the water and wondered if the ripples it created might, in some atomic form, eventually nudge the beaches at Coffs Harbour, travel up gorges and waterfalls and shudder along Dumaresq Creek where it bisected my hometown.

I felt no desire to go back.

I shook my head to dislodge the shame that accompanied this thought and forced a subject change by asking myself out loud what I was looking forward to. "See Hailee again," was one source of excitement. "Not be cycling for a while," was another, connected to the first.

I picked my way down to the shoreline, dived in and swam back into the world. I approached our little camp — bicycles leaning against one another, a pile of sandy panniers, three sleeping bags laid out side-by-side, clothes draped over bushes in the dunes, Jamie strumming his ukulele as he sang "Happy Birthday," Robbie frying pancakes over the stove. It felt like coming home.

# CHAPTER 30

Silence reigned at the edge of Highway 200 as Robbie, Alejandra, Jamie and I stood watching the boy swaying in the gutter. Blood dripped from his mouth and fingers, seeping into his jeans or the concrete at his feet. He grunted or snorted at intervals. Jamie crouched beside him, searching his pummeled face for any sign of recognition that we were there. Robbie stood back, the color drained from his face behind a leaden expression, glancing from the boy to the road and back again. Alejandra stood near Jamie, speaking to the boy in the soft, cooing voice you'd use on a restless infant.

What kind of life had led him to this moment? We'd already established that he'd likely fallen unnoticed from the back of a moving vehicle. But to be left here by passersby? This was a symptom of something bigger. With a hollow feeling in my guts, I wondered what waited for him in his future — or whatever was left of it.

A few more vehicles stopped over the next 20 minutes and though we could convince no-one to take him, we extracted several promises to call an ambulance once they found a cell signal.

Half an hour went by. Our friend — as we now called him — stopped his groaning and quieted down. Jamie caught him with his good eye closed, toppling to one side.

"We can't let him sleep." I heard fear in the big man's voice as he held the boy up by his shoulders, the first time anyone had touched him. We stirred into action again.

Robbie and I took Alejandra's phone, mounted our bikes and followed the highway east to find a cell signal and call an ambulance ourselves. We sped off the hill, crossed a scrubby flat and then climbed

165

toward a notch in another range running perpendicular to the coast. Beaches and headlands glowed below us, bordered by the inky ocean. As Robbie and I labored into the ascent a large, unfamiliar breed of black-and-yellow bird appeared in the air several feet off my shoulder. It winged quietly alongside for a few hundred meters, stopping in a tree every now and then to let us catch up. I pushed harder on the pedals.

Motion felt useful, and it felt good to be useful. Now, between hoping that our winged companion wasn't some messenger from the kid's newly departed soul — and checking Alejandra's phone for a signal — I now found myself thinking that, for the first time, I was on an adventure of real consequence. Had he known that his medical emergency had inserted the first ever moment of life-and-death drama to some pampered foreigner's life, our friend would almost certainly have been unimpressed. But I focused on the task at hand and ignored an inner surge of excitement at being swept up in events bigger than some contrived challenge of my own making.

"If somebody did this to him on purpose, it could be dangerous to help," Alejandra had said after the woman in the first truck had finally offered to "dar parte" and tell the police about him. "You never know who might be watching."

Robbie, Jamie and I had exchanged glances at that, recognizing in those words the black cloud of violence Mexicans euphemistically called "la inseguridad," *the insecurity.* We had never seen this violence in person. The closest we'd come was glimpses of its aftermath, and always relatively distant — bodies splayed on front pages of the Durango papers, the gordita stand mutterings of a "war" recently won and lost in apparently tranquil Yahualica de González Gallo — like smoky tendrils recoiling over the horizon. We never understood the direct causes of any individual death, or that alleged war, or the infamous disappearance of 43 college students en route to a demonstration in the nearby state of Guerrero (plenty of faded banners still wondered "Where are the 43?" seven months after the fact) but no-one doubted their ultimate cause. This, of course, was the shifting trade routes that sent criminalized narcotics north into the United States' insatiable maw, the absurdly violent struggles over their control and the ripples of corruption and crime they created.

But to us, the stories remained stories. They never felt real. While it was impossible to dispute that violence was occurring somewhere, it always felt far away — a dark smudge dancing just outside our field of vision. And everyone was so open and unguarded, so relaxed in one another's company, so quick to invite strangers — "desconocidos," literally "unknowns" — like us into conversation or even their homes. The lush forests and gorgeous coastline flanking Mexico's mountainous spine, the high pastoral fields and dusky deserts risking to volcanic tumult as we pedaled south, the rambling toddlers and canoodling teenagers and happy pensioners in every plaza, the wry jokes and easy smiles — this was no war zone.

As I pedaled, I conjured the image of the boy, bloodied and bruised, still shuffling in the gutter, and in my mind's eye I saw a puff of black cloud brooding over his bowed head. It was unlikely that he had anything to do with smuggling, narcotraficantes, any of it. To the bike gang — three Australians and a chilanga from Mexico City — he was just a kid in need of urgent care. But to the passengers in that truck, he may or may not have been an example of what happened to those who crossed certain boundaries. The mere possibility of involvement by some thuggish form of authority — a local gang, highway bandits, perhaps even the police — was enough to pervert natural human decency.

We rolled out of the pass and Robbie stayed by the highway while I rushed along a dirt road to a village called Zonjal, nestled at the foot of the range. I ditched my bike in the dusty, deserted main street and ran into a store to brief the señora inside and enlist her help. She phoned the police in Salina Cruz, a small city to the east, and they assured her that they would send an ambulance.

My task completed, I bought snacks and bottles of cola from the señora and pedaled back out of town. Robbie and I sat beneath the cooling boughs of a parota tree, watched sunbeams streaking overhead as the bush darkened around us, and waited.

The ambulance, when it arrived, was a van mounted with flashing lights speeding up toward the pass. Minutes later, a second ambulance flashed by. Someone had called after all. The ambulances soon rushed back toward Salina Cruz together and through the rear window of the first we could see a paramedic working away at what we assumed was our friend.

It was dark by the time Jamie and Alejandra joined us. Last they'd seen him, the boy had been conscious as he'd gone into the ambulance. With permission from the señora who had made the phone call, we made our camp on the basketball court at Zonjal's small primary school. We cooked our usual bean taco feast with all the fixings and drank beers to belatedly celebrate my 11,000th kilometer, which had come and gone during Robbie and I's race to find a phone signal earlier that afternoon. But it was a subdued night for the usually raucous bike gang. Before they'd taken him away, the paramedics had told Alejandra that our friend would be treated at the civil hospital in Salina Cruz. When she called the next day, however, the hospital refused to give any news without proof that she was family, and we didn't even know his name.

It took another two days of sweaty riding to reach Salina Cruz, a scalding hot and treeless port town where we stopped in the central plaza to gorge on tlayudas and cold aguas frescas. We took turns watching the bikes and fielding the usual questions from curious townsfolk ("Where did you start? How much does the bike weigh?") while the others sat in an internet cafe sifting through emails, social media notifications and Couchsurfing requests. We also looked for references to our friend in the local media but found nothing. We did find the hospital's website, but the listed address was across town, out of our way. Then we found a cinema, which wasn't out of our way, and suddenly the prospect of two hours' worth of popcorn, fizzy drink, air-conditioning and superhero adventures overrode all other plans.

"What are we going to do anyway?" Robbie asked reasonably. "Have him say 'thank-you?' And that's if they let us see him in the first place."

So we left Salina Cruz and found the cinema in a mall outside town. The sun was low when the movie finished, so we asked a security guard to let us camp on a patch of dreamily soft turf at the edge of the parking lot. With clean bathrooms and an air-conditioned supermarket nearby, the spot promised luxury urban camping at its finest.

"All I ask is a little something for a drink," the guard replied.

This turn of phrase confused me, and I looked to Alejandra for an explanation. "¿Algo por el refresco?" I repeated, but she was already reaching for her wallet.

The guard, who called himself "Chinksy," asked that we refrain from building our tents until the mall closed at 10 p.m., so we loafed in the parking lot cooking dinner and drinking beer. We talked about the beach we'd camped on the previous night and the sea turtles we'd seen there, about the mountains that waited for us in Chiapas, several days ahead. We told Alejandra to call in sick for another week, to forget about Mexico City and ride on with us into Guatemala and beyond, and through it all she said nothing, just laced her fingers in front of her and sighed, grinning. When we didn't let up, she changed the subject.

"Guys," she said, looking each of us in the eye in turn. "Back before Zonjal. With our friend, the boy. We did something amazing that day."

"Maybe," Jamie said in a small voice, exhaling smoke and tapping his cigarette into the gutter. "Fuck I hope he's okay. I mean, what if he really was involved in… something? It'd almost be like we were just delaying the inevitable."

"Whether or not he did anything is beside the point," Robbie said evenly. "The fact is, he was incredibly lucky we saw him. For whatever reason — and I'm sure they had their reasons — nobody else felt like they could help him. But we could. And we did." He reached over and took the cigarette from Jamie, whose unfocused eyes bored into the gutter between his knees. "Maybe he made decisions that got him into that mess, maybe not, I don't know," Robbie went on. "I don't think it matters, to be honest. What I do know is that we got him out of immediate danger."

To me, the whole affair was ancient history by now. Bicycle touring has the habit of packing many small adventures into each day, and had long since warped my sense of time. Days felt like weeks, and the concept of a month had become meaningless.

I'd seen some beautiful things since Zonjal — starlit beaches, sea turtles, the coming mountains looming up ahead — but I only remembered looking at them for a while, as if in a museum, and then pedaling away.

Later, once the parking lot had cleared out, Jamie and I held jousting competitions to prove the nimble bicycle's superiority over the clumsy shopping cart.

"C'mon, guys," Chinksy complained. "Don't make me lose my job over this."

"No mames, Chinksy," we taunted. "You need another refresco or what?"

# CHAPTER 31

We woke at 5:30 the next morning to the sound of shopping carts screeching and clanking beside our tents. This, we later agreed, was Chinksy's fitting revenge for our shenanigans the previous evening. We made good time across a flatland of half-hearted agriculture to the town of Unión Hidalgo, which proclaimed itself the "Tierra de las mujeres bonitas" — *The land of pretty women.*

We stopped for supplies at an abarrotes where, in the drowsy and deserted streets at the peak of the day's heat, our bikes nevertheless attracted a crowd.

"I can't understand this accent at all," I muttered in English to Alejandra as the crowd chatted among themselves.

"They're speaking Zapoteco," Alejandra whispered. "I knew it was still spoken down here, but I've never actually heard it in person before."

The language — which had a staccato rhythm similar to Mandarin — was the native tongue of Benito Juárez, who became the nation's first indigenous president in 1861. We learned this from a genial man named Virgilio, who waded through the crowd and introduced himself with a politician's grin, handshakes and backslaps.

"Señor Juárez never even learned Spanish until he was 12 years old," Virgilio said in Spanish. "But let's not dwell on the past. Is there anything I can do for you right now?"

"We're just looking for a place to camp..." I began.

"You absolutely must stay through the weekend," Virgilio interrupted. "We're having our annual Fiesta de San Isidro, and there's going to be a parade and a big celebration."

My heart sank. This was more information than I had wanted. The date of my rendezvous with Hailee was fast approaching and I was all for cycling on toward Tuxtla Gutiérrez, where I planned to take the bus to meet her in Cancún. I glanced around us — the wide concrete streets of Unión Hidalgo were blindingly hot, and the flat, stagnant countryside around it didn't offer much relief. The weekend was five days away. Five days? Here?

"What'd he say?" Jamie asked, nodding at the expectant Virgilio. When I translated news of the festival, Jamie's eyes lit up.

"Get fucked," he said. "I bet this town knows how to party."

Virgilio understood the English word "party," and he latched onto it.

"Oh yes," he cut in, pointing a finger at Jamie and nodding at Robbie and me. "On Friday there is a parade, and on Saturday the party starts at eight and carries on until the next morning."

I looked to Alejandra, who had been chatting with a couple of ladies nearby.

"There's going to be music and fancy dress," she smiled.

"Well, la chica, el muchacho and I make three out of five," Virgilio announced, thumping Jamie on the back. "You're staying for the weekend. I know just the place."

As Virgilio gave Alejandra the directions to a camping spot on the outskirts of town, Rob gave me a sympathetic nudge with his shoulder.

"Notice how Virgilio gave himself the bike gang's deciding vote there?"

"Kind of muscled his way in, didn't he?" I sighed.

Robbie tilted his head to catch my eye. "You okay?"

"Yeah. I just… yeah," I sighed again. To the crowd's amusement, Jamie had swapped his bike for someone's three-wheeled ice-cream cart and was taking a lap of Unión Hidalgo's modest plaza. "I suppose this could be fun."

"It's going to be weird, at the very least," Robbie said, watching Jamie. He turned to me again. "We'll get you to that bus on time, mate."

Virgilio's directions took us through a dusty cemetery where the tombs of multiple family members resided together in crypts like little pastel-painted chapels. These were arranged sidc-by-side in streets, a little town of the dead neighboring the living. The campground was a balneario — a concrete pool — run by a woman named Silvia and her husband, Pedro.

"Señor Virgilio sent us here," Alejandra began. Silvia grumbled something inaudible, but told us we were welcome to stay so long as we ate one meal per day at her adjoining restaurant.

Silvia and Pedro's home was on a plot of land out on the scrubby coastal plain behind a large saltwater lake, hemmed in by bush on one side and cattle paddocks on the other. Their house was small, made with tin sheets, timber and cinder blocks, and abutted by a large tin roof covering an assortment of plastic chairs and tables. Families from Unión Hidalgo came to Silvia and Pedro's place to while away hot afternoons — the kids swam in the pool while the parents sat in the shade drinking light beers and eating in the open-air restaurant. Chickens and turkeys of all ages strutted or scurried around our ankles, and every few days we watched Pedro take an elder away, hang it by its feet from the barbed wire and quietly slit its throat.

Silvia then plucked and butchered the bird beneath a parota tree at a wooden bench piled with tortillas, ears of garlic, stacks of tomatoes, avocados and canisters of spice. She worked at the bench with her daughter — also named Silvia — for most of the day. In the evenings Pedro would drag a bed outside onto the grass. They slept under the stars while we occupied the hammocks strung under the tin roof. I woke each morning to Silvia's thunderous farts.

We swam in the pool each morning while the water was still clean — Pedro drained and refilled it after the last guests left each night — and waited out the hottest part of the day reading or chatting with Silvia while she cooked. She had been attending the festival for 60 years. When she had first attended the much-discussed party, men and women were not allowed to sit together. If a man wanted to speak with a woman, he had to venture up front to ask her to dance. Any private conversation would then take place on the dance floor, in full view of the town.

"It was like this until about twenty years ago," she said. "My daughter was in the first generation that wasn't separated."

"Do you think it was better before, or now?" Alejandra asked.

"To be honest, it's mostly the same," she said. "Modesty was more important when I was a girl, but we still found ways to drive the muchachitos crazy. And at least now they can learn something about each other before the whole town decides they're an item."

"Virgilio said they would have turtle eggs at this party," I piped up. He had confirmed the presence of this illegal delicacy when we had run into him again in town the day before.

"Virgilio says a lot of things," Silvia said evenly.

"How long have you known him?" Alejandra said.

"We dated for a while," Silvia chuckled now. "In high school."

This caused a few whistles and whoops, which Silvia batted away.

"What happened?"

"Nothing. He's always loved to talk, our Virgilio. I couldn't get a word in myself." As Alejandra relayed this latest bit of gossip to Robbie and Jamie, Silvia watched a shirtless Pedro pushing a wheelbarrow of earth towards the pool, where he was building a mound to soften the effect of the concrete jutting out of the flat grass.

\* \* \*

The Festival for San Isidro, patron saint of agriculture, began the next day. The people of Unión Hidalgo massed along their town's main thoroughfare, where the parade started with a calf led on a rope. A child of about seven sat on the calf's back and when it took off, spooked by the noise of the crowd, the boy fell heavily onto the pavement.

"He's okay!" the boy's father yelled after a moment of concerned silence, holding his dazed son aloft. The people roared approvingly.

A procession of trucks, tractors and cattle followed, towing trailers decked out in bunches of flowers, ears of corn, sacks of beans, heaps of mangoes and images of Isidro, an 11th century Spanish peasant credited with several farm-related miracles. Ladies and girls of all ages sat in the trailers wearing quilted blouses, heavy skirts and flowers in their hair. They threw fistfuls of snacks and chili-coated candy into the crowds. Marching bands followed, and between the soundtrack of screaming trumpets, barrumping tubas and swirling clarinets, the bushels of strange herbs and flowers, the bobbing heads and braying voices of the cattle and the elegant men and women on horseback, I imagined myself on some backwater planet of the Star Wars galaxy. I understood none of the symbolism and reveled in my own confusion.

After the first four trucks, the flying candy became toys, balls, masks and then fly swatters, strainers, saltshakers and bags of rice that would explode on outstretched fingers and shower the crowd with their contents. The loot had all been donated, I was told, by a local businessman. Kids scurried between knees after plastic bowls and bags of oats, then handed the winnings off to their parents, who smiled shyly at the back of the crowd.

One truck carried two little girls of about seven, dressed in gowns and tiaras and handing out bouncy balls. One tossed her gifts into the jostling crowd with abandon, but the other sat with perfect posture, hands in her lap, eyes scanning the faces around her. She ignored the outstretched arms and friendly begging until suddenly she would spot someone who, in her mind, seemed especially deserving. She would then bend down, retrieve a ball and gracefully pass it into their waiting hands, a benevolent princess taking her job very seriously.

Finally, the largest float of all arrived, a tower on wheels. At its top stood a boy in a black suit and pale green satin shirt. Behind and above him, a girl of about 14 squeezed into a matching green satin gown and tiara. She was the reina — the queen of the festival — and she flung plastic cups and toys at the crowd with dainty gloved hands.

The next evening's party was a more genteel affair. The town's prominent families arranged themselves around a large dance floor in one of Unión Hidalgo's smaller plazas and a brass band of ancient musicians played traditional favorites for the crowd's dancing pleasure. Virgilio was there, beaming so hard his cheeks must've ached. Robbie, Alejandra, Jamie and I struggled to control our Hunger around the gigantic dinner buffet.

Silvia's daughter had dressed Alejandra up in the traditional local outfit of quilted blouses and long, heavy skirts decorated with images of blue, orange and purple flowers.

"You look great," I told Alejandra as I led her to the dance floor.

"I look hot!" she replied.

"Oh! Ah, yeah! It's a stunning outfit."

"No I mean I'm literally quite hot. I've never sweated so much in my life!"

Later, I sat in a corner of the pavilion watching Robbie, Jamie and Alejandra dance. I saw Robbie scan the crowd, grab a couple of beers and then make his way towards me.

"Having fun?" he asked, taking a seat and handing me a bottle.

"I've never felt further from home," I said, feeling tipsy and philosophical. "But only in the physical sense."

"Ohh, tell me more." Whenever I wanted to talk about so-called "deep shit," I could always count on Robbie to listen.

"This," I waved my new beer at the party, the women swirling their floral dresses and waving paper fans at their faces, the waiter boys in red satin vests, the shifty men slurping turtle eggs at the margins, the old cathedral looming over all. "It's so different to anything I've ever known. But this feeling? A strange place with my friends, the bikes, the chat? It's home."

"What's going to happen when you go to meet Hailee?" Robbie asked. "Is she going to feel like home?"

"I have no idea," I said truthfully, and took a mouthful of beer. Less than five minutes out of the cooler, it had already gone warm in the heat. "What about you? You and Jamie are going to have some fun together, I think."

Robbie took a deep breath and followed my gaze to the dance floor. Jamie stood head and shoulders above the crowd and was provocatively wiggling his bum between two of Silvia's cackling nieces.

"I hope so," he said. "I'm pretty nervous about that. He sure knows how to bring the fun. But I can't help but feel responsible for the guy."

"You've just got to send him off to Steffi in one piece," I said. "Get him to Cancún. Your mission, should you choose to accept it."

"And then what?" Robbie wanted to know. "Are you coming back to the bike?"

I'd been fixated on the moment of Hailee's arrival for so long, I hadn't considered what might happen after.

"I assume so," I said. "But I can ask you the same question: When are you gonna find something else to do? You've said that you're not going all the way to Patagonia with me. What's your next adventure, Rob?"

A weight seemed to settle briefly on Robbie's face. He shrugged it off, took a sip from his beer and nodded toward the dance floor. Silvia's nieces had caught Jamie between them and were now grinding against our friend from either side.

"Right now I'm wondering if Jamie needs a rescue, or if Alejandra wants a drink," he said.

"And then?"

"And then I'll take a last look at the buffet," he winked, and disappeared into the crowd.

# CHAPTER 32

Throughout the preceding months — starting somewhere around Guanajuato — I had strived to fulfill a lifelong goal: to grow a mustache. I wanted a thick, Zapata-like caterpillar nestled along my upper lip, and the manly authority that I imagined it would bestow upon me.

After bidding Alejandra goodbye at a dusty bus terminal near the border with Chiapas, we'd spent several days climbing into the foothills of this mountainous new state. Now, in the bathroom at our Couchsurfing host's house in a middle-class district of Tuxtla Gutiérrez — and with a day left until my bus over the mountains to meet Hailee in Cancún — I pondered the result of months' worth of not-shaving.

I certainly had a mustache, for I felt it shivering like a coastal heath in a sea breeze with each nasal breath. In the last couple of weeks, several enterprising follicles had even managed to curve over my upper lip and dip into my mouth, like roots seeking moisture.

But despite all the tactile evidence, visual proof of this mustache was sparse. The fine hairs tended to appear only when I tilted my face just so to catch the light. I was leaning over the sink, running my fingers up and down my upper lip to reassure myself that it really was there, when I had a thought.

"Should I shave before I see her?" I said, loudly enough that Robbie might hear from the lounge room. He wandered in, surveyed my upper lip and thought for a moment.

"You have to realize that you're meeting her in the land of mustaches," he said. "Suppose that she's got a little bit of a thing for facial hair. And suppose you shave yours off. So she flies all the way down here to see you and before long, she realizes that she's hanging out with the only guy in this entire country who can't grow a decent mustache."

"Uh-huh," I murmured, looking in the mirror again.

"In that case, every other man is more attractive than you," Robbie concluded.

Jamie's ukulele strumming from the verandah was lost in a sudden gale of laughter.

"Listen good, Quinno," he called. "The man's a fucken scholar."

"On the other hand," Robbie went on, ignoring Jamie's heckling, "if you do turn up with a mustache, well, at least you're on a level playing field."

"And if she doesn't like it?" I asked, eyes still fixed on the mirror.

"Tell him, Rob!"

"Oh, that's easy," Robbie grinned. "You shave it off right then and there. You see? Win-win. You can't grow your mo overnight — but you can get rid of it."

A fresh hurricane of giggles stormed in from the verandah.

"Jamie, this is serious!" I yelled, then turned back to Robbie. "Alright, the mustache stays. But what about sleeping arrangements? My bus will get to Cancún eight hours before her flight, and I'm in charge of finding accommodation. Isn't it a bit presumptuous to book a double room? And if so, does it then send the wrong message if I put us in a dorm?"

Jamie had started strumming again and Robbie walked away. "I already told you," he called from the lounge. "She's flying all the way down here to see you. What do you think she's coming for?"

\* \* \*

In the morning I said goodbye to Robbie, who I would see in a month, and Jamie, who would take off for his own romantic date with destiny before I would see him again. We wished each other luck and tailwinds. I listened to the rumble of the bus engine and snatched episodes of shallow sleep before gasping awake again in the canned air.

We nosed into central Cancún's steely bus terminal around midmorning the next day. I washed in the station's bathroom sink and reassembled Baxter, fitted him with the bags and rolled into the street. The day had a surreal quality to it. I felt unmoored without hills on the horizon and groggy from the overnight ride. Sparkly sunshine cut the air like a beam, giving the streets a more glittery feel than Chiapas' humidity-filtered light.

I rolled Baxter heavily from hostel to hostel looking for places with both dorms and private rooms available, unable to make a decision and wanting to keep my options open. I tried and failed to comprehend that Hailee was, at that moment, in the air and headed my way, bridging a gap that had taken me seven months to cover by bike. As the appointed hour approached I found the park where we had agreed to meet, propped Baxter in a prominent spot and tried to settle my nerves with a book while I waited.

* * *

I recognized the way she walked — a sort of speedy amble — and her mane of curls. She wore loose elephant pants, a pair of Chaco sandals (Tommy had also owned a pair) and a t-shirt that had become dotted with sweat.

*Well*, an excited voice whispered in my brain as I stood to greet her, *here we go.*

Hailee and I hugged briefly — "Give me a second, I'm very sweaty," she said — and then sat together on the bench while she cooled down. The park had been hard to find, and she'd spent an hour lugging her backpack around in the still afternoon heat before she found me.

She was brimming with energy. She had received her bachelor's degree only days before and was untethered from a school or family home, truly loose upon the world for the first time in her 22-and-a-half years. Her parents, sisters, grandparents, an uncle and an aunt had made the trip to attend her graduation where, among other things, she'd taught her grandparents to "shotgun" a can of cheap beer. She recounted the afternoon she'd spent explaining the existence of dating apps to her parents — and then informing them that a person she'd met on Tinder was now inviting her to Mexico.

"Weren't they worried about you?" I imagined a typical Anglo-American couple aghast at the news that their eldest daughter would soon disappear into darkest Mexico — "Don't they chop people's heads off down there?" — to see a man she'd met on the internet.

"Oh, as soon as we get Wi-Fi I'll have to call them," she said. "But I talked them through it all. They're very supportive."

I sat and listened, watching my memories of her return — the way she threw her head back when she laughed, the way her eyes turned from green to steely blue when she fixed them on mine. I tried to concentrate on making witty comments. We talked all the way to the hostel I had picked and then out to a taquería, a bar and then a plaza, which had filled with holidaying families from all over the country as the evening cooled. We were still chatting as we moseyed back to the hostel, and I wondered somewhat frantically whether we had enough conversation to fill an entire month.

It wasn't until we reached the room that we tried silence for the first time. She sat back against the headboard of the bed, watching me. I made myself hold her eye and willed away an urge to fill the moment with more chatter. I felt my thoughts — which had been dancing in overdrive all evening — begin to resettle into the contours of my brain, and found that it was easy to sit in that silence. She watched this happen, smiling slightly, and suddenly I found myself looking back on the preceding gulf of seven months like a mere puddle, skipped over after a spot of rain.

\* \* \*

Several days later, I lay face-down on a beach. A midday breeze whipped sand across my body. The sound of it in the coconut palms overhead muffled the shouts of children in the water and banda horns galloping from a small boom box further along. The families who came out during the day to barbecue would begin packing up soon, once the lanchas arrived to ferry them back to the mainland.

A day earlier, our plans to hitchhike to a town called Valladolid had gone slightly awry when a drunk picked us up and tried to take us back to Cancún to party with him. After finally convincing him to let us out, Hailee and I had been wandering aimlessly on foot when a young man pulled over and said he was on his way to Valladolid. His name was Irán, and the reggae rhythms and air conditioning inside his company car calmed our unease after the dicey situation during our last ride.

Irán told us about his hometown up on the Yucatan peninsula's northern coast, called San Felipe. Sea cucumbers were currently in season, he said, and diving crews had converged from all over southern Mexico to make their fortunes offshore. Irán's father was a veteran diver, and each year the young man worried about his dad's safety. The divers went down 10 or 20 meters, sometimes more, he said.

"They go with scuba tanks?" Hailee asked. Her Spanish had been rusty for the first few days, and still carried the Italianate rhythms and softened consonants she'd picked up during her study abroad program in Buenos Aires. But as her confidence returned, she began taking the lead on these conversations with new acquaintances.

Irán smiled and shook his head. "They take a hose," he said, "hook one end to an air compressor, put the other in their mouths. If they lose the hose, they can drown. And if they come up too quickly, they get very sick."

Hailee winced. "That does sound dangerous," she said. "My dad used to fish for tuna and salmon in Alaska, but they had nets, skiffs and winches, not air compressors and hoses."

"¿Verdad?" Irán smiled in the rearview mirror. "I saw a TV show about that, they say you can make good money on those boats. You're right though, about the sea cucumbers. It is dangerous. Four men have already been lost this season.

"San Felipe is a beautiful town," he changed the subject after a heavy pause. "There's this island just offshore, with white sandy beaches. Flamingoes. You can hire someone to take you with a boat — no more than 60 pesos — and we used to camp out there all the time. I have never understood why we don't get more tourists."

Hailee glanced at me, eyebrows raised, then turned back to Irán.

"If we wanted to check it out, how might we get there?"

Now, I looked out at the small strait between our island and another, a couple of hundred meters away. Lanchas pushed through small swells in the channel, taking divers from San Felipe out to the sea cucumber fields. I saw the air compressors, coolers and coiled hoses at the feet of rope-muscled men.

I watched them pass and then glanced down at Hailee, who was asleep beside me. White sand was gathering in her hair and in drifts around her arms, but her face was peaceful. I opened my book and as I began to read, her foot found mine. It moved up and down my calf, just saying "hello," and then returned to its own towel.

\* \* \*

The Zaci cenote fills one of Valladolid's central city blocks. It is essentially a large hole bored at an angle into the Earth, a haven from the Yucatan's deadening midday heat. Large black fish swam in the brackish water, a portal to the underground fissures, cavities and cave networks running through the Yucatan's limestone bedrock like a big hunk of Swiss cheese.

After an introductory swim, Hailee decided she wanted to jump from one of the platforms on the wall of the cenote (pronounced "se-NO-teh"), some ten meters up. There was a long silence between the scratch of her feet leaving the rock and the crash as they hit the water. This, of course, meant that I had to jump as well — though it took me much longer to climb over the railing and step off into the air, and the adrenaline of the freefall tugged fearful and somewhat embarrassing noises from my chest.

"Well," she said with a sly grin as I pulled myself up onto the rocks beside her. "That... well, that was something."

The romance that had been growing between us inside my tent and cheap hotel rooms was flush with new excitement. But this — sitting around talking shit, ribbing each other and watching the world — was as easy and comfortable as old friends.

At some point, three men descended into the cenote and sat on a ledge, watching us jump.

"You're crazy," one said as I walked past. "And she follows you in your madness."

"You've got it wrong," I replied. "It's me following her."

Meanwhile, Hailee was chatting with a trio of teenagers. One girl, who was about 14 or 15, quietly asked if there was any secret to surviving the drop.

"Step out with conviction, keep your arms by your side and your legs together," Hailee said. "Would you like me to go first? Or do you think you've got it?"

The girl said she would go alone. She had been very serious and solemn throughout their conversation but once she leapt the first time, snapped her feet together as she hit the water and surfaced, she allowed herself a small smile.

Hailee jumped next and, after a quick debriefing session, the girl loped up the steps toward the jumping platform again — prompting groans of dismay from her friends. Hailee swam over to the ledge where I was sitting.

"I wonder what her parents will say when she tells them some gringa taught her to jump off high ledges into mysterious deep water," I said as she pulled herself up to sit beside me. The girl was now standing on the ledge, taking mid-air pose requests from her friends.

"I don't think anybody needs to worry about her," Hailee said. "I'm more worried about whoever gets in her way."

And all I could think was, *Who is this woman, and where did she come from?*

# CHAPTER 33

"So the Zapatistas are like a separate country, or something?"

"Kind of." Hailee pursed her lips, summoning a semester's worth of public university education from her mind's library. Her childhood love of historical fiction — which covered everything from *Little Women* through *Pillars of the Earth* and *Outlander* to *Jane Eyre* — had combined with her passion for the Spanish language to draw her into classes about Latin American history. "They're a kind of loose confederation of rural communities, which they call 'caracoles,'" she said.

We'd seen signs for caracoles — literally *snails* — complete with painted pictures of spiral shells in the countryside on our way into Chiapas.

"They're a rural indigenous land movement. In January 1994 they went into rebellion against the Mexican government to protest NAFTA," Hailee went on. "I'm pretty sure the trade agreement took effect the same day. The government was already intruding on a bunch of indigenous land rights and attempting to privatize the farm collectives they call 'ejidos.' NAFTA was the final straw."

"They went into armed rebellion over a trade deal?"

"Well, they weren't actually fighting for very long. But the Zapatistas were pretty much correct about NAFTA. It totally wiped out the profit margins for small independent farmers down here. That jump-started mass migration from the southern states up to the new factories they built on the Mexican side of the northern border, or into the United States itself. I wrote my thesis about Central American migration into the U.S.," she added. "Down there, many of the same dynamics — plus prolonged civil wars fueled in part by U.S. policy — have uprooted a lot of people."

Hailee turned to the window of the minivan. We were ascending out of the basin cradling San Cristóbal de las Casas, a rainy city of colonial-era streets lodged high in the rainforest-clad sierras of southern Mexico.

"I love my country," she said after a pause, still watching the world streaming by outside the window. "It's my home. I believe in it. I believe in its people. The fact that we're allowed to learn about the crimes of our government and corporations is the embodiment of some of our highest ideals. But over the last four years I've also learned a lot about the crimes and mistakes my government has committed in places like this."

Clouds enveloped the minivan. Muddy villages crowded the roadside, which had turned claustrophobic in the mist. Gangs of machete-wielding workmen climbed in and out of ancient trucks. Children and old timers watched the traffic. The village women's lurid skirts and embroidered blouses provided splotches of color against the wisps of mist and humid greens of the forest lurking at the edge.

"That's why I'm excited to visit this Zapatista village," Hailee said after a while. "Because they run their society in a kind of radical adherence to democratic principles. You're aware that everyone's probably going to be wearing balaclavas when we get there, right?"

"I thought that was just their leader — Subcomandante… something?"

"Marcos. Except he goes by a new pseudonym now. 'Insurgente Galeano,' I think. But it's not just him. They have to hide their identity from outsiders, because the government is definitely out to get them. And they also use the masks to prevent any one personality from dominating administrative proceedings. Each community is run by an elected council — half men, half women. And everyone wears balaclavas to mask their identity."

As the road rounded a steep hillside, the van pulled over and the driver looked back at us. "Oventic," he announced, and we climbed out into the mist.

Two men in balaclavas manned a checkpoint. Behind it, a dirt road led down the hillside into the village. Neither man spoke Spanish, and it took a while for them to find someone in the village who did. When this third man arrived, he took us through a questionnaire reminiscent of the prickliest of border crossings. He then led us into a wooden hut, where we sat for another interview with a young man in a balaclava.

After 20 minutes the interviewer assigned us a guide — a man in a soccer jersey and a balaclava — whose job was to guide us away from the mountainside village's homes, hospital and school and toward the photo-ready trinket markets and murals glorifying nature, indigenous culture and the peasant rebellion leader from whom the Zapatistas take their name. We asked the guide questions about the Zapatista movement and how they ran their society, and to each question he answered: "No sé. La verdad es que no sé." *I don't know. The truth is that I don't know.*

"When did you join the Zapatistas?" I asked, growing impatient.

"Last Sunday," the man said.

"I don't blame them," Hailee said later as we stood by the road, waiting for a ride. "The government has never stopped trying to sabotage them. Paramilitaries, the works. They're right to be suspicious of outsiders, and I guess they've recognized that most of us are really only looking for photos, anyway. Seems like Oventic's just a place to funnel curious tourists."

After a few minutes of waiting, Hailee flagged down a pickup truck headed back to San Cristóbal and we climbed in the back. As we rolled down out of the mountains, I stole glances at her as she watched the winding mountain road and its drifts of cloud, tramping laborers, rickety tractors and lethargic dogs stream out from underneath and beside the truck, the world appearing at the edges of her vision and receding into the center, her eyes half-closed and a contented smile on her face.

"What?" she said when she caught me looking.

We had been together for almost three weeks by now, with just over a week left before she would leave Mexico. Although the quick timeline made no sense — a week in the Bay Area, seven months of sporadic text messaging and now three weeks of travel — I felt an emotion which, in my head, I had found myself referring to as "love." So when I conjured the image of saying goodbye and her getting on a plane, I couldn't picture what came after that moment.

Lying awake at night while she slept warm and soft beside me, I had run simulations in my head. It had taken me ten months to ride from Vancouver to Tuxtla Gutierrez, which was only about a third of the distance to Patagonia. My funds were dwindling, and I would need to find work soon. At this rate, it would take another two years to reach the goal I had set for myself.

Whatever this was with Hailee, I couldn't stomach the idea of it ending once she left Mexico. I was sure she felt the same way. I also couldn't ask her to wait for me while I kept pedaling toward Tierra del Fuego. But if I stopped cycling and abandoned the journey I had built my life around these last two years, what would come next? Just weeks earlier, I would have dismissed such thoughts as sacrilege.

As she waited for an answer in the back of that truck, all of this rumbled across my mind like a Brisbane thunderstorm. I opened my mouth to address it — the "L" word, the scary future, the big "what now?" — but at the last moment some brain cell lunged for the control panel and slammed a red "ABORT" button, and I heard my voice veering into safer territory.

"You're going to roll your eyes at this one, but it still blows my mind that, theoretically, we could ride this truck all the way back to your place from here."

She looked out at the receding mountain road again. "It's true. Pretty crazy." It wasn't the first time I'd brought up the possibility of overland travel from the Chiapas jungle to, say, New York City or the Arctic Circle. "Are all Australians as obsessed with borders as you are?"

"I don't think so," I replied, remembering Robbie's increasingly bored responses to my border-themed diatribes. "But they should be. It drives me crazy. We've both got passports that can take us virtually anywhere. Anytime you go on a road trip, aren't you tempted to drive deep into Canada, or down into Central America?"

"International road trip, I like that."

As we reentered San Cristóbal, hopped off the truck and wandered toward our hostel, the conversation morphed into a fantasy planning session for a grand North American van trip.

"We could start in Alaska," I said. "Go across Canada and see all the provinces."

"I've always wanted to see Prince Edward Island," Hailee said, "ever since I read *Anne of Green Gables*."

"Then you've got the lower 48, and then 32 Mexican states," I said, drawing an imaginary line with my finger.

"You're not thinking of an RV, are you?"

"I think it would have to be a van. Cheaper to run. Easier to camp out on city streets."

"Woow," Hailee sounded stunned. "But wouldn't a van just feel… I dunno… too *luxurious* for you?" I caught her mischievous smile. She already knew how to push my buttons.

"Get outta here." I nudged her shoulder, and she cackled.

"In all seriousness though, I want an electric van," she said after a moment. "Cover it in solar panels. Makes you go slow."

"Might be a while before either of us could afford that."

"Hey, you're going to tell me what I can and can't afford on my fantasy road trip?"

Several days later, we were stuffed into another minivan picking its way along another mountain road beset with more tall rainforest, headed back toward the Yucatan via more Mayan ruins. It was pouring rain outside, and the van's windows had all fogged up. Every few minutes, an old woman seated up front rubbed a clear space on the windshield in front of the driver.

"Weeks ago, just before we crossed out of Puebla, we stopped at an abarrotes to get dinner supplies," I was saying. "When we got back to the bikes, this little gecko was perched on Baxter's handlebars. We started riding again and he just hung out there for, like, half an hour or so until the next break. I stopped to pee and when I came back, he was gone."

"That was his stop," Hailee said.

"I suppose so. But in that time I'd become so attached to the idea of him coming with me to Patagonia. Robbie was talking about knitting him little beanies for when it got cold."

Hailee nodded knowingly. Though she had never met Robbie, Jamie, Alejandra, Simon, Tommy, Olga, Pablo or Miki, she'd heard enough stories by now to feel as if she knew them.

"Maybe we'd need an animal to take with us on the van trip," I added, returning to my favorite topic of conversation of late.

"A dog would be lots of fun," she said, "but maybe a bit large for a van."

"And I suspect a gecko would get lost in all the gear."

As the minivan rounded a bend in the road, the driver swore and stomped on the brake.

"¿Señor? ¿Qué pasa?" a woman asked from the backseat.

"Hay paro," the driver sighed.

"What's a paro?" I whispered as Hailee and the rest of the passengers groaned.

"A strike or protest," she said. "Someone's blocking the road. Used to happen all the time when I was in Argentina. A handful of people roll some rocks and old tires onto the highway, and nobody gets by. Once, I was stuck on a bus for ten hours waiting for one of these to clear. The protesters had their reasons, but I'd gone a bit crazy by the end."

The driver turned and addressed Hailee and I directly.

"I'm sorry about this," he said. "I love my state with all my heart. But sometimes life here in Chiapas can be… complicated."

Eventually, word came down the growing line of stranded vehicles: the demonstration would not end anytime soon. However, enterprising minivan drivers from the next town along were waiting behind the protesters and would be happy to complete the rest of our route. We disembarked, shouldered our packs and joined a procession of trudging travelers in the rain.

The protesters were a sad lot, standing around in the road getting wet. They watched us pass with faces like forlorn street dogs. They had a banner announcing their cause, but we couldn't read the slogan because they'd converted it into a makeshift shelter against the rain.

"How about a turtle?" Hailee said suddenly, once we had passed the group and were traipsing up the road toward a swarm of minivans and beckoning drivers. "For the van trip, I mean. One of those freshwater turtles with the stumpy little legs?"

Several more days went by, Mayan temples and waterfalls and miniscule taco stands interspersed with the stop-start lethargy of public transport travel and blissful evenings curled together. We were wedged into a taxi now, having returned to the main highway after a detour to the remote Mayan ruins of Calakmul. Vines and trees still covered many of the old pyramids, giving them the appearance of naturally occurring hillocks in the otherwise flat jungle.

"We'd have to stop pretty often," I said.

"Huh?"

"For the turtle."

"Oh," Hailee smiled. "So she could swim?"

"Yeah. Pond pit stops across North and Central America."

"Isn't turtle's blood a favorite ingredient for witches' brews?" she wondered.

"We'd have to stay away from Salem, then."

"I've always been fascinated by stories of witches," Hailee said. "Even though I know they were usually hunted down because a woman living alone in the forest freaks everybody out, apparently. But hey, I want to learn some spells and potions."

I was seated in the middle of the back seat, with Hailee on my left and a small man on my right. He had introduced himself as Yoshi back at Calakmul, but he and his girlfriend — flicking through her phone in the front seat — had stayed silent in the subsequent hour of travel and I assumed they didn't speak English. Now, however, Yoshi piped up.

"The ancient Mayans were very good at potions," he said.

"Oh yeah?" Hailee leaned over, immediately engaged. "I didn't know that."

Yoshi nodded furiously. "They were potion masters. Advanced scientists also, and theologians and astronomers. But especially good with potions."

Yoshi was writing a PhD on the ancient Mayans, he explained, and had come to Central America from his native Japan to see the cities and temples left behind by the people he'd been studying. He pulled out a map of the region covered in scribbled notes.

"I started in Honduras, then El Salvador, Belize, Guatemala and now Mexico."

"It looks like you're trying to visit every single Mayan site," Hailee said, peering at the map.

"We've seen a *lot* of ruins," his girlfriend replied from the front seat, making deep eye contact with Hailee for a moment before absorbing herself back into her phone.

"I want to see them all before I go home," Yoshi half-whispered, gazing at the map.

"So what's your theory, then?" I asked.

"For why they disappeared?"

"Yeah, what do you think?"

Though Mayan culture lives on, the classical civilizations that built the great ruins of Chichén Itzá, Uxmal, Palenque, Tulum, Tikal and others collapsed in the years leading up to 900 AD. The cause of this collapse and catastrophic depopulation remains one of the great unsolved mysteries of history and archaeology — but Yoshi had a theory.

"Like I said, Mayan priests were very advanced potion masters. Chemists, also. They had centuries' worth of knowledge that we still do not possess. And at some point in the 850s, they became masters of alchemy," he said. I felt Hailee stiffen by my side. Now she was really listening. I was looking forward to our post-conversation debrief later on — Hailee always noticed details that I missed.

"You mean, they learned how to create gold from lesser metals?" I said.

Yoshi nodded earnestly.

"How would that explain a civilization's collapse, though?" Hailee asked.

"It didn't collapse," Yoshi said. He was excited now. "It's more correct to say that they disappeared. You see, alchemy gives you great powers, far beyond turning metal into gold. Personally, I believe they used this power to ascend from Earth. Alternatively, it's possible that extra-terrestrials arrived to take them away once they had perfected the technique."

"You mean, leave this dimension?" I said. "Travel to nirvana, something like that?"

"No," Yoshi wrinkled his nose. "They moved to another planet. Another galaxy entirely. I myself have seen detailed plans for Mayan spacecraft."

"How many more sites do you have left to see, Yoshi?" Hailee asked.

"About 50," he said. In the front seat, I saw his girlfriend's jaw muscle tense.

"So the girlfriend's leaving him soon, right?" I said later. We were lying under a fan in a Chetumal hostel, waiting for night to relieve the blazing hot afternoon outside. In these lazy moments with her weight against me I felt simple and sunny happiness, like a glass of water catching the sunlight.

"Who knows, man," Hailee murmured sleepily, nuzzling into my neck. "She's stuck with him for this long. What I really want to know, though, is what his professor's going to say when they read that dissertation on Mayan space travel. I mean shoot, I want to read it myself."

Our next stop was Lake Bacalar, the so-called "lake of seven colors" in the Yucatan's south-eastern corner. The clear fresh water glittered against its white limestone bed, and we lingered on its shores for almost a week.

One afternoon, we followed a track to a submerged cenote ringed with jungle palms at the lake's southern end.

"We could go to Alabama, Mississippi, Louisiana, follow the Gulf around into Texas and then Tamaulipas," I trailed off dreamily. We were planning the fantasy van trip again.

"I have that cousin I've always wanted to visit in New Orleans," Hailee said. "And my uncle used to live in the Florida Keys. It's supposed to be cool down there."

"I really want to go back to the Huasteca too, I feel like Robbie and I only barely scratched the surface…"

"The thing is…" Hailee interrupted, then trailed off. But I knew what she was thinking.

"… I would do it," I finished her thought.

She was nodding. "Yeah."

We walked in silence until we reached the cenote. Her flight and whatever lay beyond were less than a week away, and this was as close as we'd come to actually addressing it head-on. We dived into the water and swam out into the center of the submerged cave, where the water was deep and blue enough to unnerve us if we treaded water for too long.

"We still haven't talked about what's going to happen after I leave here," Hailee said once we'd returned to the shore. She hung her towel from a branch and turned to look me in the eye. "I'm still not sure where I'll live, what I'll do for work. But if you want to be a factor in my decision making, well, you can."

* * *

"I want to finish on the bike, instead of as a backpacker," I said. "It wouldn't feel right any other way."

It was now late in the evening. We were sitting up in my tent by the shore of the lake, plotting out a new future, arranging our lives to make space for whatever was growing between us. In a week, Hailee was headed off on the second phase of her post-graduation travels in Southeast Asia, while I would link up with Robbie to meet some friends in Cuba. After Cuba and another stretch of Central American cycling, I would see Hailee again in two months' time.

I took a deep breath and said, "You sure you're up for this?"

She was sitting cross-legged under the light of a head torch, which dangled from the roof of my tent. It cast severe shadows over her soft face, but she wore a wry smile. "I am," she said. "Are you?"

Until now, I had been giddily admiring the possibilities posed by this newly opened pathway. But there was something about the intensity in Hailee's eyes that now shunted me irretrievably toward wherever it might lead.

Way back on some drizzly stretch of Oregon's Highway 101, Miki had observed that "passion is very unstable," an irrational rush of chemicals to the brain. To the outside observer, it might have seemed as if Hailee and I were rearranging our entire lives around passion's heady first rush. Saying that we loved each other was one thing. The logistics involved in allowing ourselves to pursue that love was quite another.

After her travels in Southeast Asia, Hailee would likely return to the Bay Area. So far, the job applications she'd been firing off for months had only yielded one offer — a sales role at a large technology company. The very idea of it left a bad taste in her humanitarian mouth.

"But what else am I going to do?" she said. "Move back in with my parents, waitressing and slogging on with applications for who knows how long? At least this way I'll still have my independence and can plan the next move from there."

The next logistical question — where was I going to live? — was actually quite simple. For starters, this entire plan was made immeasurably easier by my birthright citizenship in the United States. And seeing as though we were planning to rearrange our lives based on a grand total of five weeks together between Berkeley and southern Mexico, we saw no problem in continuing the trend and moving in together right away.

"No point beating around the bush," Hailee shrugged. "Let's see whether it'll work or not."

We both enjoyed the irony that our next great adventure involved a monogamous relationship and, eventually, day jobs and a share house in the Bay Area suburbs.

So that was that. We would meet in San Francisco in two months' time. We spent the cool hours before dawn lying in my tent.

"We're really going to do this," Hailee smiled. Her eyes bulged, her eyebrows arched.

"We are," I grinned back.

For the first time, I felt swept away by something much larger than myself. In one direction, I knew, lay more roads, warm beaches, humid forests, lonesome fears and ecstasies, friendships and relationships as fast and fleeting as chemical pyrotechnics.

In the other direction, an entirely different adventure waited. This, too, would be a journey through landscapes — with less variety, but the kind of depth that came with repetition. More importantly, it would take me into another mind. I would find this journey stranger than any physical trip, physically easier and yet increasingly complex as I glimpsed third, fourth, fifth and sixth dimensions of a soul that seemed to make room for me as I wandered deeper in.

I was choosing the latter, and it felt good. After 24 years of aggressively defending my independence, always choosing the route that took me further away from the people I loved, it felt strangely liberating to let go. The effect was a little like floating in a river with little idea of what waited downstream, only knowing that the sensation of moving with the current felt good. I was willing to follow this feeling and the person who inspired it wherever she took me, startled to realize that I had discovered religion and, furthermore, to learn that it wasn't geology or all-you-can-eat buffets or even bicycle touring — it was, of all things, love.

# CHAPTER 34

"Eventually we did get Jamie out of hospital, but it was slow going through those mountains heading out of San Cristóbal," Robbie was saying. "And by the time we made Playa del Carmen, it was my turn to get sick."

We were sitting on a municipal bus heading out of Cancún, rumbling through the outskirts of town towards the resorts.

"What'd you have?"

"A doctor said it was a combination of typhoid and salmonella," Robbie said.

"Jesus." I sat back and looked him up and down. Come to think of it, Rob was a lot paler than I remembered. Skinnier too, though that was normal for long-term cycle tourists. "So no fun for you in Playa."

"Jamie had fun. He shacked up with this rich chilanga in her hotel room on the beach."

"What about Steffi?"

Robbie shrugged. "Dunno. But he sure was having fun with this woman. We tried and failed to leave town three days in a row."

"You what?"

Robbie closed his eyes. "Don't ask," he said, shaking his head. He reopened his eyes. "But we did make it to Cancún in time for his flight. Last I saw him, he was still wearing one of those evil-smelling t-shirts that he'd hacked into a tank top. He hadn't showered in days. I felt sorry for whoever sat next to him on that plane. Then I went camping in an abandoned building and got infested with ticks."

"Ticks?" I was appalled. "Shit Rob, you can't catch a break."

"I think I've tweezered them all now," he said, then paused. He sucked in a deep breath and locked eyes with me. "It's been a big month. I'm excited to go to Cuba and not be cycling for a little while." Outside, the suburbs of Cancún had morphed into the manicured lawns and Vegas-style monuments of the Hotel Zone, where tourists barricaded themselves against the beach and away from the scary outside world.

"Are you still feeling this… disease combo you've got going on?"

"Starting to get over it. That kind of illness, it gets into your mind. It hijacks your thinking." But with antibiotics he was starting to feel himself again. "My brain seems clear for the first time in quite a while."

The bus pulled up at Playa Delfines, the one stretch of public sand in the Zona Hotelera. We wandered towards Listerine water across the white sand, which was cooling as the sun prepared to set behind the dunes. We sat and toasted cans of Tecate to Jamie's success in European love before, at last, Robbie asked the question I dreaded: "So, how'd it go?"

For as long as I'd known him, Robbie had always loved watching people in public places having what he called "real conversations." By this he meant long, involved discussions between people who were heavily invested in what the other had to say, who were passionate in their responses, who appeared to be uncovering some truth together. He loved the drama of it, a possible turning point in someone's life taking place in real time. It was one of the reasons he loved Latin America: so much of life takes place in the street. He would point them out from across a plaza — two old women gesturing at one another on a park bench, or a pair of young travelers staring intensely and nodding hard — and, having quit his life in Australia and come to the Americas on an open-ended cycling plan, he was especially happy to have a good Life Chat.

So a friend was about to unexpectedly settle in a foreign country and move in with a woman he'd only physically been with for five cumulative weeks? Robbie lived for this shit.

"I don't know," I said, winding down my tale. "I don't know if any of this is a good idea, or if it's all going to end in tears. All I know is that Patagonia will always be there. I can always get back on the bike. But this thing with Hailee isn't over, and I can't keep going down this road south without first knowing where the other one leads."

Robbie sat on the sand, the dregs of the day's sunlight glowing purple in the wispy clouds overhead, and beamed.

"I knew it!" he cried. "Holy shit mate, that's so exciting." He pulled me into a hug.

"I'm sorry I'm leaving," I mumbled. "I've been wondering what you're going to do, now that you'll be on your own and all."

"I've been thinking about that, too."

"But I only just told you I'm leaving," I said, confused.

"I had an inkling something like this might happen," Robbie winked. He looked out at the water again and took a deep breath. "I came over here because I wanted to hang out with you. It didn't really matter where we went — though, obviously, this has been great," and he waved his arm in a way that encompassed the white sand beach, the crystalline water, the whole dang country between here and Tijuana. "You know I like to keep my people close. That's why I get all weird when, say, a bunch of ants chase you, Jamie and Simon away from a palapa and I end up sleeping on my own.

"These last six months have been the best of my life," he went on. "But it's all coming to an end, now. My brother's gone, Jamie's gone, soon enough you'll be going away, too. And seeing as there's no-one left to ride with, I guess I've got to start figuring out what the hell I do now."

"It's all a big adventure, mate," I said, clapping him on the back. "And it's your own."

# CHAPTER 35

My finger hovered above the mouse for a second and then, with a deep breath, I clicked. In an instant, signals coursed out into the ether, data centers acknowledged the request, banking systems conducted invisible transactions. A confirmation message appeared on the screen: I'd be flying from San Salvador to Oakland in 24 days' time. The capital of El Salvador was more than 1,000 kilometres south of Robbie and I, who were still up on the border between Mexico and Belize. I dashed off a giddy message to Hailee letting her know when and where I'd be arriving ("See you soooon!") and then Robbie and I plotted a rough cycling route that cut through the upper half of Belize, spanned the length of Guatemala from north to south and then crossed into El Salvador.

"Nothing left to do but to do it," Robbie smiled.

It had been a month since we'd been on the bikes, a month of rum drinking, salsa dancing, plaza sitting and beach lazing throughout the western half of Cuba with some old friends we'd met back in Bogotá. Eventually we left Havana, where timber, paper, steel and rubber are reused over and again, and arrived back in gleaming Cancún, where everything is plastic and serves a single use on its inevitable journey to landfill. We lubricated chains, inflated tires, calibrated gear shifters and checked brakes, then took off on the hot highway cutting through the jungle towards the border.

Being the only main road through the north of Belize, we'd expected the industriously named Northern Highway to be a bustling thoroughfare of trucks and buses and rest stops, stalls and highway noise, the usual Latin American scene. Instead, we found a quaint country lane meandering through the scrub that coated the country's gently undulating countryside. At most, around 400,000 people live in Belize, and most of them live in the central cities of Belmopan and Belize City. This left the rest of the country remarkably undisturbed by human habitation.

"Do you think everyone got a bit tired of hearing about Hailee while we were in Cuba?" I asked as we rolled through the slow town of Orange Walk. We were passing businesses with names like "Happy Store" and "Friendship Hardware." Pedestrians wished us a "G'marnin'" in a languid English creole. Wooden houses built on stilts had appeared among the standard Mexican-style bungalows. Cane fields ringed the town.

"I'm not sure about that," Robbie said in a diplomatic tone. "But I'm very excited for you. I've never lived with a woman — I'd love to live in the same city and catch up once or twice a week to hear how it's going."

"If only," I said. Many of us move across countries to be with a lover — why not do the same to be close to a friend? But moving to the United States is absurdly difficult for anyone who did not luck into a bonus citizenship like I did, so Robbie would continue on the road south. There was talk of Simon joining him again, and of taking a Spanish immersion course in Nicaragua.

With few towns, mountains or beaches to distract us, Robbie and I settled back into the rhythm of life on a bike, joking that we had returned to our day jobs after an extended Cuban holiday. On the first night, the sun timed its departure with the full moon's rise, glowing white and cold like a lamp overhead. Dogs barked at intervals, a cock crowed at 3 a.m. It felt like old times.

Northern Belize had been full of Spanish speakers and Spanish place names — San-this and Santa-that — but this changed as we entered the heart of this former British colony. Here, we encountered place names of such devastating Englishness that we imagined a lady of high Victorian society, parasol in hand and servants for her luggage, touring the territory on a mission to rename various towns and villages. Hattieville, Ladyville and (my personal favorite) Teakettle all bore evidence of her work. Like James Cook on the east coast of Australia, she also appeared to have named geographical features of the landscape based on little more than the various moods that had seized her during her trip — there was soaring ambition at Mount Hope, an attempt at what might charitably be described as "19th century-style political correctness" at Indian Church and murmurs of dark deeds at Revenge.

She summoned all her descriptive powers at Roaring River, and at Silk Grass I suspected she had indulged in the sort of meadow romp that Hailee might have recognized from her old novels.

On our second Belizean afternoon, three little boys approached us from a raised house on the bank of a river at Burrel Boom and said that yes, we could swim and camp here if we pleased. Mom would be home soon.

Their names were Gerardo, James — pronounced "Jeeyums" — and little Emerson. They spoke English to us and a Spanglish creole to one another, a mix I could follow but not speak.

We had seen "tapir crossing" signs all day, and I asked if the boys had ever seen one. James claimed his uncle shot them. I asked about chupacabras, the mythical demon dog of Central America, and James said his dad had once hit one with his car. I asked what other fantastical creatures lived in Belize, and Gerardo mentioned mermaids.

"Mermaids?"

Emerson grinned, but his older brothers were nodding furiously.

"You can recognize the bad ones because they have black tails," James said. "They tip boats over. That's why we don't swim in the ocean."

"Any other creatures?"

"Jesus!" Emerson squeaked, and James shoved him.

"Jesus don't live in Belize."

"Where, then?" Emerson wanted to know.

"Up there," James said, and for a moment we all gazed at the cloud-flecked sky.

Mom soon arrived and the kids disappeared inside for dinner, leaving Rob and I to eat and wash the day's grime away in the river. I left the fly off my tent to breathe better in the hot, still night, and was in the middle of a dream involving Hailee and a strong sense of restful bliss when I woke to drops of rain on my face. In the ensuing scramble I managed to put the tent's fly on inside-out and was soaked in the process.

Robbie was in the same situation, but he cackled at the storm.

"I love it," he called as I grumbled. "It breaks the heat."

As I pegged out the fly, I fantasized about chilly weather, a warm bed and clean sheets.

Small hills appeared as we pushed west toward Guatemala and we began to feel apprehensive about crossing another border. The usual warnings began: Guatemala was poor. Guatemala was dangerous.

Guatemalans were desperate and capable of anything. So when we finally met someone who said otherwise, we latched onto his advice.

"They're nice enough over there," a barbecue restaurant owner said on our last morning in Belize. We had camped out the back of his farmhouse restaurant the night before, and he and his wife had invited us in for breakfast with their toddler son, who was squawking "I dropped my cuchillo!" and "Juguemos con mi toy car!"

"It can get a little crazy at times," the restaurateur added. "Get away from the border today if you can, be careful and you'll be fine."

We pushed through to the frontier in a spitting rain. We were rolling down a hill in no-man's land towards Guatemalan customs when I attempted to click Baxter's rear shifter into a higher gear. As I pushed the lever, something popped and crunched inside the shifting mechanism. The chain didn't switch gears and the shifter, upon closer examination, was busted. Changing gears was impossible.

So after officially entering Guatemala, we rode up into the town of Melchor de Mencos, a warren of concrete and timber splatted onto a hillside. The bike stores in town were closed for Sunday, so we found a petrol station and set up shop under an awning near the bathrooms, out of the intermittent rain, to try fixing the shifter ourselves.

A group of men sat around a table by the station's front door, chatting over tall cans of Gallo beer. Every now and then one would drift away to the bathroom, offering a friendly "buenas" as they passed. A shining white sedan pulled up and while an attendant filled it up, a middle-aged couple approached to ask if we were okay. They were from Quetzaltenango in the country's mountainous south, members of a light-skinned upper crust who looked almost as foreign as we did among Melchor's working-class Mayans.

"Be careful," the man said after the usual pleasantries. "Guatemala is a beautiful country. But out here," he cast a wary eye to the men at the table, "there are problems."

By this time, we'd cracked Baxter's shifter open and found the insides had virtually disintegrated — it was certainly beyond our skill to repair. Riding in the hills surrounding Melchor required the ability to change gears, and so we would have to stay overnight and find a replacement shifter once the stores opened in the morning.

We were putting the pocketknives and Allen keys away when another of the drinkers came by, a short fellow in an old Houston Texans cap and brown polo shirt. He stared as he passed, pissed in the gutter, then paused beside me on his way back to his friends.

"¿Gringos?" he hissed.

"Australianos," I replied.

"We don't like gringos here," he said. That got my attention. This wasn't your average Interview. Whenever people warned us of dangerous locals, they always spoke in the third person — "they," not "we."

"I was in the United States for three years," he went on. "Gringos don't like me, and I don't like them. And I'm not the only one. You better be careful. Somebody might kill you."

He said this slowly and clearly, making sure we understood. His use of the word "kill" — *matar* — seemed so extreme that we assumed he wasn't quite right in the head, and gave him the usual treatment we reserved for the rare aggressive or deranged Interviewer: "Okay, bueno, sí, okay, hasta luego," and off he went. We waved at his back as he stomped away.

A few minutes later, I watched as he approached Robbie from behind, put his hands on Oscar and then slammed the bike onto the pavement.

Robbie stepped back and my voice broke as I yelled "¿Qué haces?" I felt every pair of eyes in the intersection fix on us.

"¡No! ¡Les quiero! ¡Aquí!" he shouted, huffing between words. *I don't want you here.*

Righteous indignation ballooned inside my chest and I advanced on the man, shouting that I was sorry about how he'd been treated in the United States but that it obviously had nothing to do with us. I suddenly felt it was important to point out that we weren't proper gringos: "¡Otro continente, cabrón!" Once I had finished spitting this at him, I noticed the man's friends congregating around us. Several motorists were watching from their cars and the shotgun-toting security guard — a fixture at all Guatemalan gas stations, we later learned — was ambling over as well.

We were at the center of a circle now. The bike tipper took advantage of my pause to repeat that we should not be here and I repeated that we weren't even gringos and then summoned my best bogotano street snarl to call him a "racista hijueputa," which I immediately realized went too far and, in any case, came out sounding considerably less intimidating than I had hoped.

"You just don't like gringos because they're gringos?" I concluded.

"Sí," was the haughty reply and, well, there really was no arguing with that.

Several of his friends pulled him away while others helped Robbie replace the scattered contents of his panniers. One of the friends gently grabbed my arm and looked me in the eye.

"Andate," he said. "Please, it's better if you go," and it was the pain in his voice that convinced me to back off.

"Welcome to Guatemala, eh?" Robbie muttered as we rolled away, and we said nothing more of the incident for the rest of the day. Had the fearmongers been right, for once? What if they had always been right, and we'd been exquisitely lucky this whole time? We'd barely been in this country for two hours — was that man an outlier, or a warning of things to come? I had come back from Cuba for a month-long farewell cruise to see out a year of bicycle touring, not abuse and threats from traumatized ex-migrants in backwater border towns. When I remembered that I would be leaving Rob alone in El Salvador — which had a particularly unpleasant reputation on the international scene — a sense of guilt settled heavily in my gut.

The trouble, of course, was that my broken shifter prevented us from simply riding out of Melchor and leaving those bad vibes behind. We found a small hotel and barricaded our gear inside, then walked over to the main plaza. It was full of plaid shirts, cowboy hats and high-heeled boots, the air smoky and thick with the scent of sizzling chicken and thin cecina steaks. This was a familiar, friendly scene and we had already settled the night's anxiety-ridden question of "Where Are We Sleeping Tonight?" but I felt on edge. I constantly scanned the crowd for the short man in the Houston Texans cap, and when we went to bed we piled our bags and bikes against the inside of the hotel room door.

# CHAPTER 36

We found a bike store to replace the shifter in the morning, and once we had scurried out of Melchor de Mencos we found Guatemalan riding to be rather enjoyable. There was very little traffic and after the hills along the frontier, the landscape settled into bucolic scenes of lush forests interspersed with wide fields of thick grass and little homesteads.

The only downside in those early Guatemalan days was the revelation that the country was in the midst of a presidential election. Mexico's midterm campaigns had dragged on for months during our time there, culminating in an election night of firecrackers and shouting during Hailee and I's journey from mountainous Chiapas back into the Yucatan. Now the billboards and posters, the speeches and loudspeakers and childish campaign slogans were back — and it appeared that Guatemala observed this democratic ritual with even more fervor than its northern neighbor. Every political party had its own theme song, and cars overloaded with comically large loudspeakers plied the streets of every town and village delivering inane jingles about justice and victory and popular will directly into the ears of the suffering populace.

"My theory is that they're trying to deafen the voters," Rob said as one of these dilapidated vehicles screeched along an otherwise tranquil street in the lakeside colonial town of Flores. "That way, nobody can hear the competition when they show up tomorrow."

But Guatemalan political parties are not content to assault the ears alone — they are also after your eyes. Every conceivable surface was painted with the two-tone colors of this party or that. Roadside trees bore the red-and-white of the Renewed Democratic Liberty party; rocks and boulders had been splashed with the green-and-white of the National Unity of Hope party; and abandoned buildings proudly exhibited the red, white and blue of the National Convergence Front. In the villages, political agents had taken their cues from Pepsi and Coca-Cola and bought off entire communities with fistfuls of quetzals (the local currency, named after a striking local species of green-and-red bird), painting their houses and storefronts with slogans and primary colors.

Guatemala had called this particular election because its former president and vice president were both now answering allegations of corruption in court. The eventual victor would be a former comedian and political novice called Jimmy Morales, whose campaign slogan said more than enough about the sad state of democracy in a country where, by some accounts, fully 50 percent of government funding disappears before it reaches its intended target: "Not corrupt, not a thief."

Having experienced two elections on the continent in the space of several months, Robbie's expert traveler's advice was to avoid any municipality, province or nation state in the Americas where people are scheduled to vote. This wasn't a government travel warning about unrest and political violence, but a recognition that rigors of New World campaigning may drive the hapless traveler to the brink of insanity.

"This is to protect the politicians from travelers, not the other way around," Robbie explained. "If you're not used to it, this shit can send you over the edge."

\* \* \*

Guatemala is divided into two distinct geographic sections. One straddles Central America's volcanic spine, a maze of mountains and valleys stacked one on top of the other, villages speckled throughout, with white politicians and businessmen alternately running or embezzling the country from its capital, Guatemala City. The other is defined by the state of Petén, the country's largest, which forms a panhandle poking up at the Yucatan between Chiapas and Belize. Petén is almost as flat as the Yucatan, with the occasional patch of jungle left between big tracts of ranchland and even bigger fruit and palm plantations. The general lack of picturesque colonial towns and mountainous landscapes means most foreign travelers see Petén through the window of a speeding minibus, on their way to its main attraction: the legendary Mayan ruins of Tikal.

It felt good to be on the road and moving again. We entered a Guatemalan outback south of La Libertad, and the land became a flat disk of pasture bordered here and there by lines of twisted tree limbs and barbed wire. The cattle looked healthy, but the street dogs did not. Broken-legged, hungry-eyed beggars would watch us eat, it seemed, just to torture themselves.

Palm-thatched roofs and wooden houses, torn t-shirts on barefoot children, machete men riding old mountain bikes to jobs on huge Dole plantations — Guatemala felt poorer, rawer than the nations to its north. Hospitals, police stations and schools were all thin on the ground in Petén, and those we did see appeared barricaded against the people they were supposed to serve.

In some ways, the Guatemalan government remains an occupying power in Petén. The country's 36-year civil war, which ended in 1996, saw an attempted genocide of indigenous nations by Guatemalan armed forces — equipped, of course, by the United States throughout this period. Efraín Ríos Montt, a general who took power in a 1982 coup, oversaw the bloodiest phase of the war. His daughter, Zury Ríos, was now running for president as head of the VIVA party, and we saw her blue-and-white colors alongside all the others. The younger Ríos had married U.S. congressman-turned-lobbyist Jerry Weller in 2004, a year after participating in her father's campaign to retake the presidency.

Petén endured the worst of this madness. We saw military bases everywhere. Its people endlessly warned us of "gente mala" — bad people. One evening, a nuggety little farmer named Diego approached to tell us that we were setting up our tents on his land.

"I'm happy to host you," he said, "but I feel responsible. Better if you come closer to the house." There were gente mala about.

At a petrol station in La Libertad, we watched a carwash at work. The diminutive leader of the gum-booted crew carried a black assault rifle hanging off a shoulder strap, and the sheer impracticality of the spectacle made Robbie and I giggle — the weapon kept scraping on the concrete and knocking over buckets — because it was easier to ignore the more unsettling implications. That evening, camped by a creek, we heard six pops in quick succession coming from the opposite direction of the military base we'd passed that afternoon.

"Firecrackers?" I whispered from my tent. Robbie had grown up on a farm, making him the authority on distinguishing different types of cracks, booms and pops.

"Gunshots," he replied in a low voice. I slept flat on my stomach, hugging the ground.

A rainstorm soaked us out later that night, and in the morning we hung sodden clothes, blankets and tents off the exposed pylons and bits of rebar protruding from an unfinished bridge crossing the creek. The new bridge had been "under construction" for years, according to one man who was setting up a barbecue nearby for his soon-to-arrive family. The interim solution was a makeshift bridge of felled logs packed with earth, which wobbled when you walked on it, and would also soon need replacing. Someone had covered the unfinished concrete structure beside it with the colors of the Renewed Democratic Liberty party, which would go on to win a majority in Guatemala's congress. Its presidential candidate, the pasty-faced Manuel Baldizón, would soon be arrested in Miami after fleeing corruption charges in Guatemala City.

But despite the signs of a desperate and neglected people on edge, we found no gente mala on our ride through Petén. Women in long skirts washed clothes in the creeks and slapped them dry on boulders or chunks of concrete that had fallen off crumbling bridges. Everyone was quick to smile, yet shy and respectful of our personal space. The only Interview we encountered in Petén was a man in La Libertad who approached simply to ask: "¿Por qué en bicicleta?" *Why on a bicycle?*

We heard the word "gringo" more in one day of Guatemalan riding than we ever did in Mexico. The word has angry historical connotations in Mexico and at best it is a slightly endearing, slightly disparaging nickname strictly reserved for Americans. But every foreigner in Guatemala is a gringo, and we soon forgot our disturbing encounter in Melchor amid the smiling faces of dozens of miniature cheerleaders who lined the highway in village after village to watch us pass.

It wasn't clear to us how often foreign cyclists had traveled Petén's Highway 5, but the kids sure were good at the art of Gringo Spotting. Sometimes a hut would be hundreds of meters from the highway, on a hill across a shallow valley, and still there'd be some kid jumping and waving and hollering "greengo, greengo" in a chirpy little voice. The cry would precede us through town, sending bewildered señoras and young mothers wandering out to see what the fuss was about, then breaking into broad grins as they returned our "buenas tardes," the hordes of kids chasing our bikes and screaming with laughter whenever I rang Baxter's bell in greeting.

While most of Petén's bridges were crumbling or out of service, it appeared nobody had even bothered to build one across the wide Rio de la Pasión, which divided the small city of Sayaxche. Instead, travelers rode a wooden barge fitted with a pair of outboard motors mounted on the downstream corners. Once it had loaded up with cars, lorries, buses and cyclists, a bloke would hop on the appropriate motor and guide the creaking vessel across.

South of Sayaxche, the road entered proper jungle. Carcasses of the black, red and white coral snake (the *culebra coralillo*) littered the roadside. The jungle was filled with giant palms and covered with a dense canopy, which soon gave way to mile upon mile of palm plantation — some 50 or 60 kilometers of it. Beyond Los Pozos my odometer clicked past 12,000 kilometers. We sat in the palms and drank large cans of Gallo beer to celebrate another thousand kilometers.

"Probably your last one, eh?" Rob said.

Lying in bed that night, I looked up at the walls of my tent lofting in a tiny breeze and thought about home. I realized that, while making plans with Hailee, I had never considered going back to Australia. It was filled with people and memories that I loved but here in my tent, listening to the bird and bug calls, the mysterious grass swishings and twig crackings in the night — this was also home. Riding Baxter in unfamiliar country was home. Sitting in a field at twilight, sharing rice and beans from a pot with my best friend was home. Soon, Hailee would be home. These were homes I had made for myself.

Toward the end of the straight lines that defined the plantations of Petén, a row of mountains loomed up ahead — a solid wall to the south-east with higher, darker ranges behind. As we pedaled toward it, Rob looked over his shoulder with a wild look of adventure in his eyes.

"Mountains again," he said.

I felt ready for them. The next morning, the highway sneaked in through a gap in the range flanked with white cliffs.

"This is where we enter Rivendell," we agreed, but really we were only entering the state of Alta Verapaz and with it, Mountainous Guatemala. After a pleasant morning's ride meandering in a steep-sided valley, the road pitched upward toward the small city of Chisec and didn't stop climbing for a long, long time.

In the afternoon, we spied a rusty sign advertising a balneario five minutes down a dirt track. Balnearios had always been kind to us in Mexico — a pool to bathe in, space to camp — so we rode to a gate where a woman emerged from a farmhouse to take a small entrance fee.

"You're free to camp by the water, stay as long as you like," she said. "Watch out for the children, they're very curious."

Instead of a concrete hole in the ground, this balneario turned out to be a deep bend in a river. The water slipped down a series of small cascades and then congregated in a wide pool of the clearest pale blue before chattering down some stones at the far end. Huge trees hung out over the river, and a pack of small boys gathered to watch a scrawny kid named Wilson scale the trees and leap into the water. A constant procession of villagers came down to fill vessels — jerry cans, ceramic jugs, plastic buckets — while older women scrubbed and beat clothes on the rocks downstream.

That evening saw another iteration of an increasingly common ritual Robbie liked to call "Dinner with Friends." "Dinner with Friends" occurred when curious villagers or farmers gathered around to watch in fascination as we broke out our portable stoves and pots to cook a plain dinner of rice, beans, vegetables, hot sauce and perhaps a piece of meat, if we were lucky.

"Welcome back to 'Dinner with Friends,'" Robbie said in English to the mob of boys, aged between eight and 12, who had gathered around the picnic bench we had chosen for our kitchen. "Glad to have you all with us this evening."

"Always a treat," I added. "Now, tell me Rob, what's on the menu tonight?"

"Well, it's a bit of a hodge-podge tonight, as is often the case when you're unexpectedly having 'Dinner with Friends.'" Robbie was rooting around in his food bag. "Sometimes you've just got to throw together whatever you've got in the panniers."

"And what have we got in the panniers tonight, Rob?"

"An entire cabbage," Robbie said, dropping the yellow mass on the table with a thump, "which should go well with this coconut oil, as well as these two-minute noodles and that can of refried beans you've got over there."

And so we began, with the boys hissing and chatting in the local Mayan language. Only two of them spoke Spanish, so they translated questions from their peers — mostly to ask if they could try on our helmets, hats and sunglasses. Their only other request was for shampoo, and this was ventured so timidly that Robbie couldn't find it in himself to refuse and handed over his only bar of soap.

# CHAPTER 37

The country swelled beneath our wheels as we wound our way south, deeper into the ridges and folds of the continent's volcanic spine, and at some point we began climbing a mountain that simply never ended. It took us out of the jungles and into an altitude where all the slopes around us — many of which floated across some fog-filled abyss — were coated in a fuzz of corn. This was the same sense of dislocation we'd experienced in the Huasteca, where the land became a three-dimensional thing hiding entire worlds in unseen valleys, hillsides and riverbanks directly above or below us. Higher sierras appeared in the distance, a patchwork of crops and wild forest. Kids yelled "¡Gringos!" and told us we had a lot of climbing to go.

Not long after entering the country, I noticed that Guatemalan men often said "hello" with a whistle, one of the world's more charming forms of greeting. I hadn't detected any system or distinct meaning for different kinds of whistles, but everyone had their own signature style. As we pushed up through a thick patch of forest, I approached a group of wood carriers resting by the roadside. The wood carriers were boys and men who carried chopped firewood in a sling hanging from their forehead down their back, and sold their handiwork to feed cook fires, kilns and small ceramics factories, machetes sticking from the load as they trudged. I'd been rehearsing a high-low "*tweet-tweeet, tweet-tweeet*" that I'd heard from an old guy back in Petén, and I tried it now on the wood carriers. A discordant chorus erupted in immediate reply as everyone sounded off with their own signature whistle.

Online maps showed two possible routes to Antigua, a colonial city in the country's south. Both seemed excessively long. One looped east as far as the Honduran border and the Caribbean coast before cutting all the way back into the country's center. The other went west past Lake Atitlán and Quetzaltenango. But by zooming all the way in on his offline maps app, Rob found a third way. It was a faint line cutting almost directly south, which linked up with more roads on the northern edge of Guatemala City that would then pop us neatly into Antigua.

"It's probably a shitty road," Robbie said. "Up for an adventure?"

I was up for getting there as quickly as possible, and this third route would definitely be the shortest, distance-wise. However, as promised, it was a punishing road. It turned to rutted gravel not long after we left the bustling provincial city of Salama, and stayed that way.

At a small town just over a rocky mountain pass, we ended up camping in the front yard of one Señora Ilda. She lived in the center of a small roadside village and so, predictably, our nightly camp-cook-eat-sleep ritual turned into another session of "Dinner With Friends."

"Dinner with Friends" was usually a fun way to spend an evening. We never felt deserving of any special treatment, but it was impossible not to feel smitten with the crowds of villagers — adults and children alike — turning out to inspect our gear, ask questions and engage in a bit of lighthearted teasing. Any alien spaceship crew looking to break up a long trans-galactic voyage would surely enjoy a break in the friendly, isolated and intensely beautiful communities of rural Guatemala — so long as they don't mind being called "gringos."

However, every now and then this friendly attention became quite intense. The next morning, for example, we awoke in Señora Ilda's front yard to find that the local primary school was right next door, and virtually the entire student body had turned out to watch us eat porridge.

"It's our first 'Breakfast With Friends,'" Robbie said.

About 50 children gathered around, too timid to approach and yet unable to look away. We'd been a bit facetious with Ilda's cheeky teenage son Torino the night before, and we now regretted it as he flitted through the crowd filling the students in with his insider's information.

"They're from Australia, which is one of those disconnected states like Hawaii or Alaska. They said they usually travel by kangaroo, but the kangaroos are taking a break in Playa del Carmen so they're riding the bicycles instead."

Later, we stopped to drink a morning beer in celebration of Robbie's 8,000th kilometer. Then, as we descended into a wide basin cut with a maze of miniature valleys and ridges at its bottom, I steered Baxter into a pothole and blew out my front tire.

"Got a fucking plane to catch," I muttered to myself as I ran my fingers around the inside of the tire, looking for the puncture's source.

"What's that?" Rob said.

"Nothing."

The landscape was cut by a river called the Motagua, which we'd heard was a "difficult crossing." We soon discovered why. The river had flooded four years earlier, washing away the bridge that had once joined Salama to Guatemala City and was now listing in the riverbed 50 meters downstream from its foundations. It was possible to drive through the river in a four-wheel drive, but the buses didn't dare. They simply dropped passengers off to make their own way to the far bank, where another bus waited to complete the journey. One enterprising bloke had lashed planks of wood to an inflated inner tube and for a few quetzals he ferried the elderly, the young and the precious souls who didn't want to get their feet wet.

"Four years, and the idiots never bothered to replace the bridge," I complained grumpily as we de-bagged the bikes and prepared to wade in.

"Corruption mate." Robbie was shaking his head.

"Oh yeah, fuck 'em," I agreed vaguely.

"Fuck him, you mean." Robbie nodded at the raft operator, who was pleading with a pair of gray-haired señoras to "please be careful." The intrepid ladies appeared to be ignoring him and whooped every time the river lapped their bare feet. One reached down and splashed her friend.

"Him?" I dreaded Robbie's attempt to cheer me up.

"Sure," Rob said darkly. "You haven't heard? The river rafting lobby runs this country. Old mate's business depends on that bridge staying unbuilt, so he sends in his lobbyists to scratch a few backs. It's how the world goes 'round."

Rob remained straight-faced until the women joined forces and began splashing the hapless raft operator together.

"¡Señoras, por favor!" the man shouted over fresh cackles from his passengers.

We forded the river on foot and had ridden less than a kilometer when I felt Baxter's right pedal flex under my weight and, with a clunk, it and the crank connecting it to the bike fell off completely. We combed the gravel for the bolt that had either jiggled loose or sheared in two. After twenty minutes, I gave up and sat in the dirt with my head in my hands. I thought about the remaining distance between here and San Salvador, the remaining ten days until my flight, the new life waiting for me. No more chopping onions with a pocketknife. No more squatting in the dirt or endless sweating, no more "Where Are We Sleeping Tonight?" or "Dinner with Friends." Just a woman who made my pulse quicken.

"Got a fucking plane to catch," I muttered again.

By this point, a portly gentleman in a large cowboy hat and shiny grills had appeared and was helping Robbie look for the bolt. I felt them glancing at me, but I didn't care. I was laying in the dirt now and, having abandoned all pretense, had decided to wait for a bus.

"There's a village just down the road," the cowboy said. "You'll find a motorcycle workshop on the main street, I'm sure they'll be able to help you out."

So Robbie pulled me to my feet and we walked the bikes into the village. It was pretty, nestled a safe distance up the riverbank. An excitable mechanic promised to fix Baxter and a lovely restaurateur cooked eggs, beans and tortillas while we waited in her flower-filled garden.

We sat together in silence. I watched Rob's eyes roving from the flower-laden vines spilling over the garden wall, past the street dogs poking a nose in to inquire about food, to the kitchen door and its homey smell of frying tortillas and the sound of conversation. His smile exhibited a supreme sense of contentment.

"I know you're hurting," he said at last. "But you've got to admit: this is brilliant."

Later, when the bus roared through town on its way to Guatemala City and the driver slowed to raise his eyebrows inquiringly, I didn't hop on.

* * *

From the Motagua there was nowhere to go but up, and so we followed the winding gravel road up switchbacks, through dry dusty hillsides covered in a fuzz of brown scrub. When we stopped to rest, we watched rainstorms dangling beneath mountainous cloud banks as they swept silently over a pass we'd crested two days earlier, then climbed toward us in a rising roar of wind and water. When we reached the town of Chuarrancho, strung out along a ridgeline at the summit, we could see Guatemala City smudged across a wide basin to the south.

211

"I'm in the mood for a shower, not 'Dinner with Friends,'" I said as we rolled into town.

Robbie nodded. "I was going to say the same thing."

But when we asked around, we learned that the town didn't have a single hotel to its name. We pushed on into the dimming afternoon.

"How far is San Raymundo?" I asked a grocer, a sturdy Mayan wearing a red velvet shirt, a long green skirt and beaded necklaces forming a colorful rope hanging down her chest.

"Unos veinte," she said. *Twenty kilometers.*

"They have hotels there?"

"Sí… yo creo que sí."

"Is it uphill?" I asked despite myself.

"Sí," she said again, grinning at our glum resignation. "You two are going to arrive very late." She looked at the sky. "Looks like it's going to rain again," and her chuckle soon settled into a motherly expression of amused pity. "Ay, chicos. May God take care of you."

The road meandered on through the gathering gloom until we pulled up outside a ramshackle house with two men chatting out front. Was there anywhere around here to camp?

"Nothing special," said the younger of the two. "But there's a roof here if you want it."

His name was Armando, and this was his finca — a country farmhouse he kept for weekends when he could escape Guatemala City. After showing us around, he left us with his caretaker, a man whose felt hat had a large hole at the crux of the crown and brim. He called himself Gamín, the name bogotanos give to street vagrants and petty criminals.

There was a charm to the property. The outhouse was made from old car doors, and the yard was full of healthy chickens and dogs. The kitchen was a large wood-fired stove in the backyard, and Gamín helped Robbie cook a big caldo soup of vegetables and half a chicken for dinner, while I read a copy of *Return of the King* Hailee had brought to Mexico for me. After dinner, Gamín made tortillas and coffee. He talked us through local crop rotation practices, agricultural traditions and communal rituals collectively known as "milpa," and listened intently to stories of our route through Petén into the mountains. We talked about our siblings: my sister at university in Melbourne and another on her own European gap year; one of Robbie's brothers still in his hometown and Simon now back in Papua New Guinea; Gamín's siblings spread between Guatemala City, nearby villages and the distant United States.

"Do you miss the ones you don't see often?" Robbie asked.

"Always," Gamín replied. "But if I know they're happy, that's usually enough."

It was dinner with a friend, rather than "Dinner with Friends."

That night, I lay in a pile of blankets on the verandah listening to the sound of rain thrumming on the roof overhead, smacking leaves and dripping juicily into puddles and impromptu streams. My body eased into the ancient relief that comes from being safe, warm and dry under a tin roof on a stormy night.

I thought about the day: the broken bike, endless climbing, dirt roads. Then I thought about Leo and his dog Sassy Max, who I had met during the long ride to the Grand Canyon, and his story about his first outing in the mountains.

"I met this young feller," Leo had said. "He told me, 'You put yourself out here. Nobody else did it for you. You got here by yerself. So you can keep going.'"

I had often repeated this story to Robbie if he was feeling low. It was a satisfying and — I thought — rather inspiring anecdote: "You got yourself here, nobody else. So you can keep going."

This was a common theme among cycle tourists, a kind of pleasant surprise and inspiration that came from the realization that one was capable of cycling across continents. Always the odd ones out, cyclists tended to think of themselves as solitary figures covering improbable distances under their own steam.

"Everyone's on their own adventure," as Joff had said.

But now I wasn't so sure. I had done the pedaling, yes, but I wouldn't have made it through this day without the mechanic and his spare bolt, or that señora and her heavenly lunch, or Señora Ilda and half her village or even the rafter and his unruly passengers.

Thinking about all the people who had appeared with advice, water, directions, shelter or conversation soon had me reaching days, then weeks and months back until their ranks swelled into the hundreds. There were many who had done very little — just faces offering smiles, a word of encouragement, a cheer from a passing car — but if you added up all those acts, those little pushes, this collection of strangers had carried me all the way from Vancouver to the outskirts of San Raymundo.

I reached further back, cycling through faces in my mind's eye: the "why on a bike?" guy from La Libertad, the barbecue restaurateur near the Belizean border, Agustín and his family, Alejandra and her cyclist-crowded apartment, Tuly and her daughters, Walker and his daughters, the Grand Canyon visitor who helped me shed my fear, Stella and Ray, the first guy to ask "Where're you goin'?" outside Vancouver. I saw in their faces the landscapes that gave shape to their lives, forests and streets and mountains and deserts and pasture blending and melding together into a single unbroken community.

I wasn't some lonely adventurer and my trip wasn't some Herculean solo effort. To be a cycle tourist, I now realized, was to be a privileged repository of human goodness, like a basket that people plucked from the river to add a piece of themselves before sending it on downstream. And if I had learned one thing in this slow journey it was that no matter where I was, it was remarkably easy to make my way so long as I found my fellow humans there.

The realization that the single greatest achievement of my life was actually more of a group effort (someone had to build all those roads in the first place!) pooled like molten lead in the back of my skull. James, the English cyclist who'd first inspired me to start this trip, had never mentioned all the people who'd helped him on his own journey. For 12 months I had bought into the Solitary Man Theory, convinced myself that each milestone was further proof of my own strength and ingenuity, a conquest, a notch on my belt. But in a single day the road had shown that I had always traveled with others. Worst of all, I had just spent nine months telling the one person who had carried me more than anyone else that he was completely on his own, as if that were something to celebrate.

# CHAPTER 38

Cycling atop the mountainous portion of Guatemala was like riding on the country's roof, a rolling, sunlit landscape of pasture and pine bordered by the tips of clouds and volcanoes peeking over a near horizon. We reached a deep cut in the landscape and followed the road as it pitched downward, weaving back and forth like skiers across a wide highway into Antigua, Guatemala's stately colonial capital. The city reclined in a wide valley overlooked by three volcanoes: Las Aguas on one side and the twins Acatenango and Fuego on the other.

Baxter and Oscar rattled on the city's cobblestoned streets as we sought a cheap hotel — even the hostels were too expensive for my withered savings — when a lanky German leapt out at us from the footpath.

"I am alsoh traffelling by bye-sickle!" he cried, which made us instant friends. We fell into a discussion about our respective routes into the city as wealthy American tourists, leggy European backpackers and brightly dressed Mayans ambled by. Christoph pointed out the volcanoes towering over the city, and we discussed the possibility of climbing Acatenango together. One of the more popular hiking tours out of Antigua took travelers camping near its summit. From there, it was said, the booms and flashes of its active neighbor, Fuego, were observable — and all from the comfort of one's tent.

The trouble was the cost. The cheapest package went for USD$90 and as cycle tourists, superior to backpackers in every way, we felt it was beneath us to pay so much to have our hands held up some piddling volcano. So there were logistics to figure out — mainly finding a bus that would drop us at the trailhead — and over dinner we briefly plotted out the expedition before turning to the more serious matter of comparing notes on our cycling journeys thus far.

Christoph had started all the way down in Ushuaia, at the far tip of Patagonia — the same place that I, once upon a time, had claimed as my goal. Like me, Christoph was 24 years old and close to the end of his trip, just a month out from his ticket home from Cancún.

"Central America is great," he said around a mouthful of oily cecina steak, "but zer South is sumzing different altogether. Big deserts. Dirt rohds. Many days wissout seeing anybody."

He spoke of solitary cycling in the high Bolivian salt flats and days-long climbs in the Peruvian Andes. As he spoke, I pictured myself doing the same. I imagined lonely nights under huge skies on the altiplano, pedaling past jagged Patagonian peaks, hanging with photogenic backpackers in Ecuadorian surf towns. It was as if those places had sent Christoph as an envoy, and through him they were beckoning, urging me to keep going. It made me uncomfortable.

Once Christoph had wrapped his tale, Robbie and I told him about our respective starting points, which prompted the inevitable follow-up: "And where will you finish?"

This was always a tougher question for Robbie than for me. I had recently switched "Ushuaia" for "San Salvador" — the new destination was much closer than the former, but at least it was a real place on a map. All Robbie could ever say was, "I don't know."

"You don't know?" Christoph was intrigued.

"I came to ride with him," Robbie explained, nodding at me. "But he's leaving soon."

"So you came here wiss an open-ended plan? Now he is leaving, still you don't know?"

"I was originally planning to ride to Ushuaia," I interjected. This drew the spotlight off Robbie — I knew he hated these questions, which might just send him down yet another existential rabbit hole — but I also enjoyed telling this new story of Hailee, our travelers' Tinder love and the rash life decisions we had made together.

Christoph, however, seemed unimpressed.

"So you started wiss zis goal," he said. "And, I'm sorry, but you're giving it up for a woman? Who you just met?"

"It's true," I shrugged, trying to laugh it off. But Christoph's scrunched brow seemed to demand a deeper explanation. "Look," I added, "the road south will always be there. But whatever this is, with Hailee? This woman? It can't wait."

Christoph leaned back now, nodding.

"Well, I wish you luck," he shrugged, taking a swig from his beer. "But for me, I'm not so sure I could begin something so massive, only to give it up so soon. You are a long way from where you started, sure. But you are also a long, long way from Ushuaia."

Now it was Robbie's turn to intervene. "I think what he's saying is that his journey has taken an unexpected turn," he said to Christoph. "He's chasing something new."

Christoph nodded again and stroked his blonde beard pensively. He let the matter drop. But the conversation had rattled me and later, back at our hotel, I brought it up again with Robbie.

"Is this a cop-out?" I asked. "I mean, I did set out to reach Patagonia, after all. Should I not commit myself to completing that goal?"

Robbie took a moment to think, and then said, "Back in Brisbane, all you used to talk about was Vancouver and Ushuaia. They were in every conversation. You were gonna start in one, ride a bike to the other. Vancouver and Ushuaia. Ushuaia and Vancouver. Very impressive, and all that."

"Sure set expectations a bit high," I mumbled.

"Maybe. Whatever," Rob went on. "My point is: since we've been out here I've barely heard you mention either one. What does Vancouver or Ushuaia really mean to you now?"

"A beginning and an end. They define the whole thing."

"Sure, maybe they do if you draw a line on a map. But think about this for a second. You've been cycling almost a year now. Was that all you did, just ride a bike from Point A to Point B? Does that really define what you've done?"

"I mean, it literally does define what I've done…"

"Oh, sure," Rob rolled his eyes. I had rarely seen him so worked up. "All we've *literally* done this whole time is wake up, ride bikes, eat shitty camp food, fall asleep in some farmer's field, get up the next morning and then do the same thing all over again."

"So what's your point?"

"My point is that whatever you've been doing for the last year can't just be defined by where you started and ended. You haven't been single-mindedly pedaling straight for Argentina — you've been meandering all over the place, living this life on the road."

He had hit on something there. During the first few months of cycling, the dream of reaching distant Ushuaia had drifted away as the landscapes immediately behind and in front of me filled with crowds of new people and places. It was the oldest travel cliche: the journey's the thing. The points at either end were meaningless, regardless of how far apart they were — though I later made a big deal of not making a big deal when it emerged that my meandering route south had actually covered more kilometers than Christoph's northbound beeline.

Cycling had given our lives a rhythm, breaking a seemingly gigantic task into a series of repetitive and eminently achievable goals for each day: find food, find water, find shelter, decide where to go and start pedaling. It moved us to the margins of civilization, with time and space to observe the creatures and landscapes around us, how each shaped and melded with the other, the graceful and sometimes-harsh interdependence of all species and the madness of humans who seemed to have lost touch with that basic knowledge, their culture so disconnected it could produce the myth of the solitary cyclist.

I tried to express this to Robbie.

"You like the slowness of this life, the perspective it gives you," he summarized. "Surely that is more important than a couple of points you drew on a map back before you started all this?

"You're about to walk back into civilization," Robbie continued. "You're gonna be immersed to the eyeballs in a relationship and a job and plans for the weekend. You won't have the same time to sit and watch the world with new eyes, and there's a chance you go back to letting your unconscious, prejudiced mind fill in the blanks for you. But surely there's a way you can carry some of this life — observing your surroundings as new and strange, giving and receiving little kindnesses and all that — into the next phase that you're about to begin?"

\* \* \*

Robbie, Christoph and I successfully reached and then scaled Acatenango, though we walked straight into a blistering storm near the summit. We dived into Robbie's tent and spent 13 hours wedged together listening to wind tearing through the saddleback and thunder booming as if giants were playing bocce with the boulders outside. We saw no lava, and we heard no eruptions. The wind and fog remained in the morning but the rain had subsided, so we staggered up to the summit and stood around shivering, unable to see further than five meters or so in the dirty gray clouds clustered around the mountaintop.

Then, for a few seconds, the fog lifted like a curtain and we beheld the ocean of craggy peaks below, Lake Atitlán winking in distant sunshine and Fuego smoking off Acatenango's high shoulder. There was a lot of hooting and cautious leaping about — the wind was still viciously strong, and nobody wanted to be blown away — and within a minute another batch of fog swooped up and took possession of the summit. We set off back to the road, agreeing that the journey had been worth it.

# CHAPTER 39

The boy stood with his back to the observer, shoulders slumped, staring up at a high concrete wall. Cartoonish bones littered the dirt around his bare feet. On an expanse of green hills beyond the wall, I glimpsed airplanes, cars and houses with swimming pools surrounding a gleaming white city. A caption below the mural read, "El sueño norteamericano es la tumba de muchos migrantes." *The North American dream is the tomb of many migrants.*

The Salvadoran border town of Cara Sucia bustled around me: visa offices, fried chicken restaurants, Western Union branches that specialized in remittances. Home to 6 million people yet just 270 kilometers long and 142 kilometers wide, El Salvador is the most densely populated country in Central America. More than a million Salvadorans live in the United States, driven away by a combination of poverty, gangs, the violent residue of civil war and the creeping destruction wrought by climate change. As we neared the border from the Guatemalan side, we heard the same things Canadians had said about Americans, that Americans had said about Mexicans, that Mexicans had said about Belizeans and that Belizeans had said about Guatemalans: "It's dangerous down there."

Gang violence has become an epidemic in El Salvador, much of it imported by migrants radicalized in American prisons and then deported back to their country of origin. We met one middle-aged man, Manuel, who lived in a beach town that seemed cheery until we learned how local gang rivalries restricted his movements.

"I'm not involved with them in any way," he said. "But as a resident of this town, I can't walk or drive five kilometers east along this beach."

"Why?"

"Because that would mean crossing a border into another group's territory," he shrugged. "One that is feuding with the gang that controls this town. The kids don't recognize me up there, so they'll give me problems."

These unsettlingly common complaints notwithstanding, our impression of El Salvador improved as we pushed deeper into the country. Its dense population manifested itself in the masses of strolling ladies, cycling laborers, giggling teenagers and barefoot kids meandering up and down Highway 2. An abundance of fellow cyclists was one of the more pleasing features of cycle touring in El Salvador. Most carried machetes and little else on their way to and from work in the cane fields. Others brought family members or friends. Our record sighting was a family of five mounted on a single bicycle — Dad pedaled and steered from the saddle, Mom sat on the top bar propping a baby daughter on the handlebars while two sons straddled the rear rack.

Ever since the gecko back in Puebla, Robbie and I had long talked about picking up a baby chicken, goat or pig and taking it along as a sort of cycling companion, fattening it up until, one day, we could celebrate some milestone with a barbecue. Well, we saw plenty of Salvadoran cyclists who appeared to have been collecting baby humans. There were babies on bicycles everywhere, balanced on the handlebars or lined up on the rear racks. Up to four children often crowded a single steed. Late in the afternoon of that first day in the country, we spotted a teenage cyclist with a slightly different passenger. Wedged between his arms, on the horizontal top bar was an ancient little man with sunken cheeks and toothless gums. Robbie turned to me.

"Now, there's a cyclist that got too attached," he said, his face grave. "Let his baby get too old."

On the second day we turned off the main highway and headed for the coast, where the road climbed toward the ocean's edge, rounded the cliffs high above a headland and then descended inland again, like a tropical Oregon coast. Sometimes there was a town nestled in the nook or bay between promontories, but often there wasn't — just a family sitting at the roadside with a pile of watermelons for sale. One such family insisted we take an entire watermelon, free of charge. They watched as we tried to strap it to Baxter's rack, then winced as one when it inevitably fell and split on the highway. So we sat with them in the shade and chatted, spooning greedily at the pink flesh.

That evening we reached the surfer's outpost of El Tunco, where I used a Wi-Fi connection to call Hailee. My flight was just two days away, and she had made plans for us to stay with a friend for the coming weekend. There it was, that new life swirling together and taking an alien shape just beyond the threshold of an airplane. Hailee sounded excited over the phone, and I felt giddy.

She had also found us a house to live in. Rooms in San Francisco, Oakland, Berkeley and any other recognizably cool Bay Area locale were far beyond the financial reach of a humanities graduate and her nearly broke new boyfriend. But after a long and frustrating process, she had found us a room in the basement of an old family home, with eight housemates, in a suburb called Burlingame. I liked the full cheeked, rounded sound of the name, complemented by the street: Broadway.

"How American is that!" I squeaked when I told Robbie the news. We looked the place up online. "I'm gonna have a kitchen and a backyard and everything!"

There was even a diner down the street. Robbie grinned so hard his ears almost fell off.

"Ho-ly shit, mate," he said, shaking his head.

San Salvador's airport is 50 kilometers outside the city itself. This had two happy consequences: we would avoid the notorious capital altogether, and instead spend my last evening camping by a beach. In the late afternoon we rolled along an esplanade of tightly packed beach homes called Playa Pimentel, playing "Where Are We Sleeping Tonight?" one last time. We spotted an older couple sitting at a table in a sandy beachside lot and, with a glance at one another, pulled up to ask if there was anywhere nearby that we might be able to camp — meaning, of course, "can we camp here?"

The couple turned out to be mother and son, Tito and spunky little Miti. They were Salvadoran expats who, funnily enough, now lived in the Bay Area. Tito lived in San Mateo which, he said, was just down the road from Burlingame.

"You're so far from home," he kept saying.

Their small beach house was across the road, and they insisted we camp in their front yard. After a dinner of tortillas, freshly caught fish, lemon and homemade salsa with Miti, Tito, their caretaker Eduardo and his family, Robbie and I bought beers and sipped them on the beach in the light of a crescent moon. It was quiet. We talked in patches about his route for the next few days and his plan to ride through Honduras to Nicaragua, where he wanted to take classes to improve his Spanish.

Later, as I slipped into my tent, Robbie returned to the beach. When he came back and unzipped his own tent, I heard sniffling.

"You 'right?"

222

"Yeah," he said. "I'm just... I'm just sad. I'm going to miss you."

"I'll miss you too," I said. "Hey, please don't not sleep all night. Give me a yell if you're stuck awake."

"I'll probably be keeping you up all night, then."

The sand was soft under my tent, and I slept soundly all night.

* * *

In the morning we rose, swam, bought eggs, scrambled and ate them, swam again, packed up, bid our hosts goodbye and then rode to the airport. Robbie and I chatted from time to time, riding side-by-side on the quiet road through fields and villages, the only sounds coming from the slap-slap-slap of women playing hot potato with the masa for the day's tortillas, and the hum of our wheels on the road.

We hung around outside the airport for a little while, but eventually Rob had to get going. My flight wouldn't leave until one o'clock the next morning, but he still had to play "Where Am I Sleeping Tonight?"

So we took a photo together and said a few things that felt formal and awkwardly scripted, mostly because they'd already been said so many times before. Good-lucks and see-you-soons and thank-you-for-everythings. I hugged him and I watched him ride away, freshly ocean-washed Rob in his grubby blue riding shirt, sandals and straw hat, gallant Oscar beneath him, rolling through the manicured airport grounds, back to the business of seeing the world from the saddle of a bicycle, back to familiar rituals in unfamiliar places, to making himself vulnerable to the world and trusting that it was good. He didn't look back, and I felt more pride for him than I will ever feel for myself.

He disappeared into the traffic and I, smiling as bravely as I could, spun on my sandals to face the airport. Feeling like my feet had lifted from the ocean floor, I let the current carry me into the steel jaws of the terminal and its unearthly air conditioning.

# ACKNOWLEDGMENTS

This book tells the story of a formative year in my life. The process of its creation, however, tells the story of my life in the years since.

*The Guest* sputtered into being across a handful of chapters typed out on a work laptop during long, crowded Caltrain commutes between a San Jose job and our basement bedroom in Burlingame. After a year running in the Bay Area rat race, Hailee and I quit our jobs and poured our meager savings into plane tickets to Australia and a camper ute we named Steve. We spent the next year emptying our minds of the world and refilling them with each other. I wrote the first full draft of this book sharing eucalyptus shade with Steve in an old camping chair, bathing in the song of kookaburras and rosellas, charging my laptop off a weathered solar panel and a deep-cycle battery as we made our way around the continent.

I wrote the second draft after Hailee's visa ran out and she'd gone back to America. I stayed at my Mom's house in my home town: Armidale, New South Wales. I worked at a fishing, boating and camping store during the day and typed for most of the night in my sister's old bedroom.

After four long months of that, I joined Hailee in the U.S. I wrote, edited and unsuccessfully pitched the third draft to agents and publishers as we started yet another new life in Seattle. Shout out to the Ballard writing crew (now the Wallingford writing crew), who were standing by with encouragement and advice at plenty of key junctures.

In May 2021, six years to the day since she'd landed in Cancún, I proposed marriage to Hailee in Gas Works Park. We tied the knot two months later and then moved to the Boston area, where she started grad school. During this time I wrapped up the final edits and finally, five years after I'd started, began readying this thing for publication.

Thanks to everyone who offered guidance along the way: Ally, who read the early drafts long before I had any business showing them to anyone and then, several years later, urged me to overcome my Aussie aversion to displays of real emotion; Alison, who asked pertinent questions about bike touring logistics and helped me figure out what this book was all about; Jon, who inducted me into the Church of the Lucid Dream and who convinced me to stop waiting for some publisher or agent to choose me — "Why not just choose yourself?"; Eva, whose cover design turned the paperback into a bonafide work of art; Hailee and Robbie, who were the first to read this thing from cover-to-cover in the weeks before, during and after a trip to Corsica together, and who have graciously supported my five-year attempt to render them within these pages.

So much love to my parents, who raised me to go out and get lost in the world. Brotherly bear hugs to my sisters, who quietly kick arse and take names. I love you all.

Eternal thanks to Robbie. The world would be a much better place if we all had friends and adventure compañeros like you, Señor Dark Horse.

And finally, infinite love and gratitude to Hailee, *The Guest's* biggest supporter and believer through all these ecstatic years. You see and bring out the best in everyone you meet. Waking up next to you every day is the clearest manifestation of Quinten Luck there is. I will always love you.

Quinten
*October 2021*

Printed in Great Britain
by Amazon

79702669R00133